Contemporary
Catholic Thought

Contemporary Catholic Thought

Faith, Hope and Love in the Modern World

EDITED WITH AN INTRODUCTION BY

Barry Ulanov

SHEED AND WARD · NEW YORK

ACKNOWLEDGMENTS

"God Of My Life"; quoted from *Encounters With Silence* by Karl Rahner, S.J., with the permission of The Newman Press.

"Reason and Faith"; quoted from *An Essay in Christian Philosophy* by Dom Illtyd Trethowan with the permission of Longmans, Green & Co., Ltd.

"The Sources, Heart, and World of Faith"; quoted from *I Believe* by Jean Mouroux with the permission of Sheed & Ward, Inc.

"The Value of Belief in the Trinity"; quoted from *Belief in the Trinity* by Dom Mark Pontifex with the permission of Longmans, Green & Co., Ltd. Copyright by Harper & Row, Publishers, Inc. Reprinted by permission.

"The Unknown God"; quoted from *Science, Religion and Christianity* by Hans Urs von Balthasar with the permission of The Newman Press.

"The Mystical Body and Contemporary Humanity"; quoted from *Morality and the Mystical Body* by Emile Mersch, S.J., with the permission of P. J. Kenedy & Sons.

"The Pastoral Idea in the History of the Liturgy"; quoted from *The Assisi Papers* by Josef A. Jungmann, S.J. Copyright by The Order of St. Benedict, Inc., Collegeville, Minnesota.

"Modern Forms of Christian Life and Art" by P. R. Régamey, O.P.: quoted from *Towards A Living Tradition,* ed. Justus George Lawler, published by Pio Decimo Press.

"Towards a Theory of the Catholic Intellectual" by Pedro Lain Entralgo, translated by Joseph L. Caulfield; reprinted with permission from *Cross Currents*.

"Psychologists Versus Morality" by Jean Rimaud, S.J., translated by Leon King and Gerard de Vissant; reprinted with permission from *Cross Currents*.

"Pessimism and the Eschatological Consciousness"; quoted from *Men Against Humanity* by Gabriel Marcel with the permission of The Harvill Press Ltd. Permission also granted by Henry Regnery Company and by La Colombe.

"The End of the Modern World"; quoted from *The End of the Modern World* by Romano Guardini with the permission of Sheed & Ward, Inc.

"The Virtue of Charity"; quoted from *Love of Our Neighbor* by Albert Plé, O.P., with the permission of Templegate Publishers.

"Love Your Neighbor as Yourself"; quoted from *Spirituality of the New Testament* by W. K. Grossouw with the permission of B. Herder Book Co.

"Truth and Human Fellowship"; quoted from *On the Use of Philosophy* by Jacques Maritain with the permission of Princeton University Press.

"Love and Belief"; quoted from *Christ and the Western Mind and Love and Belief* by Karl Adam with the permission of Sheed & Ward, Inc.

"The Growth of the Divine Milieu"; reprinted from *The Divine Milieu* by Pierre Teilhard de Chardin, S.J., by permission of Harper & Row, Publishers. Copyright by Harper & Row, Publishers.

"Our Temptations Concerning the Church"; quoted from *The Splendor of the Church* by Henri de Lubac, S.J., with the permission of Sheed & Ward, Inc.

"God of Wrath or God of Love?"; quoted from *Love and Violence* by Philippe de la Trinité, O.C.D., with the permission of Sheed & Ward, Inc.

Contents

Contemporary Catholic Thought

Introduction

FOR most of us, the value of the contemporary is its closeness to our own experience. Whether person, thing, or event, whatever lives alongside us confirms our own existence. This is how we know what we know, beyond any theory, beyond any system of cognition, beyond any epistemology, no matter how carefully worked out. This is how we know that we know, this is how we know that we are.

To proclaim something as contemporary, then, is not simply to fill in a gap in time, to bring a chronology up to date. It is to give witness to existence, our own witness, not somebody else's. There is nothing remote about the events or people or ideas we call contemporary. They come out of our own lives. They speak our language. "Know all men by these presents," we say: "Know all men by those present."

And as it is for other people, other events, other ideas, so it is for contemporary Catholic thought and contemporary Catholic thinkers. They also are our witnesses, we also are theirs. We speak to each other out of a common experience, in a common language. And this, to begin with, unites us in a very special way, no matter how close or far away our interests and our convictions may be.

Catholic thought in our time is very much of our time. It shares the sense of crisis which pervades everything of any seriousness written in our time. It reflects the outrage of sensitive men of any time at injustice, but an outrage exacerbated in our time by the particularly ugly offenses against human dignity committed by the totalitarians of nation, state, race, religion, class, and creed. "It is a sin," said the Archbishop of Durban, South Africa, just a few years ago, speaking of Apartheid, "it is a sin to humiliate one's fellow man."

Catholic thought in our time is deeply involved in the perplexities and paradoxes of our scientistic age, aware of its miracles,
aware of its morasses, and constantly concerned to provide some
means with which to endure both, some means that is genuinely
meditative and not, like so many of the other ways of responding
to our time, merely manic-depressive, shouting with jubilation at
every orbit of the earth by an astronaut, groaning with misery at
every circuit by a cosmonaut, and each day facing apotheosis or
extinction.

The deliberations of psychologists, sociologists, and philosophers
about the nature of the self have not escaped Catholic thinkers.
They have, indeed, made their own contributions to them. None of
them is disposed today, like some of the more confident pulpit
oracles of a few years ago, to dismiss an entire field of knowledge.
No one now consigns psychology or psychoanalysis to the dust-
heap with a facile wave of an adjective. Very few identify comparative religion as the work of the devil. Psychology has in fact
entered the seminary and psychoanalysis is practised by many
Catholics with distinction. And, as a few centuries ago the Jesuits
were among the first to recognize the benefits to Christians and
Christianity of the close examination of religious experience different from theirs, of Indian and Chinese modes of revelation, so
once again today Catholic scholars, priests and laymen both, are
very much involved in the complexities of the Eastern religions.
Their involvements, like those of the psychologists, are not easily
dissipated, either. They are not engaged in order to disengage
themselves. They make no quick judgments, but rather quite incomplete discriminations, which they are content to leave that
way. They recognize, as at least one priest, the Passionist Father
Thomas Berry, has put it, that "the Christ experience" must be
universal, that under Providence some special insights must have
been given every civilization, every religion, even without the fullness of revelation that accompanied the Incarnation.

No discipline stands today altogether apart from Catholic
thought. No matter what the biases of those working in a given
field, even if they make up the majority, there are some Catholics
who can work with them, alongside them, collaborating, if need
be, without sharing the biases, but neither shattered by them nor so

conscious of them that they cannot work in peace. Thus there are Catholics among the latest Oxford reformers, the therapeutic grammarians, whose addiction for ordinary language and abhorrence for obfuscation threaten to make philosophy lucid once again. There are Catholics in anthropology, demography, biochemistry, and genetics, working with the highly efficient tools now available to specialists in these fields, plotting the complexities of primitive societies, making population surveys, facing the possibilities of an ovum developing without fertilization from a sperm (parthenogenesis), or a foetus growing up outside the womb (ectogenesis), or a foetus being moved from womb to womb, without the eviscerating fears with which all the world believes Catholics are inevitably afflicted in the face of these ancient conflagration issues. There are Catholics working everywhere that reason works its way without making it impossible for faith to work its way, which is to say everywhere.

What is more, Catholics have been able to work in all these areas of the intellect, and to work well, in spite of the harrowing cries that go up with such predictable frequency these days. Always, it seems, they must be reminded of their obligation to be leaders, of their responsibility to exercise an influence commensurate with the proportion of Catholics in the population. Hooray for the pluralist society, they are asked to shout, but let it never be so pluralist that the singularity of Catholics fails to stand out. Remember, remember, remember, they are nagged at least three times a year, whenever Catholic journals run out of other things to print, remember that we—or rather, you—must be zealous for intellectual influence, leadership, inspiration, excellence, etc., etc., etc., in terms following the general outlines of that spirited call to the convolutions of Monsignor John Tracy Ellis, "The American Catholic and the Intellectual Life," delivered in 1955 as a paper at the annual meeting of the Catholic Commission on Intellectual and Cultural Affairs. Another cleric asks, "Where are our Oppenheimers? Where are our Einsteins?" The voice of the intellectual-rouser is heard in the land. If the Catholic intellectual, duly roused, answers "Here! Present!" too boldly, too loudly, there is always the chance that there will be a further response, and from a very high place, saying with something less than notable originality, "Who do these intellectuals think they are anyway?" A long time ago the word went out that the Church thrives on oppression; each generation there are new volunteers for the role of oppressor, anxious to see to it that the Church continue to thrive in the ancient way.

The fact is, of course, that the Church does thrive on all the difficulties that afflict it, that afflict humanity. It does so not because it prospers as the result of exploiting indignity and suffering, but because of its endless resources of mercy. This, as Cardinal Newman says in the splendid cadences of his *Grammar of Assent,* is how Christianity "at present . . . is so mysteriously potent, in spite of the new and fearful adversaries which beset its path. It has with it that gift of staunching and healing the one deep wound of human nature, which avails more for its success than a full encyclopedia of scientific knowledge and a whole library of controversy, and therefore it must last while human nature lasts. It is a living truth which never can grow old." And so the Church faces misery with mercy, faces suffering and sin and every impotence and affliction of humankind with the several mediations of the Incarnation. But the mediations that it offers are always offered in familiar terms, contemporary terms, in the vernacular of body and soul into which each day the Church makes new translations. Newman's words on this theme, which directly follow those quoted above, are justly famous. They could, in substance, be called the Church's binomial theorem, for these words explain how, in just what way, Christianity is both old and new:

Some persons speak of it as if it were a thing of history, with only indirect bearings upon modern times; I cannot allow that it is a mere historical religion. Certainly it has its foundations in past and glorious memories, but its power is in the present. It is no dreary matter of antiquarianism; we do not contemplate it in conclusions drawn from dumb documents and dead events, but by faith exercised in ever-living objects, and by the appropriation and use of ever-recurring gifts.

Our communion with it is in the unseen, not in the obsolete. At this very day its rites and ordinances are continually eliciting the active interposition of that Omnipotence in which the Religion long ago began.

Few men in the history of ideas can have served one epoch so
well in another as by anticipation, prediction, and example Newman served the twentieth century in the nineteenth. To an astonishing degree, the texture of Catholic thought in our time reflects his
personality and his thinking, and in ever-widening spectra. As his
thinking tended to be unsystematic—not anarchical, of course, and
certainly not chaotic, but rather disposed to follow the least divaga-
tion of the human person, any stray feeling or impression—so the
same thing may be said of much of the most compelling speculation in current Catholic thought. As he was, by every special kind
of training and all the marks of his own temperament, inclined to
look to the Fathers of the Church for almost every kind of enlightenment and understanding, so are most of the outstanding
theologians and philosophers of the present-day Church. They follow him, too, in preparing translations or helping others to do so
from the Greek or Latin of the Fathers into the modern vernacular
tongues, although few can match the bite and brawn of his prose.
Like Newman, the founders and directors and editors of *Sources
chrétiennes,* to name just one distinguished series, men like Henri
de Lubac, Jean Daniélou, and Jean Leclercq, have been particularly concerned to make the Fathers widely available to their contemporaries in clear modern translations. For in doing so, they
have been able to bring into bold relief the good news of the gospel
and its reception by the first generations of Christians and all the
practises which surrounded it. They have been able to communicate, by the most direct transmission, the fervor and the dedication and the depth of insight of those remarkable men who had, in
addition to their own large gifts, the historical grace of living contact with the first witnesses, the early popes, the proto-martyrs,
and all the other holy men who drew their inspiration from the
apostles at no more than third or fourth remove. The Fathers were
in reach of the men who knew our Lord, who had been touched
by Him directly. It is that exalted connection that gives such unmistakable unction to their writings and recommends them so
warmly to Newman, to Leclercq and Daniélou and de Lubac, and
to all those in our own time—and how many there are!—who
prefer the warmth of human contact to the cool precisions of
scholastic formulas. This is how, for many of us, it is easiest to

understand, not simply to accept, the fact of the Apostolic succession.

Newman stands in relation to our time as St. Augustine did in relation to his. Both men were masters of the method of digression, circling round and round a subject, allowing almost anything that came into their mind in the course of reflection on a theme, if it seemed in any way apposite, to settle there for a moment, for a phrase, for a clause, or for several paragraphs, if need be, and almost always as a result to deepen their understanding and therefore that of their readers. Though not a professional rhetorician, as Augustine was, Newman certainly was a master of language, soaked in Scripture, non- if not anti-scholastic, and endlessly open to the guidance of other wise men, ancient and modern. That great openness of Newman's can be attributed to many sources, to many things: to his perambulations among the Fathers, and especially the Alexandrians, to his intense participation in the polemics of the Oxford Movement, to his ardors both in the establishment and the development of the Oratory in England, and certainly to the spiritual combat which ultimately led to his conversion. And yet something else, already mentioned, may be more significant in explaining Newman, in explaining his openness, in explaining his faith, in explaining his great claim on the modern imagination— that is the place of Scripture in his life. He asserted that place fairly early in his career, in 1838, in a long essay, a small book really, on "Holy Scripture in Its Relation to the Catholic Creed." It is worth examining in its entirety as one of the most remarkable of the Newman exhibits, with its rich display of biblical understanding and its anticipation of modern Scripture scholarship, in and out of the Church, Scripture scholarship purged of its first uncontrolled enthusiasm for the so-called Higher Criticism but not without its proper respect for the critical apparatus and historical methods which together have revealed so much of the richness beneath the surface of the Bible. But the special moment for the modern reader is the ending of the work. There Newman expatiates on the theme of scepticism and religious faith: "Doubt and difficulty, as regards evidence, seems our lot; the simple question is, What is our duty under it?"

In answering his own question—the central question of modern man—Newman invokes the parable of the talents: "Do not those who refuse to go by the hints and probable meaning of Scripture hide their talent in a napkin? and will they be excused?" Scripture insists that in these things we have a positive obligation to go by faith. No matter what arguments are brought against "its own inspiration, its canonicity, its doctrines," no matter what the objections, no matter what methods or apparatus, Scripture "has provided against them, by recognizing them." And thus it insists on the way of faith, "because it knows that, unless we believe, there is no means of our arriving at a knowledge of divine things." The evidence is heavily on the side of revelation: "if we will determine that no evidence is enough to prove revealed doctrine but what is simply overpowering; if we will not go by evidence in which there are (so to say) a score of reasons for Revelation, yet one or two against it, we cannot be Christians; we shall miss Christ either in His inspired Scriptures, or in His doctrines, or in His ordinances."

We have, Newman points out, an illustrious precedent. After the discourse of Jesus on the bread of life (John 6), many of his disciples leave him. He asks the twelve who are closest to him, "Will you also go away?" And Peter answers, "Lord, to whom shall we go?" Newman's point is that Peter did not have the alternative of what in our time has been called the "existential vacuum," what Newman described as the "negative state of neither believing nor disbelieving, neither acting this way nor that. . . ." Peter had to make a choice: "If Christ could deceive him, to whom should he go? Christ's ways might be dark, His words often perplexing, but still he found in Him what he found nowhere else,—amidst difficulties, a realization of his inward longings." And so Peter elects to stay, for, as he says to Christ, "Thou hast the words of eternal life."

In that choice, in those words, Newman finds all his faith, all his hope, all his love. He puts the interior drama of Peter into new words. The speech he gives the "fervent Apostle" is the critical one that Peter had to make, when confronted with the choice between scepticism and faith. It is the significant statement Newman made when offered the modern choice of no choice. It is the choice modern man makes when he rejects the void, when he re-

fuses nausea, when, for all its modishness, he turns down ship-
wreck and accepts instead the vision of eternal life. Thus, Newman's Peter speaks:

We will stand by what we believed and knew yesterday,—what we
believed and knew the day before. A sudden gust of new doctrines,
a sudden inroad of new perplexities, shall not unsettle us. We *have*
believed, we *have* known: we cannot collect together all the evidence,
but this is the abiding deep conviction of our minds. We feel that it is
better, safer, truer, pleasanter, more blessed to cling to Thy feet, O
merciful Saviour, than to leave Thee. *Thou canst not* deceive us: it is
impossible. We will hope in Thee against hope, and believe in Thee
against doubt, and obey Thee in spite of gloom.

These words—what might be called Peter's Magnificat—draw
from Newman an answering and an echoing statement. In two
paragraphs, he draws faith and love together, asserting the primary
position of love in human life as in divine life. Love, as he explains
in a footnote, is the necessary prerequisite for faith. The love
which precedes and leads to faith is, of course, "not evangelical
charity, the theological virtue, but that desire for the knowledge and
drawing towards the service of our Maker, which precedes religious conversion." But it is a love of great stature, for that "inward acceptance of Revelation on the part of individuals," which
is what this love becomes, is not in any way apart from or hostile
to reason. The love here described, the love which is antecedent to
belief, is rather "a sovereign condition which is antecedent to belief," "a sovereign condition without which Reason cannot be
brought to bear upon the great work in hand."

And so, by means of love, all is made compact and given purpose, all: the world before faith, the world after faith; the Church;
the human condition. Starting with a pious affection or merely with
good will, we end, in this sublime motion of mind and soul, with
the great disposition of the affections which a deep faith inevitably brings with it. And thus a testament of faith becomes an
act of love. Newman's 1838 Credo, elicited by his meditations on
Scripture, deserves reproduction in full. For what it contains, it is
brief enough.

Now what are the feelings I have described but the love of Christ? Thus love is the parent of faith. We believe in things we see not, from love of them: if we did not love, we should not believe. Faith is reliance on the word of another; the word of another is in itself a faint evidence compared with that of sight or reason. It is influential only when we cannot do without it. We cannot do without it when it is our informant about things which we cannot do without. Things we cannot do without, are things which we desire. They who feel they cannot do without the next world, go by faith (not that sight would not be better), but because they have no other means of knowledge to go by. "To whom shall they go?" If they will not believe the word preached to them, what other access have they to the next world? Love of God led St. Peter to follow Christ, and love of Christ leads men now to love and follow the Church, as His representative and voice.

Let us then say, If we give up the Gospel, as we have received it in the Church, to whom shall we go? It has the words of eternal life in it: where else are they to be found? Is there any other Religion to choose but that of the Church? Shall we go to Mahometanism or Paganism? But we may seek some heresy or sect: true, we may; but why are they more sure? are they not a part, while the Church is the whole? Why is the part true, if the whole is not? Why is not that evidence trustworthy for the whole, which is trustworthy for a part? Sectaries commonly give up the Church doctrines, and go by the Church's Bible; but if the doctrines cannot be proved true, neither can the Bible; they stand or fall together. If we begin, we must soon make an end. On what consistent principle can I give up part and keep the rest? No: I see a work before me, which professes to be the work of that God whose being and attributes I feel within me to be real. Why should not this great sight be,—what it professes to be—His presence? Why should not the Church be divine? The burden of proof surely is on the other side. I will accept her doctrines, and her rites, and her Bible,—not one, and not the other, but all,—till I have clear proof, which is an impossibility, that she is mistaken. It is, I feel, God's will that I should do so; and besides, I love all that belong to her,—I love her Bible, her doctrines, her rites, and therefore I believe.

Those words are Newman's. They bear the unmistakable stamp of his person. But they set the tone as no others could half so well —except perhaps other passages by the same writer—for a collection of Catholic thought in the middle of the twentieth century.

For one thing that is constant in the Catholic writing of our time, as it is constant in all the writing and thinking of our time, is a preoccupation with love. Love in all its guises—love secluded, love sequestered, love bewildered; love aroused and exposed and altogether open to the eye; love baffled and frustrated and quite misunderstood; fleshly love, spiritual love, and love which is both and a good deal more than the sum of all its parts—love is always before us today. The problems of love. The mystery of love. We have opinions to go on and obiter dicta on which to stop. We have endless thoughts, endless words, a stream of material, now sluggish, now vigorous and charging, with which to deal.

It may be said that this is the way it has always been, for love, like life and death, is the constant preoccupation of men. All would like love to fill all their days. When has it ever been different? The answer is, Never and always. Love has, of course, been central to human thought from the beginning. But all the more because it is at the center of men's lives, it wears the clothing of the epoch. The most universal of things, it is also the most particular. In love is the essence of the contemporary. Love sports the fashions of the times, speaks the language of the day, changes, changes, constantly changes. And so in our day it is Freudian, Frommian, Jungian; it affects the modes of existentialist discourse; it is distilled in sociological and anthropological essences; it stands warily and hungrily at the edge of lonely crowds; it bounces merrily around the beaches and bursts through the huts of the Polynesians; and it stands exposed in the simplest and most chaste monstrances ever designed to hold it firm on the altars of churches of the same modality of design.

Love does look different in the modern church. Not because everywhere it dons the trappings of modernity. Le Corbusier has designed only a few churches, Niemeyer not many more; Matisse's vivid elegances float unconfined throughout only one chapel; Cocteau has scrawled his way through no more than a pair of churches; the great bold stance of Rouault, Léger, Picasso, Bazaine is not yet contagious among pastors. But the liturgical movement, at least the foster parent if not the natural father of modern art in the churches, has almost everywhere been infectious. The least nimble of presiding priests has tried out a dialogue mass, has tickled the throats of his congregations with a *missa cantata,* has at least once or twice made an attempt at an offertory procession or bullied a curate or his tallest altar boy into the office of lector. The least adventurous of bishops have accepted the letter, if not the spirit, of the new eucharistic legislation that permits evening mass, and on Holy Days of Obligation or First Fridays or both have called for 5 or 6 or 7 P.M. masses. Eastern rite liturgies have been sampled with clear pleasure at schools and colleges and even at a neighborhood church from time to time. The sacraments have found among many a new efficaciousness; their understanding has ceased to be mute; in this way, at least, love looks different, love sounds different, in the modern church.

But liturgy is not all, as even the most ardent liturgist will admit. Nor is the constant pushing, probing, and proclaiming of the place of the layman in the Church, that natural corollary of a concern with the liturgy and a larger, deeper, more perceptive participation in its measures. Something more significant still is responsible for the great changes in the modern Church: the concentration on love—a concentration so intense that it may one day become what it has so long looked like becoming, a revolution, a revolution of love. That significant "thing" is a crisis, the crisis of faith.

Newman's prophetic words are the best possible summation of the crisis of faith. Modern man is faced, as no man has ever before been faced, with a vacuum, "neither believing nor disbelieving, neither acting this way or that. . . ." Oh, we all know that there have been terrifying moments before now. Man has seemed on several occasions to have the weapons of total destruction in his grasp. But never before has extinction seemed such a logical, such an inescapable consequence of a long series of inexorable events. And never before has man been so generous in his anticipation of annihilation with a philosophy of the void so complete, a scepticism so thorough that he stands utterly empty in the face of his own being, seems almost to deny his own being.

Confronted by such a depletion of faith and hope, the modern Christian cannot simply tonelessly affirm his own belief in terms of the rote measures of the catechism. Besides, he himself feels the tug of the void. Of all the contagions none is so quickly epidemic as despair. And so the Christian falls sick too, is tempted too by the nostrum of no nostrum, by the panacea of calculated apathy. The crisis of this illness is the crisis of faith. In it, the Christian must examine as he never has before the resources of his faith, the meaning of his faith, the way he has discovered God and redis-covered Him and may continue to find Him. He must look, as he never has before, at the language in which he reasons about his faith, if he reasons at all. He must make up his mind about language where language is most important: the way it makes possible (or does not) some discourse with and about God, some cogitation about being, some assurance about his own existence, some as-surance of existence itself. He must make up his mind.

In the course of this exploration, this terrifying exploration which calls everything into question, the Christian dies many times, in great torture, and comes alive many times, not without torture. He imitates Christ in the most direct way possible: he takes up His Cross.

This too is not new. Christian witness has always been a martyr-dom in both senses of the word. The saints have frequently shown the marks of scourging, of the thorns, of the nails and the spear. The new stigmata are not always so obvious. In them the flesh is made word, and the anguish draws—or at least seems to draw—more adjectives than blood. But the anguish is real, whatever its marks may be, and it results, as Christian anguish always does, in a renewal of faith, in a deepening of hope, and in a new con-sciousness of love. Faith comes now not from formulas but from a re-experience of one's relationship with God or perhaps the first real experience of that relationship. One verbalizes now with one's own words, not with other men's words, and one finds valuable only those testimonies of faith which reflect a real experience of faith. And so one welcomes with special warmth such discourses on the mystery of being as Gabriel Marcel's, which are so in-sistently autobiographical; they speak to one's condition, they speak of one's condition.

Hope, too, must in the same way be grounded in experience. That is why the modern Catholic turns so often, with such open-ness, to the world in all its shapes, all its signs, all its societies and all its religions, and finds in all these things, in all these beings, acceptable modes of revelation. They will not and cannot substitute for his faith. But they can supplement it. And more important, they constantly demonstrate to him the presence of God, moving with stubborn love wherever anything moves, wherever anything is. Nothing is so productive of hope as this understanding, that the missionary goes out into the world to confirm and to deepen love, not to introduce it.

From every examination, every speculation, every meditation of this kind, love emerges. Wherever the Christian goes in faith, however and whenever hope develops, love comes along too. If ever anything were necessary to demonstrate the interchangeability of the three theological virtues, this would do it. Faith, hope, and love in this are exactly like the three Persons of the Blessed Trinity. We know each best through the others; we find access to any one Person through any one of the others. Every experience of the Christian in our time suggests these facts; his every experience demands them. And when all is said and done, it is the demand that matters, far more than the suggestion. For what contemporary Catholic experience—and thus contemporary Catholic thought— proclaims is the urgent need of man for God, the besieging hope of man in God, the demanding love of man for God. Faith, as Newman said in 1838, and Christians say again and again today, "is influential only when we cannot do without it. We cannot do without it when it is our informant about things which we cannot do without. Things which we cannot do without, are things which we desire."

The profound conviction that underlies almost every significant piece of Catholic writing in our time is that faith, hope, and love are things we cannot do without, and therefore things we desire. Joining the insights of St. Thomas Aquinas and Sigmund Freud, a not impossible combination, as I think we are beginning to understand, we realize that our desire for faith, hope, and love (and especially the last) is of such an urgency, is so compelling, that our every act is motivated by it. That means that even our shabby acts, our slobbery ones, our sinful ones, are motivated by this desire. Whatever we do, however we act, there stands behind the doing and the acting the impulse to the good, the drive to love, the desire to rest finally in love itself. All of which is another way of saying that somehow we have discovered the faith which in turn produces the hope that love of some kind may be ours. However clumsy our notion of love may be, however dim our faith and hope, we have enough of all three to move with them toward them.

With them toward them—this is the mysterious way of the theological virtues, that you need them to get them. It is another way of saying "You would not seek me if you had not already found me." It is, of course, altogether appropriate that there should be such a confusion of tenses and apparent inversion of the proper sequence of events. We are working here with the most disturbing of all sequences of events, when eternity enters into time, as it does every time we make the slightest motion, of thought or action, in the direction of faith, hope, and love. Thus the Catholic writer today dealing with the world around him—with things, with ideas, with people—never stops at the limits of the world, whether the world is viewed in terms of the planet earth or in terms of the largest possible construction of the universe. The extra-territorial rights of the Christian give him at all times a piece of eternity. If the Incarnation, the event upon which Christianity rests, makes sense, it does so because the words of the Incarnate God, "Before Abraham was, I am," make sense.

And so, wherever he goes, whatever he deals with, the Catholic thinker goes in and out of time. He moves directly into the areas of faith, hope, and love or he contemplates the adumbrations, anticipations, and echoes of them to be found in the ancient Greeks and Romans; the Hindus, the Buddhists, the Confucians, the Taoists; the formulations about the microscopic world of physicists; the splatterings in the macroscopic world of painters, sculptors, and architects. The grandeur of that motion out of time into eternity and back into time again has perhaps never been so apparent as in our time, for it has never before described so wide an arc. We go far, far outside ourselves. We go deep, deep inside ourselves. That is the orbit of contemporary Catholic thought.

Prologue

GOD OF MY LIFE

KARL RAHNER, S.J.

I SHOULD like to speak with You, my God, and yet what else can I speak of but You? Indeed, could anything at all exist which had not been present with You from all eternity, which didn't have its true home and most intimate explanation in Your mind and heart? Isn't everything I ever say really a statement about You?

On the other hand, if I try, shyly and hesitantly, to speak to You about Yourself, You will still be hearing about *me*. For what could I say about You except that You are *my* God, the God of my beginning and end, God of my joy and my need, God of my life?

Of course You are endlessly more than merely the God of my life —if that's all You were, You wouldn't really be God at all. But even when I think of Your towering majesty, even when I acknowledge You as someone Who has no need of me, Who is infinitely far exalted above the lowly valleys through which I drag out the paths of my life—even then I have called You once again by the same name, God of my life.

And when I give praise to You as Father, Son, and Holy Spirit, when I confess the thrice holy mystery of Your life, so eternally hidden in the abysses of Your Infinity that it leaves behind in creation no sign that we could make out by ourselves, am I not still praising You as the God of my life? Even granting that You had revealed to me this secret of Your own inner life, would I be able to accept and realize this mystery if *Your* life had not become *my* life through grace? Would I be able to acknowledge and love You,

Father, and You, Eternal Word of the Father's Heart, and You, Spirit of the Father and the Son, if You had not deigned to become through grace the triune God of my life?

But what am I really saying, when I call You *my* God, the God of my life? That You are the meaning of my life? the goal of my wanderings? the consecration of my actions? the judgment of my sins? the bitterness of my bitter hours and my most secret joy? my strength, which turns *my own* strength into weakness? Creator, Sustainer, Pardoner, the One both far and near? Incomprehensible? God of my brethren? God of my fathers?

Are there any titles which I needn't give You? And when I have listed them all, what have I said? If I should take my stand on the shore of Your Endlessness and shout into the trackless reaches of Your Being all the words I have ever learned in the poor prison of my little existence, what should I have said? I should never have spoken the last word about You.

Then why do I even begin to speak of You? Why do You torment me with Your Infinity, if I can never really measure it? Why do You constrain me to walk along Your paths, if they lead only to the awful darkness of Your night, where only You can see? For us, only the finite and tangible is real and near enough to touch: can You be real and near to me, when I must confess You as Infinite?

Why have You burnt Your mark in my soul in Baptism? Why have You kindled in me the flame of faith, this dark light which lures us out of the bright security of our little huts into Your night? And why have You made me Your priest, one whose vocation it is to be with You on behalf of men, when my finiteness makes me gasp for breath in Your presence?

Look at the vast majority of men, Lord—and excuse me if I presume to pass judgment on them—but do they often think of You? Are You the First Beginning and Last End for them, the One without whom their minds and hearts can find no rest? Don't they manage to get along perfectly well without You? Don't they feel quite at home in this world which they know so well, where they can be sure of just what they have to reckon with? Are You anything more for them than the One who sees to it that the world stays on its hinges, so that they won't have to call on You? Tell me, are You the God of *their* life?

I don't really know, Lord, if my complaint is just or not—who knows the heart of another man? You alone are the reader of hearts, O God, and how can I expect to understand the heart of another when I don't even understand my own? It's just that I can't help thinking of those others, because—as You well know, since You see into the depths of my heart, O Hidden God from whom nothing is hidden—often enough I feel in myself a secret longing to be like them or, at least, to be as they seem to be.

O Lord, how helpless I am when I try to talk to You about Yourself! How can I call You anything but the God of my life? And what have I said with that title, when no name is really adequate? I'm constantly tempted to creep away from You in utter discouragement, back to the things that are more comprehensible, to things with which my heart feels so much more at home than it does with Your mysteriousness.

And yet, where shall I go? If the narrow hut of this earthly life with its dear, familiar trivialities, its joys and sorrows both great and small—if this were my real home, wouldn't it still be surrounded by Your distant Endlessness? Could the earth be my home without Your far-away heaven above it?

Suppose I tried to be satisfied with what so many today profess to be the purpose of their lives. Suppose I defiantly determined to admit my finiteness, and glory in it alone. I could only begin to recognize this finiteness and accept it as my sole destiny, because I had previously so often stared out into the vast reaches of limitless space, to those hazy horizons where Your Endless Life is just beginning.

Without You, I should founder helplessly in my own dull and groping narrowness. I could never feel the pain of longing, not even deliberately resign myself to being content with this world, had not my mind again and again soared out over its own limitations into the hushed reaches which are filled by You alone, the Silent Infinite. Where should I flee before You, when all my yearning for the unbounded, even my bold trust in my littleness, is really a confession of You?

What else is there that I can tell You about Yourself, except that You are the One without whom I cannot exist, the Eternal God from whom alone I, a creature of time, can draw the strength to

live, the Infinity who gives meaning to my finiteness? And when I
tell You all this, then I have given myself my true name, the name
I ever repeat when I pray in David's Psalter, "*Tuus sum ego.*" I
am the one who belongs not to himself, but to You. I know no
more than this about myself, nor about You, O God of my life,
Infinity of my finiteness.

What a poor creature You have made me, O God! All I know
about You and about myself is that You are the eternal mystery
of my life. Lord, what a frightful puzzle man is! He belongs to You,
and You are the Incomprehensible—Incomprehensible in Your
Being, and even more so in Your ways and judgments. For if all
Your dealings with me are acts of Your freedom, quite unmerited
gifts of Your grace which knows no "why," if my creation and my
whole life hang absolutely on Your free decision, if all my paths
are, after all, Your paths and, therefore, unsearchable, then, Lord,
no amount of questioning will ever fathom Your depths—You will
still be the Incomprehensible, even when I see You face to face.

But if You were not incomprehensible, You would be inferior to
me, for my mind could grasp and assimilate You. You would belong to me, instead of I to You. And that would truly be hell, if I
should belong only to myself! It would be the fate of the damned,
to be doomed to pace up and down for all eternity in the cramped
and confining prison of my own finiteness.

But can it be that You are my true home? Are You the One
who will release me from my narrow little dungeon? Or are You
merely adding another torment to my life, when You throw open
the gates leading out upon Your broad and endless plain? Are You
anything more than my own great insufficiency, if all my knowledge leads only to Your Incomprehensibility? Are You merely
eternal unrest for the restless soul? Must every question fall dumb
before You, unanswered? Is Your only response the mute "I will
have it so," that so coldly smothers my burning desire to understand?

But I am rambling on like a fool—excuse me, O God. You have
told me through Your Son that You are the God of my love, and
You have commanded me to love You. Your commands are often
hard because they enjoin the opposite of what my own inclinations
would lead me to do, but when You bid me love You, You are

ordering something that my own inclinations would never even dare to suggest: to love *You*, to come intimately close to You, to love Your very life. You ask me to lose myself in You, knowing that You will take me to Your Heart, where I may speak on loving, familiar terms with You, the incomprehensible mystery of my life. And all this because You are Love Itself.

Only in love can I find You, my God. In love the gates of my soul spring open, allowing me to breathe a new air of freedom and forget my own petty self. In love my whole being streams forth out of the rigid confines of narrowness and anxious self-assertion, which make me a prisoner of my own poverty and emptiness. In love all the powers of my soul flow out toward You, wanting never more to return, but to lose themselves completely in You, since by Your love You are the inmost center of my heart, closer to me than I am to myself.

But when I love You, when I manage to break out of the narrow circle of self and leave behind the restless agony of unanswered questions, when my blinded eyes no longer look merely from afar and from the outside upon Your unapproachable brightness, and much more when You Yourself, O Incomprehensible One, have become through love the inmost center of my life, then I can bury myself entirely in You, O mysterious God, and with myself all my questions.

Love such as this wills to possess You as You are—how could it desire otherwise? It wants You Yourself, not Your reflection in the mirror of its own spirit. It wants to be united with You alone, so that in the very instant in which it gives up possession of itself, it will have not just Your image, but Your very Self.

Love wants You as You are, and just as love knows that it itself is right and good and needs no further justification, so You are right and good for it, and it embraces You without asking for any explanation of why You are as You are. Your "I will have it so" is love's greatest bliss. In this state of joy my mind no longer tries to bring You forcibly down to its level, in order to wrest from You Your eternal secret, but rather love seizes me and carries me up to Your level, into You.

When I abandon myself in love, then You are my very life, and Your Incomprehensibility is swallowed up in love's unity. When I am allowed to love You, the grasp of Your very mystery becomes a positive source of bliss. Then the farther Your Infinity is removed from my nothingness, the greater is the challenge to my love. The more complete the dependence of my fragile existence upon Your unsearchable counsels, the more unconditional must be the surrender of my whole being to You, beloved God. The more annihilating the incomprehensibility of Your ways and judgments, the greater must be the holy defiance of my love. And my love is all the greater and more blessed, the less my poor spirit understands of You.

God of my life, Incomprehensible, be my life. God of my faith, who lead me into Your darkness—God of my love, who turn Your darkness into the sweet light of my life, be now the God of my hope, so that You will one day be the God of my life, the life of eternal love.

Faith

AMONG all the quests of our time, none has been more assiduous
than the one for identity. Our novels throb with it, our plays find
their dramatic tension in it. In search of identity—their own and
that of the race—painters and sculptors have elaborated a marvelously complex set of signs and symbols, obscure in their private languages, but clear at least in this, that they, like almost everybody
else, are looking for their identity.

In this, Catholics are no different from other people. They hunt
the same object with the same diligence. They have no more certainty of all truth than anybody else. But they are certain of the existence of truth, however much or however little of it they may discover, and they have a corollary conviction that each truth extends
and confirms some other truth immediately, and all other truth ultimately. This is the defining condition of their faith. With it, they
can move with comparative ease into the startling contradictions
and depressing conflicts of the modern world. With it, they can take
joy in a time more productive of mysteries, perhaps, than any other
in recorded history, the great mysteries constantly being turned up
by the scientists and artists, psychologists, anthropologists, and philosophers of our time.

Faith is the integrating virtue. It gives coherence to a life, and
does so no matter how dissolute the life or how destitute of the
things we have come to think of as requirements for civilized living.
Faith is its own necessity, for within its integrating motions a man
may find his own identity and something of the identity of the universe of which he is a part—and not, as the Christian faith keeps re-
minding him, so small a part at that. Some indication of his part and
the world's may be gathered from the approaches to faith in the fol-

lowing section. The perspectives are philosophical, theological, liturgical; they are scientific, they are psychological. And they are full of the excitement of the most seminal of subjects, the most rewarding of subjects, the faith that brings man so close to himself, and in himself to his maker.

In these pieces, one sees reason not so much reconciled with faith as accepted with it, accepted as its natural and normal counterpart, as Dom Illtyd Trethowan shows. With such a reasonable faith, one can look far inside oneself to make oneself capable of playing one's part and more. Jean Mouroux says it well: "The spirit . . . does not simply deepen from within, he interiorizes in order to universalize. He makes the person a perfect member so that he may be a true witness."

True witness involves a deepening of one's contemplative faculties, as much as it does a constantly expanding participation in the liturgy. Thus one examines ideas good and bad, simple and difficult, lucid and obscure, as Mark Pontifex and Hans Urs von Balthasar do, to find, perhaps, as the last-named does, that even "the frightening phenomenon of modern atheism may, among other things, be a forcible measure of Providence to bring back mankind, and especially Christendom, to a more adequate idea of God." Thus one moves, in a less paradoxical thrust, through each penetration of liturgical structure to the source of the liturgy, Scripture, and each time finds the liturgy incomparably enriched by the move.

The motion of the mind here is not always in a neat and orderly fashion. One can approach faith systematically, but faith is larger than systems; it subsumes systems; and it is not ill at ease with any of the very different systems of thought in which it is deeply involved. It faces the challenge of the space age with equanimity, or rather, it is itself challenging, if we make it so, if our temperament is steady in faith.

Steadiness in the Christian tradition is not stoicism. We go on being hurt, and worse, we go on hurting others. But we see some purpose in the pain. That is the healing strength of Christ, not to remove difficulties like a surgeon or a discoverer of wonder drugs, valuable as those contributions are, but to find a place for them in the economy of salvation, where ultimately we all—no matter what we think—seek our identity and find it.

REASON AND FAITH

DOM ILLTYD TRETHOWAN

PEOPLE sometimes talk about faith as though it were something which one contracted, like a disease, as a result of being specially exposed to it: accidents of training and temperament, on this view, account for the fact that some people have faith and others haven't. Without going to this length, an educated man nowadays will nevertheless commonly regard faith as something which can't be explained—rather like having a flair for a particular form of art or sport, but probably caused by "subjective" factors, by which it is not meant necessarily that faith is humbug but rather that it can't be usefully discussed. The first thing, then, that has to be made clear is that traditional Christian teaching is entirely opposed to the notion that there is a special faculty for faith, the notion, in other words, that it is not a matter for those powers of intellect which make man what he is. To have faith is to know the ultimate truth and to pursue it. It is supremely an intellectual affair, but this must not be allowed to suggest anything less than an activity of the whole person. We have touched already on the grievous effects of trying to safeguard religion by locking it up against reason. By pretending to elevate it, we simply make it meaningless. By cutting it off from the mind and connecting it solely with the will and the emotions, we produce a nonsensical state of affairs which can be ended only by the abolition of religion or by starting all over again. Theology may be mysterious, but it must always make sense.

On the other hand there is the danger of talking about faith as though it meant simply the acceptance of an authority on ordinary logical and historical grounds. Thus it might seem that you have only to examine the well-known proofs of the Christian Church's mission, the Resurrection of Christ and the rest of it, and you will be convinced that anything which she tells you must be true. You may not be able to see that there is any reason for asserting there are three Persons in one God apart from the fact that the Church has told you so; but that is a cogent reason for believing it. It is

pretty baffling, no doubt, but if you examine the words in which
the doctrine is enshrined you find that it avoids contradiction. There
you are, then, you have only to keep your head and you can't get
it wrong. Everything follows inevitably if you don't lose the thread.
Faith is also somehow or other God's supernatural gift, but that
is all right, our over-zealous mentor might hastily add; we couldn't
know anything much about that, and at present, anyway, you
needn't worry about it. No doubt God gives people all sorts of
extra help to bring them into the Church, but we can't be expected
to know how they work. You just want to be hard-headed and
honest, and it will be all quite simple.

But it isn't as simple as that. "Blessed art thou, Simon Bar-Jona,
for flesh and blood have not revealed it to thee, but my Father." It
is the teaching of traditional theology that an act of faith is not
only reasonable and a matter of certainty, but also something of
which the natural reason is, apart from grace, altogether incapable;
moreover it is a *free* act, a matter of choice. How are we to reconcile all these apparently conflicting requirements? Before we make
any attempt to do so we must face the further complexity that the
apologetic arguments do not work out in actual fact as smoothly
as was suggested. Most people will admit that there is a great mass
of evidence which fits in with the supposition that a revelation from
God actually occurred in Palestine nearly two thousand years ago,
and even perhaps that this evidence is not easy to reconcile with
any other proposed explanation. But can we really contend that,
if they follow up the suspicion thus engendered (as they would
seem morally bound to do, if they can), they will in normal circumstances obtain *absolute* conviction, unless they draw back in the
course of the enquiry or deliberately turn their backs on what stares
them in the face at the end of it? Can we really contend that a
purely scientific enquiry will in normal circumstances give them a
certainty? (And could we call it a "free" certainty?) We might
allow that somebody who was in a particularly favorable position
for appreciating the real strength of the evidence might be absolutely convinced by it. But we should have to allow also that there
have been people, by no means unintelligent or ill-informed and
apparently with the best will in the world, who have reached the
stage of seeing no hole in the evidence without being convinced

that no hole might appear at some subsequent date. (And for absolute certainty, we have argued earlier, we need to know that nothing could shake our conviction.) Newman, before his conversion to Catholicism, was for long in a state in which he could see no way to avoid it, but this did not mean that he could see his way to move.

There are several accounts of faith which attempt to meet these difficulties, and I shall begin with that which seems to be the most popular. It acknowledges that the apologetic evidence cannot be expected to provide us with more than a "moral" certainty. But it maintains that such a certainty is sufficient. It has not the inescapable character of a mathematical certainty, but it is more than a mere probability. Thus we are not asked to take a leap in the dark when we make an act of faith. Nevertheless in making the act we shall obtain "theological certitude," which is profounder than any logical or psychological one. A man's logical reasons for belief may be rather wobbly. "Psychological certitude," that is, a state of *feeling* in the matter, may be what you please. But "theological certitude" is what really puts us on the right lines and keeps us there. And, if we are to have "theological certitude," we must use our *wills*. The moral certainty which the arguments give us is good enough to go on if we try.

That represents the best I can do to set out a point of view which will be familiar to some readers and can be easily discovered in apologetics books by others who are interested. It seems rather obvious that it is unsatisfactory. One thing against it is that the faithful in so many cases seem to have no grounds for their faith which could be formulated logically at all. It might be replied that this is true of those who are baptized in infancy—they have "theological certitude" and so need no apologetic arguments—but is not true of converts. Yet it seems extremely doubtful whether we could claim that all converts have a "moral certainty" that revelation has occurred based on these arguments. Moreover, if "theological certitude" is required in order that a man shall really "have the faith," the apologetic arguments, although necessary no doubt in most cases to *lead* a man to faith, seem unnecessary as the explanation (or part of the explanation) of his eventual absolute conviction. In any case the whole attitude towards the question of certainty shown by this popular account of faith is, if our earlier conclusions are correct, unacceptable. "Moral certainty" would seem to fall short of absolute conviction, but yet to refer to something more than a high probability. There is an appeal to the will which may be taken to mean that conviction can be gained by the use of this faculty in some separation from the use of the intellect. And the reference to "theological certitude" as something which appears to be beyond the reach of psychological experience makes one wonder what "conviction" really means in this account.

Let us consider these difficulties in order. It is obviously true that we can have certainties which are not mathematical certainties. And it is also true that there are certainties which cannot be obtained without good will—we can decide to break off an enquiry when we begin to dislike the look of things, and we can become incapable of seeing certain things through the viciousness of our habits. But we can reach conclusions, although they are of a sort to be threatened by these hazards, with absolute certainty. I can be absolutely certain that it is my duty to help X. If this were what "moral certainty" means in this context it would be acceptable enough, but it would make the appeal to "theological certitude" unnecessary. We shall be obliged to conclude that it means something else.

For the moment, however, it will be useful to notice that we have been brought up against the notion of a "free certainty." It should not refer, as the view which we are criticizing suggests that it refers, to evidence which is capable of producing assent only if we go to meet it in some way, evidence which we are *entitled* to regard as satisfactory but which we need not so regard, for this is not a state of affairs which proves to make sense. It should refer to evidence of a sort which we are specially tempted to avoid, but which, when seen, is simply evidence—that is, it produces assent when we see it, and this assent is not refusable at the time of our seeing it. Either there is evidence for the truth of something—the mass of facts at my disposal, for example, to persuade me that Moscow exists although I have never been there. Or there is evidence which makes me only more or less suspicious of the existence of something—say, the existence of telepathy—in which case the evidence consists of various experiences of mine and reports of other people's; it makes me certain of some things, and doubtful about whether other things may not be lying behind these. Evidence, in fact, gives me, when I see it, some direct experience which I cannot avoid, and in some cases shows me that consequences follow which are equally unavoidable. I cannot make myself see these consequences except by looking at the evidence. I cannot prevent myself from seeing them when I am looking at it. Freedom is not to the point at the moment of vision, although it may be all-important in preventing that moment from arriving, or in favoring its arrival, and in banishing it from the memory if it proves embarrassing.

What, then, is this popular account of faith suggesting? We seem forced to conclude that it does after all recommend a leap, not into absolute darkness, but into something less than the pure luminosity of *evidence*. It seems to say to one: "Don't give way to foolish scruples. You can see that everything points in one direction. It would be unreasonable to expect the sort of certainty about this that you get in mathematics. So come along, now—make an act of faith, and you will feel a lot better, or at least you will *be* a lot better. And you will realize somehow more and more, as time goes on, that you've done the right thing." But isn't it saying in effect: "Open your mouth and shut your eyes"? And are we entitled to encourage people to shut their eyes like this, even in a good cause? In practice it may work out all right. For in practice, at this stage of the proceedings, there may well be evidence which is causing a perfectly genuine assent, a conviction that the thing is true. Yet it is not to be explained by mere logical arguments or historical facts, but by the direct action of God the Revealer on the human soul. That is, the proposal, fantastic as it may seem at first, which I shall develop at a later stage, when it will come (I hope) to seem plausible.

But we have still to go on with our examination of the difficulties in the popular theory. According to it, in order to obtain "theological certitude" we are entitled, it would appear, to make a *decision* on evidence which is not strictly evidence *of* revelation, but evidence which only points, however strongly, in that direction. There is the *possibility* that we might turn out to be wrong, but this gap is bridged by the *will*. It is not put like that, but I fail to see how such a conclusion is to be avoided. If it were merely a question of urging a man to take the sensible course of adopting the Christian religion as true on the ground that there was so much in favor of it and so little (relatively) against it, then there could be no cause of complaint from the philosopher's point of view. But it would not be consistent with what traditional Christians believe about faith. The act of faith which is to be made is not merely a pledging to a certain form of conduct but an act of unqualified acceptance. Although the reasons on which the act of faith is based are, on the popular theory, capable of producing only a "moral certainty," yet the act of faith itself is quite unhesitating. And this change in the situation is ascribed to the will and to the "theological certitude" which (according to some versions, at least, of the theory) enables the will to do its part if it is suitably disposed; at any rate the certitude is present (on any version of the theory) when the act is once accomplished. And we are faced with the insuperable difficulties that the will cannot move toward an object which the intellect has not presented to it, and that a certitude which is not the result of any such presentation is meaningless to a philosopher. If the theologian could explain how a will can be fixed except by some object intelligently loved, it would be another story. But this hardly seems likely.

At this point we may be told that faith is necessarily a paradoxical affair. It is the "evidence of things not seen." But this does not mean that faith both sees and does not see the same thing at the same time. It means that faith in revelation commits us to belief in mysteries, and these we do not see; but we must see the evidence that revelation has occurred, that there exists an authority which we can absolutely trust. And if the apologetic arguments do not provide us with the sort of evidence that we require, if they do not take us the whole way, then we must ask whether there can be some other form of evidence.

But first we must take a rapid glance at two other accounts of faith. One appeals to "human faith" and points out that we believe a witness because he is who he is, because we trust him apart from the intrinsic probability of what he tells us and apart from all external evidence that what he tells us is true. I refer to Cardinal Billot's "faith of simple authority," which has been described by supporters as likely to become a common opinion of theologians.

It is an attempt to show how faith can do without evidence. But it is obvious that if we "pin our faith" to anybody without evidence of his reliability we are behaving in an unjustifiable manner. Moreover there can be no question of distinguishing, as Billot seeks to do, between the authority of God and his infallibility. If the authority of God is the motive of our faith, as Billot maintains, then our acceptance of what he tells us follows logically from the fact that we know that he is speaking to us, because we also know that he is infallible. Billot sought to avoid this conclusion by appealing to "the faith of simple authority," for he wished to find a function for faith's supernatural character, and was anxious in this interest to avoid a purely logical process.

The other theory I shall call the theory of "supernatural signs," and I shall suggest that it takes us at least some distance towards the solution. It can be briefly stated as follows: The Christian Church is herself God's chief witness; we find him in her. In coming in contact with the Church we come in contact with the answer to our most deep-seated desires. We discover the true end of our being. We find God in his action on his Church, and he proves to us that she is his Church by his presence in her.

This I believe to be true, but it is, in this form, too vague to be satisfactory, and capable of explanation on very diverse lines. For example, we might take it to imply a logical argument of the following kind: Here is an institution which cannot be accounted for unless the claims which it makes about its origin are true. But this is simply an inference based upon ordinary facts of observation, and so there is nothing supernatural about it. The certainty of faith is, by general admission, supernatural—that is, it results from an intervention on God's part, enabling us to see what we could not otherwise see. Moreover such a logical inference would be beyond the capacity of large masses of people, at any rate in a form which would make the conclusion *certain;* and faith must be obtainable by all men of good will, whether they are learned or not, gifted with logical powers or not. And we cannot satisfactorily interpret the theory to mean that faith gives us logical or historical powers which we should not have without it. In other words, it is of no use to suggest that, on the general principle of grace's raising nature, faith enables reason here to appreciate an argument which otherwise would not have been appreciated.

It is surely not the function of faith simply to improve our natural processes in their own mode of working, although this may well be a by-product of faith's function. Faith would be generally understood, I think, as introducing into the situation some wholly novel feature. We cannot therefore suppose that it merely remedies nature, supplies nature's deficiencies, and that is all that it would prove to do if it merely enables us to bring to a point our apologetic arguments. For natural reason must be capable in itself, apart from accidental circumstances, of seeing an argument; if grace enables it to do so, it must be by remedying the effects of original sin, not directly as the result of an elevating process. It seems that the result of an elevating process must be the ability to see a fresh object, an object of a more elevated kind. Clearly we cannot say that faith supplies reason with unobserved facts of the ordinary observable kind. And if it does not make sense to confine its effects to the will and we are obliged to speak in the first place of its effects on the intellect, must not the object which it presents to the intellect be an object which is itself supernatural? What can this be but God himself?

It looks, then, as though, to make this theory work, we must speak more plainly than its exponents are accustomed to speak and maintain that we actually encounter in the Church God's infallible authority itself, that is, God himself. Nothing less than this, it seems, will provide us with an object capable of meeting the claims of *faith's* certainty. In no other way can we obtain an *absolute* certainty, which is genuinely *supernatural,* dependent on *moral* conditions, and in full harmony with our *rational* conclusions. But a good many difficulties have to be faced before the reader can be asked to accept that conclusion.

The chief difficulty, obviously, is to make out that such a knowledge of God exists or is even possible, for at first sight the claim will seem gratuitous. But let us begin at the easier end and consider the part played, according to this view, by the apologetic arguments. It should not be thought that to hold this view is to depreciate their force. It is perfectly compatible with this view to say that the historical facts available and the arguments which can be founded thereon constitute in themselves a case for the existence of revelation which is as strong as the case which I can make out for believing in the existence of Moscow. But a certainty about revelation gained in this way would not be the certainty of *faith,* which has other requirements. The apologetic arguments do not provide the motives of faith's certainty. What we must mean by saying that faith is reasonable, therefore, is that the apologetic arguments *lead* to faith, prepare the ground for it, set the mind working in the right direction, bring it to bear on that field in which the truth will shine out.

Theories of faith are sometimes divided into those which introduce the apologetic arguments into the motive of faith itself and those which allow the arguments no part in it. The theory of the "supernatural sign" might be interpreted to be of the first kind, to mean that the arguments add up to produce a certain weight and that a "supernatural help" then tips the scale. The view now offered to the reader takes the second line. But it considers the apologetic arguments, nevertheless, as closely bound up with the object of faith itself, for it is *in the Church* that God is found and the Church herself is the supreme argument. The Church first points us to God by arousing our interest in what we may call a purely human way (the influence of grace may be present in fact at all stages of such a process, but for purposes of exposition we may leave that on one side). We are puzzled by the Church, forced to ask questions. And then there comes a point at which the Church's life strikes us as posssesing a transcendent value; we find ourselves in the presence of something which appeals to us with irresistible force. What has happened? If I am right, the answer must be simply that we have encountered *God,* who now points to the Church as being *his.* In this way we might say that the apologetic arguments—or anyway the chief of them—always occupy the center of the stage. A man may indeed very naturally suppose that his conviction is due simply to the logical weight of these arguments, for our awareness of God is in terms of them—God's guarantee, in other words, bears upon the Church, the focus of these arguments, and we are aware of him precisely as acting in this way. We are aware of him without explicitly recognizing him. And when we analyze the situation we may find ourselves saying, "Yes, in a way, of course, I knew that all the time."

If this is so, if the awareness in question has this inexplicit character, it becomes easier to understand why others, realizing that their conviction is not to be satisfactorily explained in terms of the apologetic arguments, adopt the language of will or appeal to some activity below the conscious level, especially when the conviction takes the form of a sort of compulsion, an inability to do other than believe (an obsession, one might say, if the word had no sinister significance) for which there seems no accounting. And traditional language encourages them in this course. Take, for example, the following proposition condemned by Pope Innocent XI; "the will cannot bring it about that the assent of faith should be firmer in itself than the weight of the reasons urging assent would warrant." Pope Innocent is laying it down that the firmness of faith is not measured by the weight of the rational arguments. He might seem to be saying that the rational arguments take us part of the way and that the will must then intervene to produce faith's absolute firmness, but there is no need to take the reference to will as excluding the intellect. We are entitled to claim that the will must be following the intellect here, as on all other occasions, and that there must be some fresh evidence presented to the intellect to cause this activity of the will. Unfortunately theologians have used this language of will in a way which cannot be so benignly interpreted, claiming that the will can be given firmness to assent to an authority which is not *seen* to be an authority. That faith involves acceptance of authority is not in question; but faith's certainty is nonsensical if the authority is not *known* to be such. Believing is not seeing, but it must be based on seeing.

Part of the trouble is a failure to realize that the activities of the mind are not exclusively of a discursive character but, on the contrary, are fundamentally intuitive in the world's literal sense of "beholding." To speak of the "intellectual side" of faith would mean for most people the *working out* of arguments and *assessing* of evidences. Any operation of a profounder kind is thought to be outside the province of intellect, and so some other psychological factor has to be invoked with the disastrous result of making faith seem a matter either of the emotions or of self-deception. An appeal to an unconscious factor is, if possible, even more disastrous because a certainty of which the subject is not aware seems quite meaningless. Those who appeal to this sort of "theological certitude" are rightly anxious to avoid identifying faith with a transient emotion; but by appealing to a factor beyond the conscious level they offer a cure which is worse than the disease. To say that is not to say that the action of grace is always perceived; the virtue of faith may be present before it affects the consciousness, as the theologians tell us in the case of baptized infants, and it may have other subconscious workings. But we cannot say that it causes *certainty* by producing a firmness of assent, *bypassing* the intellect. This would be mere mumbo-jumbo, and to say at this point that the assent is intellectually justified by the apologetic arguments is to move from one horn of a dilemma to the other. Certainty is not an emotional experience, but we cannot say that it is not an experience at all. We must say that it is an *intellectual* experience, and the full import of our earlier analyses of certainty may now become apparent.

Thus we return to the themes adumbrated in the first chapter. There is a knowledge of God, available to all men, which is a gift, not to our natural powers—*some* (natural) knowledge of God, we have maintained, must come to everybody at some time—but a further gift, conditioned only by our willingness to receive it. This is the gift of faith, a *supernatural* knowledge. And we can now see more plainly what "supernatural" means. Commonly it is used to mean "spiritual" as opposed to "material," a fatal opposition which has the effect of excluding what is "material" from the sphere of religion. It ought to refer to the action of God upon our whole nature, raising it to a union with him which is begun in this life and consummated in the next. As we have seen already, such a union cannot be entered upon save with the consent of the creature. It is only when we have said "yes" to God's summons that we can receive his message, his Word, the Word who is, with the Father and the Holy Spirit, one God for ever and ever. This is the end for which we have been created.

The "supernatural end," therefore, must not be thought of as though it were something "stuck on" to human life, an extraneous appendage foreign to our nature. It is that to which our nature is in

fact *ordered*. It is an end which we cannot reach by our purely
natural resources, because these give us a knowledge of God only as
a dark background to our lives, not as the Father of lights. This
natural knowledge, it has been proposed, is in fact God's summons
to us to turn towards him, so that he may bring us into that personal
relationship with him in which is our true destiny. (The *rôle* of the
will, of the dispositions, as a condition for receiving the gift of faith
is thus vital; but the gift itself must be a gift to the intellect and,
through it, to the will.)

   "But do you really mean to say," somebody will object, "that a
man who accepts God's summons in this way will find himself a
member of the Christian Church, that he will discover God in this
Church? For that is how you were describing faith just now. Or are
you suggesting that there are two kinds of faith, an ecclesiastical
kind and a non-ecclesiastical kind?" The answer must be, although
it may seem at first merely evasive, that in a sense there are these
two kinds of faith, although all grace comes from Christ in his
Church. There may be faith although the Church is not revealed
as the depositary of God's word. It is true that this must be regarded
as an anomalous state of affairs. But the conclusion is a necessary
one and does not involve us in any inconsistency. Clearly we must
say that faith is always given to those who "do what is in them" and
there seems no reason for supposing that God delays the gift when
the subject is properly disposed for receiving it, that is, when his
intelligence is sufficiently developed and he has *turned* to God. If he
happens to be ignorant of the Church's claims, or blind to them
through no fault of his own, by reason (for example) of an inherited prejudice, we cannot expect a psychological miracle; his
union with God will be due to the Church, grace will flow from her,
but he will not recognize her as the source of it. His mind will not
be directed upon the Church so as to find God's action in her.
Where, then, does he find God acting? In the case of those who
are *ignorant* of Christianity, we must say that this supernatural
knowledge of God is in terms of his action on their own souls.

   This brings out clearly the subsidiary character of rational
demonstrations in the acquisition of "saving" faith, faith which is
necessary for salvation. What we might call the "official" procedure
is for the Church herself to be the medium in which God's word

is communicated to us. But it is God's word which gives us the guarantee that the Church is his. And his word is not bound, as St. Paul had occasion to remark. It is the bringing of our intellects into captivity to him and to his purposes for us. We cannot pretend to know how or when he communicates it to those who remain inculpably "outside the Church." It has been sometimes supposed that they receive it at the hour of death and even that they acknowledge the Church's claims at that time. All we know is that they cannot be lost to the Church, since they cannot be lost to Christ, save by their deliberate refusal to follow their consciences.

It will have become clear through these further analyses that the certainty of faith may be not only misconceived but even prevented from making its appearance by a "rationalistic" approach to the subject. A man may ask himself whether any evidence could come to light which would affect his persuasion that Christ rose from the dead. "How can I be *certain* of this?" he may say. And by seeking to pile up historical arguments he may even prevent himself from becoming certain on the false supposition that this case is on all fours with a certainty of the existence of Moscow. But if he realizes that his conviction is being brought about by something more than the weight of historical evidences, he will attend more and more to this other factor and allow it to work in him unhindered. In other words, there comes a point in the process of conversion when what matters is not learning or thinking, but praying.

Such a conclusion is a commonplace, but it is usually interpreted in an anti-intellectualist sense; that is, it is usually taken to mean that some kind of purely emotional assurance is required, because prayer itself is supposed to be essentially an emotional affair. It should be obvious that nothing of that kind is intended here, and it follows from all that has been said so far that prayer must be considered as essentially an affair of the intellect, not of the *discursive* rational faculty, but of the intellective soul precisely as intellective, or what writers on this subject call the "apex" or "fine point" of the soul. This is a subject on which something further must be said when this discussion of faith has been concluded. But some further insistence on the nature of this supernatural knowledge is still necessary.

The result which may be expected from prayer is not one which will normally be experienced *during* prayer. The business of prayer, at least for our present purposes (if not for all purposes), is to place the mind and the will in readiness for God's action upon it. This action takes place, normally, in so *smooth* a fashion (I can think of no other phrase to describe it than the Vulgate's *suaviter disponens*) that it is only in looking back over a period of time that we can realize clearly that something has in fact occurred. We find perhaps (for it would be absurd to legislate in detail for all cases) that the thought of God has become habitual; not that it is particularly appetizing or clear but that one cannot get rid of it in spite of its obscurity. And we find perhaps that the thought of God cannot be dissociated from Christianity, from the Christian Church. Or it may be simply that the case for Christianity proves one day to have become unanswerable—but not for any reason which we could assign. We could go on producing reasons, perhaps, indefinitely; but however strong they are they would never add up to *express* the attitude of mind which we now find to be ours. We now have a *point of view,* an eminently reasonable one, but one which cannot be communicated as you can communicate a technique. Prayer has produced this result, although we might not be aware that we have been praying. This may seem like a mere juggling with words. Prayer means one thing, I may be told, and thinking things out another. All I can say in answer is that prayer is to my mind a more pervasive thing than is commonly supposed. All knowledge of God, where good will is present, must partake of the nature of prayer. The pervasive character of our knowledge of God has been noticed at earlier stages of our enquiry; now that we are reaching a profounder level it may be easier to realize what we have been discussing. In our end is our beginning.

A corollary to this accout of faith's certainty must be appended here. If it is possible to be sidetracked in the approach to faith by supposing that it is all a matter of logical entailments, it is equally possible for the faithful (at a certain point in their mental development) to be under the impression that they have lost their faith, either because they find themselves unable to answer arguments which seem to tell against it, or because the doctrines of faith no longer strike them as helpful or even intelligible. They should indeed be encouraged to discover the answers. But it is at least equally important that they should be encouraged to discover—for the first time, perhaps—the presence within them of God's confirming word.[1]

So far in this chapter we have been considering the *first* act of faith. It would be a pity to end it without saying something about the developments to which it is meant to lead. For this supernatural knowledge of God is not merely a means of obtaining certainty that the doctrines of Christianity are true. It is the beginning of eternal life; it introduces us already in some sort into the life of God himself by uniting us with Christ, incorporating us into him, to use the traditional metaphor. (Here the theologian would remark that this is the effect of baptism; but baptism gives us the "virtue of faith," and it is by this, with the charity which is its flower, that we are enabled to know Christ and to love him.) This life is meant to grow. Indeed it is the whole purpose of the Church's ordinances and organization that it should grow. It is precisely this growth in which God's glorification consists. The whole sacramental system, the whole hierarchical structure, the whole code of discipline, the giving of revelation itself—all are ordered to that building up of the Church which consists in the drawing together of all its members into the unity of Christ. It cannot be too often repeated that Christianity is not just a moralism but a mysticism. The pouring out of the Spirit upon the Christian is to lead to his transformation; he is to have the "mind of Christ."

The gift of the Spirit is the worship of God. We are empowered to approach him more and more closely. This is the life of prayer. Faith, then, is the root from which all spiritual development is derived, and this development consists essentially in the deepening of our knowledge of God. This has a strange ring about it, because we are accustomed to say that religion is essentially an affair of charity. But the two statements are not inconsistent. We have already described charity as the flower of faith; knowledge which is not merely factual information but *union* is inseparable from love, but love must always be based on knowledge. And here once more we come up against the anti-intellectualist language which we had to notice in connection with faith's certainty. As there, so also here, it is usual to put all the emphasis upon the *will*. Prayer is not a vision of God, we are so often told, but a strirring up of the will, a kindling of the affections. No, it is not a vision of God, but it is an affair of the intellect; there is a growing awareness of God's action which, so far from being a process of enlightenment in any ordinary sense of that word, may rather require us to use the language of darkness if we are to attempt a description of it. The "feeling of God's absence" normally becomes intensified. But, if we are to believe St. John of the Cross, this is the inevitable effect upon us, at first, of God's approach. It is a "darkness visible," a "ray of darkness." And it is a regular stage in the soul's development, not just a matter of the cloister, but a part of common experience unrecognized for what it is owing to our unfortunate tendency to regard the "spiritual life" as a speciality.

As before, the emphasis upon the language of will seems due to a narrow interpretation of "intellectualism." That word has come, in fact, to refer simply to a narrowness. The disadvantage of this is that we have no word in regular use to refer to those operations of the soul which are deeper than discursive reasonings, for we reserve the word "intuition" for the vision of God in heaven. In their eagerness to avoid suggesting that prayer is either a matter of reasoning or an "intuition" of God, writers about prayer seize upon the will as the only faculty which, in practice, will meet their requirements. But it is surely obvious, when we analyze the situation, that what they are really doing is to point to the distinction between learning and wisdom. The union with God which is the *raison d'être* of prayer is a presence of God to the soul's "center," that is, to the intellective soul itself, and not just to one of its faculties.

Thus there is continuity between the first act of faith and the highest experiences of the mystics, and the two extremes of the process throw light on each other. St. Teresa's account of the "Interior Castle" will come to seem less remote from the life of the ordinary Christian if we can find the germ of the mystical marriage in the bestowal of faith itself. And that the first act of faith should involve a supernatural awareness of God, so obscure as to be easily mistaken for something else, will seem less strange when we realize that such an awareness undoubtedly exists, in

an unmistakable form, in the lives of the great contemplatives,
however confused their own psychological *theory* may be.

The great difficulty in this matter for the modern reader is the
widespread assumption that a "contemplative" is a freak, a peculiar
person, someone who is the subject of a quite special dispensation
which is of no relevance to the problems of the less favored. If
in fact the number of those who practice contemplative prayer is
relatively small—and it is probably much larger than external signs
would suggest—this is due, very largely, to the existence of this
prejudice, which has been encouraged by an ignorance of the traditional teaching prevalent even among professional theologians. In
our time there has been, at least among the theologians, a most significant change of attitude as a result of a fresh examination of
doctrinal sources. George Herbert had the right attitude. Although
he described prayer, at the end of his poem with that title, as

> Church-bells beyond the starres heard, the soul's blood,
> The land of spices, something understood,

he has also described it in preceding lines as

> The soul in paraphrase, heart in pilgrimage

and

> Heaven in ordinarie, man well drest.

There is nothing extravagant about this. There is no question of
levitations, corporeal visions or spectacular phenomena of any
kind. It is simply the conclusion which was implicit in our first
analysis of certainty. If metaphysics is essentially religious, religion is essentially metaphysical. To write a book on Christian philosophy and not to make prayer its ultimate concern would be the
height of absurdity, for (again in the words of Herbert's poem) it
is nothing less than

> God's breath in man returning to his birth,

and all wisdom is contained in it.

But prayer is not fully itself if it remain unfertilized by an explicit knowledge of the Christian truths, by meditation on and participation in the Christian mysteries, just as these mysteries cannot be fruitfully apprehended without prayer. This brings us to a concluding consideration about supernatural knowledge: the "light of faith," in which we are brought into our mysterious union with God, gives us the true bearing of those formularies in which the Christian mysteries are expressed. When, for example, we are told that there are three Persons in one God we must not attach a merely human sense to these words; an *analogy* is being proposed to us, and we must keep in view the object of faith, God supernaturally known, if we are to gain some understanding of it. But to pursue that subject, to show how theology is to be *understood,* would need another book.

NOTES

1. The book which I should like to recommend on the subject of faith's certainty is Fr. Coventry's *Faith Seeks Understanding* (Sheed and Ward).

THE SOURCES, HEART, AND WORLD OF FAITH

JEAN MOUROUX

CHRISTIAN Faith is specified in its entirety by Christ; it is participation in the life of a person,[1] in the mystery of his death and resurrection; thanks to this mediation it is a trinitarian faith, and a sharing in the life of the Three Persons. It could not be otherwise, since its object is Christ in whom we find the Three Persons; its source is the grace of Christ, in whom the "Author of Beatitude," the Triune God, gives and reveals himself. We can now affirm in a much deeper sense that the grace of faith is a personal grace. God is indeed the object, end and witness of faith; this formula is correct. But we now see it to mean that the object, the end and the witness of faith is God, Father, Son and Holy Spirit, revealed in Christ. Faith, then, objectively considered, is the call of the One God in Three Persons, through Christ, to a human person.[2]

So it is with faith—it is a simple act, because it is the gift of the whole man.[3] Analysis will show therein the presence of will, of thought and spiritual feelings, but all this is within the unity of one vital act,[4] the act of a person who unites himself with another person. Since the object of faith is not on the one hand truth, and on the other happiness, but a person who is both truth and happiness, the human being does not *first* have to grasp truth and then wait to be drawn to this happiness; he has simply to unite himself in one single movement to the Adorable Person who will beatify him.[5] Consequently, in the act of faith, love must penetrate and direct knowledge.

We cannot come into real contact with a person by the use of our critical faculty, by the sort of reasoning that we use to resolve problems; still less can we reach him by acts proceeding from blind impulse or animal appetite. A person is apprehended in a *spiritual contact* and by a *phenomenon of communion*. The degree of apprehension may vary enormously, and this holds good too of faith itself, whether it be unformed faith or faith informed by charity. But if the persons meet each other then there will always be this phenomenon of communion; and, in the case of living faith, the whole spiritual being throws itself open to welcome the God who calls it. In this way we can see how it is that love is the gateway to faith. We can see above all that love and knowledge are *inseparable* in this act, because both are essential activities of the human person, and because in this case the human person is giving himself to his God. In other words, it is the human being as a unity which is given, for it is neither the will nor the intellect which exists but the man, and it is this wholeness which is at work in faith, finding fulfilment in giving itself, or else mutilation in refusing to make this gift.[6]

The act of faith is obscure, firstly because it is self-revelation by one person to another, and this is always obscure to the discursive reason. The task of the latter is to understand by establishing relations and constructing its object. In so doing it works in the light, even though it may not be completely clear to itself, because it relies upon evidence which it cannot analyze, and upon principles which it cannot build up itself.[7] But obscurity to the reason is characteristic of all forms of concrete knowledge, and especially when it is a question of knowledge of persons.

The knowledge of a spiritual person is not discursive; consciousness cannot be constructed from the outside; a person does not come upon himself at the end of a series of abstract relations. The discursive function of the intellect can certainly prepare for, but cannot accomplish this grasping of a concrete existence. It cannot bring about this phenomenon of interpretation *en bloc* which is the discovery of a person similar to the "self," still less can it enter into the privacy of this spiritual person who is both unique and "social."[8]

Even supposing that the "spiritual core" of a being could reveal itself to another as Scheler wished, this would still be on a non-discursive level;[9] the existence and value of the person escape this function of the intellect—they are "obscure" to it. Further we must recognize that this perception is not the luminous penetration of an inner reality. It is much more a global grasping of a spiritual existence, a sort of *contact* and *coincidence* with the being discovered—both of them susceptible of an indefinite investigation, but in part opaque and resistant to reason.[10] It is here that the act of faith takes its place, and consequently it belongs to a sphere which is obscure and baffling to pure reason; the universe of persons is one which love alone can truly penetrate.

Thus, in the process which leads to faith and which sustains faith, the essential is this *personal quest,* this orientation of a person towards a good which can only be another person, this desire for a beatifying truth which can only be a person in whom light and love shine forth. If the soul comes gradually to interpret these signs and understand the words, if it assents more and more fully to the truths proposed, this is because through these signs, these words and these truths, it seeks and it discovers a person who calls it and to whom it replies.[11]

We *seek* a person; that is what accounts for our perception of credibility; we *meet* with a person—that explains the certainty of faith. St. Thomas gives us the principle: "Everyone who believes assents to someone's words; and thus, in any form of belief, it seems that it is *the person to whose words the assent is given,* who is of principal importance and, as it were, the end; while the individual truths through which one assents to that person are secondary."[12]

The act of faith is not only a personal act, but also a *personalizing* one. It is not an irrational complex, rooted in base impulses to personal happiness and capable of renouncing the hard lights of reason in order to indulge itself. It has its origin in an enlightened, purified and liberated spiritual appetite, and it completes the spiritual person by purifying it and by uniting it to the personal God. The transition from unbelief to faith demands a renunciation, and very often a renunciation which would make even the most courageous hesitate. What a sacrifice of our precious autonomy there is in this detachment from self, in this opening of the most inviolable "self" to Another! What an effort of spiritual purification, of humility and also of courage is needed to maintain this faith which is possessed as a living thing. This is not the place in which to consider this effort in detail, but we know well that it is a renewed and deepened gift of the self to the Infinite Being, and that it always requires lucidity, courage and fidelity. *The highest human values are immanent in the act of faith,* and this is why faith is a power of *personalization.* This spiritual effort demands an intelligible meaning and it has a rational value. An effort of personalization which is real, which brings about a life which is balanced, strong and fruitful, and which results in the slow creation of the person by himself, is something which excludes, in its origin and in its dynamism, whatever is irrational, imaginary and emotional, morbid and pathological.

Normally, Christian truth must make itself known through a Christian person; and we can describe the process by which it comes to be acknowledged. Personal commitment is the very foundation of faith, and is, in fact, faith itself. It tends by its own energy to become purer and more profound, and issues in a full faith, becoming daily more personal and richer in lucidity, reality and efficacy.

The Christian then experiences the power, the life and the joy which God gives him through faith,[13] and naturally, this shines forth in his life. That intense spiritual *élan* which is what self-giving is, raises the entire human material, informs, moulds, orientates and unifies it by its mighty form. It confers on it a significance which becomes more and more marked. Acts and thought, charity and fidelity, reveal a person wholly given to God, wholly animated by God; and thus the action and the presence of God is revealed through this person.[14] Moreover, since man is in a state of tension and desirous of communion, he will be stirred to the depths of his being when he comes into contact with another wholly given to God. His whole being will be affected by this living testimony; the organic side as well as the spiritual, the body stirred as well as the soul. The self-surrender which is seen and experienced will tend to evoke its like. The rôle of the witness is thus *to realize a presence and to transmit a call: non multa loquimus, sed vivimus.* In his own degree, he is ever sounding the "call of the Herb."[15]

The function of witness is so necessary to the Church that it constitutes a definite "state of life"; it is, too, of such moment to the believer that there is a special sacrament qualifying him for it—namely, Confirmation. In the strict sense of the word, Confirmation is the sacrament of witness; and because this demands the full commitment of the person, Confirmation is the sacrament of Christian manhood or of Christian personality.[16] The spirit is given to us to make us capable of playing our part: He does not inaugurate, he perfects the new man (as a rule); he does not simply deepen from within, he interiorizes in order to universalize.[17] He makes the person a *perfect member* so that he may be a *true witness.* Full Christian personality, in view of full Christian testimony—*this* is the meaning of Confirmation. Faith being an essential power of personalization, the ultimate ground of testimony, and the true means of Christian conquest—the victory which overcomes the world—for all these reasons the Spirit makes the Christian a person by perfecting his faith, and by adapting him to his task from within.[18] If the Christian is docile and co-operative, the Spirit will make of him a man who sees God, who touches God, and who is carried away to God—and therefore a perfect witness. This is why, when we say that Confirmation is the sacrament of witness, or of Christian personality, we add nothing to its definition but simply bring out the essential point in the statement, that it is the "sacrament of strength in faith: *Sacramentum fidei roboratae*" (St. Bonaventure). Strength of faith, strength of self-giving, strength of testimony—it is all one. Testimony is not primarily a question of *doing,* but of *being.*[19] It manifests the profound richness of the person who has given himself. It expresses the sovereign efficacy of a faith which ennobles and transforms the person, because it is itself ennobled and transformed by the Holy Spirit.

NOTES

1. Cf. the important commentary by Bonsirven, *Les Epitres de Saint Jean* (Beauchesne, coll. Verbum Salutis, 1936) on 1 John 2:5–6: "Every difficulty is resolved if we refer our relationships of indwelling in God to that relationship which is their type and principle, namely the indwelling or circumincession of the Persons in the Holy Trinity," etc.

2. (Culpable) unbelievers are "those who have not received the God and Father who called them by the Incarnate Son." St. Maximus the Confessor, *Quest. 60 ad Thal* (P.G., XC, 637 c.).

3. The unformed act of faith is not, despite appearances, simpler than the act of faith informed by charity. It is an act *imperfect in itself,* internally deficient, which can be understood only by comparison with the full and direct act of faith informed by charity. The analysis of this unformed faith is obviously useful since this unformed faith remains a wonderful grace given by God to a sinner. On the other hand, it is really only the analysis of an abnormal state of faith, a mutilated act, the act of a dead faith which is ineffective for salvation. We must take these considerations into account when we try to analyse faith in its real fullness.

4. These three do not designate three different acts of faith, but one and the same act which has different relations with the object of faith." *Summa Theol.,* 11a 11ae, q.ii, a.2, ad.3. On the actual movement of faith, cf. the famous Augustinian text of 3 *Sent.,* d.23, q.2, a.2, ad.5.

5. "Although elements pertaining to the will can be considered accidental to the acts of the intellect, they are however *essential to faith:* just as rational elements which are accidental to sense-appetite are nevertheless essential to the virtue of temperance." *De Veritate,* q.XIV, a.3, ad.10.

6. We can find yet another proof in the way in which St. Thomas replies to the question, "Is it necessary for salvation to believe anything which surpasses natural reason?" *Summa Theol.,* 11a 11ae, q.ii, a.3. Reply: Human nature is not at the summit of being, but only at a certain level; therefore it is organically dependent upon a superior nature; it is a spiritual nature, and so immediately ordered to God (*dependence upon* and *being ordered to* correspond to one another). This means: 1. The person is orientated to some further end and receptive just as much as he is subsistent and complete (because he *subsists* in a nature): 2. He is naturally receptive to a "supernatural participation in the divine goodness." 3. Where faith is concerned it is his natural desire as a spiritual person which is involved, and which God comes to fulfil.

7. Cf. G. Rabeau, *Réalité et relativité* (Vrin, 1927), p. 227, ". . . this evidence which is deceptive and humiliating for man's reason, in that what is understood is only understood by that which is not understood in the proper sense. . . ."

8. This is why a pure rationalism is led to deny the personal existence of other consciousnesses, and to make of the consciousness of another "a piece in the system of its judgments of existence." Thus L. Brunschvicg replying to M. Bresson at the *Société française de Philosophie* (1921). Quoted in Etcheverry, *L'Idéalisme français contemporain* (Alcan, 1934), p. 223.

9. Cf. especially *Vom Ewigen im Menschen* (Leipzig, 1921).

10. Cf. Delaye, *Semaine sociale de Clermont* (1937), p. 182. This is, in a sense, true of all existence; on this point see thesis by G. Rabeau, *Le Jugement d'existence* (Vrin, 1938), Chap. X.

11. This is true even of unformed faith. On this point, cf. the admirable text of St Bonaventure, 3 *Sent.*, d.23, a.2, q.1, concl.: "By the habit of faith, man's intellect is, in a certain way, rectified. . . . It is endowed with a new strength while it is submitted to the yoke of Christ, to assent to the First Truth for its own sake and above all things."

12. *Summa Theol.*, 11a 11ae, q.xi, a.1.

13. Bonsirven, *op. cit.*, p. 85: "The supreme good which (John) never tires of mentioning, under different forms, in his epistle, and which he wishes to communicate to his children, is the possession, and the consciousness of this divine power immanent in the soul."

14. This is the essential *sign* which is proper to the Church in the world. St. Gregory the Great considered it explicitly when he wrote on Mark 16: 16: "*Every day the Holy Church does spiritually what it used then to do through the Apostles.* . . . What do those faithful do, who abandon the worldly words of their old life, sing of the holy mysteries, and tell of the praises and power of their creator in accordance with their ability; what do these do except speak with new tongues? Those who take away evil from the hearts of others by their exhortations destroy serpents. . . . Those who, each day, see their neighbor growing weak in what is good and help him as much as they are able, and by their example and acts strengthen the life of those whose own activity is wavering: what are these doing if not laying their hands on the sick so that they may be cured? These miracles are the greater the more spiritual they are; they are the greater inasmuch as it is not bodies but souls which are raised up through them; and you, dear brothers, can accomplish these signs with God's help if you wish to do so" (P.L., LXXVI, 1215–1216). Cf. this echo in the work of a modern theologian:

"Not only in the sacraments and the teaching of the faith is Christ revealed to us and the celestial city unveiled, but in the whole life of the Church, in the life of all our brethren, who are also a Christophany and a means of grace. They, too, are the Lord made visible." M. J. Congar, *Divided Christendom* (Geoffrey Bles, 1939), p. 67, n.4.

15. Some profound reflections on this subject by G. Marcel can be found in *Être et Avoir* (Aubier, 1935), pp. 296–319.

16. Each sacramental character—a consecration which creates a power —plays a structural rôle in the ecclesiastical organism. The character of Confirmation qualifies a person precisely for that essential function which is the *professio fidei, Summa Theol.*, 111a, q.lxxii, a.2, that testimony born before "judges" and before the "world." But the world is everywhere, and it is always judging us. . . . Thus, there arises a question of which we cannot here treat in itself: that of the completion of the person (and of faith) by its relationship to others.

17. On this point see the profound pages of de Lubac in *Catholicisme* (Éditions du Cerf, series "Unam Sanctam," 1938), ch.xi, especially pp. 263–67.

18. *Summa Theol.*, 111a, q.lxii, a.5: "In Baptism we receive power to do those things which pertain to our own salvation, insofar as we each of us live for ourselves: whereas in Confirmation we receive power to do those things which pertain to the spiritual combat with the enemies of the faith." We shall not forget that the character of this combat is "to fight by confessing Christ's name" (*ibid.*, ad.1), and that "At Confirmation we are anointed with chrism on the forehead *so that we may show publicly that we are Christians*" (*ibid.*, a.9).

19. Gregory of Nyssa, *De Perfecta christiani forma:* "Those who profess to be Christians ought first to *be* what that name requires, and so make their lives compatible with their title" (P.G., XLVI, 256 B). It seems to us that there are few Fathers who have insisted as much as this "speculative Platonist" on the necessity of witness, and who have tried more than Gregory to establish its nature theologically. (On its *Christian* character, cf. *ibid.*, 277.)

THE VALUE OF BELIEF IN THE TRINITY

DOM MARK PONTIFEX

IT is undoubtedly hard for the average man, who has only a slight knowledge of theology, to see much value in the doctrine of the Trinity. He finds no way in which it applies to practical conduct in real life; he is apt to regard it, if not as a mere intellectual puzzle, at any rate as having no clear connection with his religion as a whole. Yet of course he is wrong, for in actual fact the Trinity lies at the root of all Christian teaching. I shall try to explain why this is so, but we can be sure from the start that the doctrine is no useless piece of information. It is incredible that God should reveal a truth with no bearing whatever on practical conduct. We are taught a doctrine, and it is for us to draw out its meaning and try to appreciate its value; we can be confident that the meaning and value are there: *credo ut intelligam.*

What, then, is the kind of value we may expect to find in the Trinitarian doctrine? One kind of value which the doctrine re-

veals is the practical effect on the souls of men caused by the
Trinity of Persons, but that is not the kind I am speaking of here.
I am speaking of the doctrine as a doctrine, and am considering
its influence on the minds of those who accept it. From this point
of view a doctrine may have religious value in two chief ways.
It may teach certain precise actions which we ought to perform as
duties of religion, as do many of the doctrines about the Church
and the Sacraments, or else it may show us the attractive power, the
beauty, of the end set before us by the Christian religion, and inspire us with a special motive for seeking this end. Plainly the
doctrine of the Trinity does not possess religious value in the first
sense, so we must ask whether it has it in the second.

The ultimate purpose of religion, from which all its value flows,
is, we all know, union with God. Union, in its most general sense,
is nothing else than perfection, since every being is perfected by
gaining what its nature desires, that is to say, by becoming united
to it. On the other hand evil as such consists in division, and a desire is evil if the union which it leads to does not lead on to ultimate
union with God, but only to ultimate separation from him, and
thus to frustration and suffering.

St. Augustine has an interesting passage on the subject of union,
when he discusses the problem of pain in animals:

Moreover the pain suffered by animals enables us to see a power in
the souls of beasts, which is in its way wonderful and admirable. It
shows us how their souls strive for unity in governing and animating
their bodies. For what else is pain but a feeling which resists division
or corruption? Hence it is as clear as possible that the soul is greedy
for unity and tenacious of it throughout the whole of its body. Neither
willingly nor with indifference, but reluctantly and with a struggle, it
meets bodily suffering, and endures the distress caused by the collapse of its unity and soundness.[1]

Union with God is, then, the ultimate value. What does this
union imply? In discussing the end for which man is made, St.
Thomas tells us at the beginning of the second part of the *Summa*
that God is the ultimate end of man, and that man's supreme
beatitude or happiness consists in the vision of the divine Essence,
the Beatific Vision, as it is called, for that alone can satisfy all his

desires. We have but an obscure notion in the present life of what
this vision implies; we can only say that "eye hath not seen, nor
ear heard, neither hath it entered into the heart of man, what things
God hath prepared for them that love Him" (1 Cor. 2:9). All
man's highest powers will be engaged and satisfied; the artist's sense
of beauty, the scientist's love for truth, the administrator's love for
order, the explorer's for adventure, the soldier's devotion to duty,
all will have full play in a higher manner than we can conceive. We
sum up man's powers as intellect and will, the former being, according to St. Thomas, the more important:

> If we consider the matter carefully, the act of the intellect which is
> vision must necessarily be more important than the delight. For de-
> light consists in the satisfaction of the will, but the will is only satis-
> fied by something through the goodness of that by which it is satis-
> fied. If, therefore, the will is satisfied by some act, its satisfaction arises
> from the goodness of the act. The will does not seek the good for the
> sake of satisfaction, for then the act of the will would be the end, and
> this contradicts what we have said. It seeks to gain satisfaction in the
> act, because the act is its good. Hence it is clear that the act itself by
> which the will is satisfied is a more important good than the satisfaction
> of the will in the good.[2]

Since union with God is man's supreme end and happiness, we
can appreciate what is meant by the love of God which leads to
it. The supernatural love of God which makes us seek this supreme
union in the Beatific Vision is called charity, the virtue which
"makes a man tend towards God by uniting his affections to God,
that he may live, not for himself, but for God."[3] St. Thomas has
a well-known passage of great beauty about charity.

> Not every love has the character of friendship, but that love has
> which is accompanied by well-wishing, when we love someone in such
> a way as to wish him good. If we do not wish good to the things we
> love, but wish their good only for ourselves, as for example when we
> are said to love wine or a horse and so on, it is not the love of friend-
> ship but of concupiscence. It would be absurd to say that anyone had
> friendship with wine or a horse. But not even well-wishing is enough
> to impart the character of friendship, for this requires a mutual love,
> since a friend is a friend to his friend. Such mutual well-wishing is

founded on some communication. When, therefore, there is communication between man and God, in so far as He communicates His beatitude to us, friendship must be founded on this communication. We are told of this communication, "God is faithful: by whom you are called unto the fellowship of His Son" (1 Cor. 1:9). The love founded on this communication is charity, and hence it is clear that charity is friendship of man with God.[4]

St. Thomas goes on a little later:

As we have said, charity is friendship of man with God, founded on the communication of eternal beatitude. This communication is not a natural gift but a free gift for we are told, "But the grace of God, life everlasting" (Rom. 6:23). Hence charity itself exceeds the power of nature. But what exceeds the power of nature can be neither natural nor acquired by natural powers, for a natural effect does not go beyond its cause. Hence charity cannot dwell in us naturally nor is it acquired by natural power, but by the infusion of the Holy Ghost, who is the love of the Father and of the Son, whose participation in us is created charity.[5]

Religious value, then, consists in the power to bring us to union with God who is man's final end, and the highest religious value consists in the power to bring us to the closest union, that is, the supernatural union of the Beatific Vision.

The question, therefore, that we have to ask is: How does the doctrine of the Trinity help us to reach union with God in the Beatific Vision? As I have said, we shall expect it to do so by throwing light on the end before us, and by giving us a special motive for seeking it. In what way does the doctrine do this?

A first suggestion that will probably be made is that the Trinity is revealed because it helps us to understand the Incarnation. There is a passage of St. Thomas which may be claimed to support this. St. Thomas asks whether it is necessary for salvation to believe explicitly in the Trinity, and replies that it is. "The mystery of the Incarnation of Christ cannot be explicitly believed without faith in the Trinity, because in the mystery of the Incarnation of Christ is contained the fact that the Son of God took flesh, that He renewed the world through the grace of the Holy Ghost, and also that He was conceived of the Holy Ghost."[6]

This, however, does not quite touch the point we are discussing at the present moment. No doubt explicit belief in the Trinity is necessary for a sufficient understanding of the Incarnation as in fact it has been revealed, but there seems no reason why we should not be able to believe in the fact of the Incarnation, simply as such, without any knowledge of the Trinity. That the one infinite Creator, as known only by natural reason, should become incarnate is comprehensible to us, so far as such a fact can be comprehensible. It is no more easy for us to understand how the second Person of the Trinity has become incarnate. Consequently this explanation does not provide a wholly satisfactory reason why the Trinity has been revealed; it does not show us the special value of the doctrine in bringing man to his final end.

The reader may feel unconvinced by this last argument. Even if the doctrine of the Trinity is not directly necessary for an understanding of the bare fact of the Incarnation, yet is it not necessary for an understanding of the effect which the Incarnation has upon man? "Blessed be the God and Father of our Lord Jesus Christ . . . who hath predestinated us unto the adoption of children through Jesus Christ unto Himself" (Eph. 1:5). Has not the Incarnation made us adopted children of God, and does not this mean that we are associated with Christ in His Sonship of God by this adoption? Is not a knowledge of the Trinity necessary to explain the position we have gained through the coming of Christ?

Yet we cannot answer the question quite in this way. St. Thomas makes it clear that we are not the adopted sons of the Father only. The second Person of the Trinity is the Son of the Father only, but we are adopted sons of all three Persons of the Trinity, who together are our Father. It is impossible that there should be adopted sons of one single Person, because adopted sons are creatures, and all God's actions outside His own Nature and upon creatures are actions of all the three Persons, and not of any one Person in distinction from the others. We are led to this conclusion both by Scripture and Tradition.

This is the difference between the adopted son and the natural Son of God, that the natural Son of God is begotten not made, but the adopted son is made according to the words of St. John (1:12), "He gave them power to be made the sons of God." Sometimes, however, an adopted son is said to be begotten through spiritual regeneration, which is freely given and not natural. Hence St. James says, "For of his own will hath he begotten us by the word of truth" (1:18). But, although in God to generate belongs to the Father, nevertheless to produce an effect in creatures is common to the whole Trinity on account of the unity of nature, for where there is one nature there must be one power and one act. Hence the Lord says, "For what things the Father doth, these the Son also doth in like manner" (John 5:19) and therefore to adopt men as sons of God belongs to the whole Trinity.[7]

It follows, therefore, that the revelation of the Trinity is not absolutely necessary in order that we should understand, at least in a general way, the work of the Incarnation in making us adopted sons of God. We must look elsewhere if we are to find a satisfactory answer to the question we are asking, if we are to understand how the doctrine of the Trinity is of the greatest significance for the whole Christian scheme.

The answer, as we have seen, must lie in the way in which the doctrine shows us the love of God for men, and how man should have an answering love for God. The supreme motive for human conduct, forming its highest inspiration, must be the love of God, accompanied by knowledge that this can attain its object. Now does the doctrine of the Trinity give us a special motive for the love of God? We can see at once that it does. Natural reason shows us God as loving His creatures, since He is the first cause and utterly perfect. Revelation takes us to a far deeper level; it shows us God, not merely as loving His creatures, but as identified with charity or love. It shows us God as three distinct Persons in one Nature, the Son proceeding by an act of knowledge and the Holy Ghost by an act of love. The doctrine of the Trinity shows us in clear terms that man's knowledge and love of God is nothing else than knowledge and love of Truth and Love themselves. "The supreme goodness of God, in the manner in which it is now understood by its effects, can be understood without the Trinity of Persons, but, so far as it is understood in itself, as it is seen by the blessed, it cannot be understood without the Trinity of Persons."[8]

Can we go even further than this; can we find a way in which this doctrine has even higher value for us? Let us look at another passage of St. Thomas, one of the most pregnant in meaning in the whole *Summa*. In answer to an objection based on the words: "God sent His Son . . . that we might receive the adoption of sons, and because you are sons, God hath sent the Spirit of His sons into your hearts, crying: Abba, Father" (Gal. 4:4–6), and arguing that it is the act of the Father alone to adopt sons, because the Son and the Holy Ghost proceed from Him, St. Thomas replies: "Adoptive sonship is a likeness of eternal Sonship, just as all that has been done in time is a likeness of what has been from eternity. Man is made like the splendor of the eternal Son by the brightness of grace which is attributed to the Holy Ghost, and therefore, although adoption is common to the whole Trinity, yet it is attributed to the Father as source, to the Son as exemplar cause, to the Holy Ghost as impressing on us the likeness of this exemplar cause."[9]

The sentence we should especially notice here is "all that has been done in time is a likeness of what has been from eternity," that is to say, all that has been created in time has its archetype in a true sense in the Being of the eternal God. This is a sentence which throws a vivid light on the value of human life and endeavor. There is nothing trivial about the purpose of human existence; it is, or should be, the working out of a likeness to the divine life in so close a way that we can be called adopted sons of God. The creature cannot be in a direct sense like the infinite Creator, but it can be like God in a true sense, though we can have only an obscure notion of what this really means. In the present life we only know God indirectly, and have only a correspondingly obscure perception of our likeness to Him. Nevertheless it is clear enough to form the strongest motive for conduct. We realize that man, though in himself a mere creature, has been so favored by God that his perfection consists in a likeness to eternal, necessary reality. The relationship which forms, so to speak, the structure of his perfection is modelled on the absolute. This conception transforms our whole idea of human history, and shows us a value and a purpose in it which is an image of eternal value and purpose.

In view of this we see at once how fundamental to the Christian scheme is the doctrine of the Trinity. We have only to reflect on the following words to appreciate this:

> In God there is procession only through an action which remains in the agent without tending towards something outside. This kind of action in an intellectual nature is an action of the intellect and an action of the will. The procession of the Word takes place through an action of the intellect. We find in ourselves another procession through the operation of the will, a procession of love, through which the loved object abides in the lover, as by the conception of the word the thing spoken or understood is in him who understands. Hence besides the procession of the Word in God there is another procession, which is the procession of love.[10]

Other doctrines teach God's love for His creatures, but the doctrine of the Trinity teaches us the ground on which this is based: ultimate and necessary reality, that is, God Himself, consists in knowledge and love between distinct Persons, in unselfish regard, in a happiness drawn from another's happiness. We use human terms to express what is beyond our full comprehension, but we are expressing the truth. It is unthinkable, then, that God should not love creatures; God creates freely and not of necessity, but, granted that He has created, He necessarily loves creation. The doctrine of the Trinity gives man the confidence and consolation of God's necessary interest in his destiny.

Moreover, since the absolute perfection of God in the Trinity is the model for created perfection, the ideal of the Christian life is derived from the Trinity. Man's relations with Christ and with Christ's mystical body, which is the whole of redeemed mankind, are all an image of the eternal relations of God in the Trinity. We saw above, St. Thomas's teaching about charity, in which he explains that it is the friendship which unites man to God, and we now see that this charity is an image of the charity which exists in the Trinity.

Let us return to the effect of the Incarnation in making men adopted sons of God. We have seen that the revelation of the Trinity is not strictly necessary in order to explain the Incarnation in a general way, but it certainly gives us a far fuller understanding of what is implied. If we only knew that the Incarnation had taken place without knowing of the Trinity, we should know God had become man and had raised man to a supernatural union with Himself, but we should not realize that this union was modelled on that relationship which exists in the heart of ultimate reality. We shall appreciate this better if we look more carefully at the promise to make us adopted sons and heirs of God, and if we see how St. Thomas works out the theology of our adoption.

A man adopts another as his son in so far as out of his goodness he admits him to a share in his inheritance. God is infinitely good, and from this it comes about that He admits His creatures to share in His goods, in particular rational creatures who, in so far as they are made to the image of God, are capable of the divine beatitude. This beatitude consists in the enjoyment of God, through which also God Himself is happy, and rich of Himself, since He enjoys Himself. Now that is called a man's inheritance out of which he himself is rich, and therefore, in so far as God of His goodness admits men to the inheritance of His beatitude, He is said to adopt them. The adoption of God surpasses human adoption because God makes the man whom He adopts fit through the gift of grace to share in the heavenly inheritance, while man does not make him whom he adopts fit for adoption, but rather chooses one who is fit for this.[11]

St. Thomas adds that man is not a stranger to God even on the purely natural level, since he receives the gift of his nature from God. But on this level he has no part in grace and glory, that is to say, in the close and supreme union which has been made possible by association with Christ. It is in regard to this that he is said to be adopted. "As by the act of creation the divine goodness is communicated to all creatures through a certain likeness, so by the act of adoption there is communicated to men a likeness of the natural Sonship, according to the words: 'For whom He foreknew, He also predestinated to be made conformable to the image of His Son' " (Rom. 8:29).[12]

As has been explained, we are not made adopted sons of the Father alone, for that would imply—what is indeed inconceivable —the absorption of a creature into the inner life of God, but we are adopted sons of the whole Trinity, our adoption, that is, our relationship to God, being modelled on the archetype in God's own

Being. This brings us back to the passage already quoted, in which St. Thomas tells us that everything which happens in time is an image of the eternal. He goes on to explain that, although we are adopted sons of the whole Trinity, yet, since our adopted sonship is modelled on the eternal Sonship, from our point of view we can regard the Father as the source of our sonship, and the Son as the exemplar cause or model on which our sonship is based, and the Holy Ghost as impressing on us this likeness to the exemplar cause.

Two more quotations and the outline we are sketching will be complete. The first explains how, as adopted sons, we are like the natural Son of God. After mentioning two ways in which any rational creature is like the Word of God, St. Thomas continues:

> . . . thirdly, the creature is made like the eternal Word of God in regard to that unity which He has with the Father. This is brought about by grace and charity, and hence our Lord prays, "that they may be one in us, as we also are one" (John 17:11). Such a likeness realizes fully the character of adoption, because the eternal inheritance is owing to those who are made like in this way. Therefore it is clear that only a rational creature is capable of being adopted, and not every rational creature, but only that which has charity, which "is poured forth in our hearts by the Holy Ghost who is given us" (Rom. 5:5), and so the Holy Ghost is called "the Spirit of adoption of sons" (Rom. 8:15).[13]

The second passage speaks of grace which causes our union with God:

> Nothing can act beyond its nature, because it is always necessary that a cause should exceed its effect. Now the gift of grace exceeds any power of a created nature, since it is nothing else than a participation in the divine nature, which exceeds every other nature. Therefore it is impossible that any creature should cause grace. Hence it follows that God alone makes a thing godlike, by communicating a share in the divine nature through a participation of likeness, just as it is impossible that anything except fire should set fire to something else.[14]

Here, then, we are brought to the highest value which the mind can conceive, nothing less than union with God of such a kind that it can be called a sharing in the divine nature. (2 Pet. 1:4.) We can, therefore, sum up what we have said about the value of the doctrine of the Trinity. Far from being a piece of detached and rather barren information with no practical bearing on Christian life, it is seen to lie at the very center of all Christian effort. For it supplies the essential motive by showing the ultimate end for man, not merely as something which will in fact perfect his nature, but as something which is, in a true sense, a close image of, a union with, the eternal and necessary. All the other Christian doctrines need the doctrine of the Trinity to draw out their meaning and significance. The Incarnation, the Redemption, the Church, and the Sacraments, all aim to bring about man's supernatural end, and this supernatural end consists in the adopted sonship of God, which we can only appreciate in the light of the Trinity.

In the section "Belief in the Holy Trinity," in the *Grammar of Assent,* Newman says, referring to the Athanasian Creed:

It is not a mere collection of notions, however momentous. It is a psalm or hymn of praise, of confession, and of profound, self-prostrating homage, parallel to the canticles of the elect in the Apocalypse. It appeals to the imagination quite as much as to the intellect. It is the war-song of faith, with which we warn first ourselves, then each other, and then all those who are within its hearing, and the hearing of the Truth, who our God is, and how we must worship Him, and how vast our responsibility will be, if we know what to believe, and yet believe not. . . . For myself I have ever felt it as the most simple and sublime, the most devotional formulary to which Christianity has given birth, more so even than the *Veni Creator* and the *Te Deum*.[15]

Thus the doctrine of the Trinity has the highest and most practical religious value. But it is not only in the directly religious sphere that this is true, but also in the application of religion to human affairs in this life. Without an adequate motive and ideal in the long run men will not work for the betterment of the human race, and if they aim at an unworthy ideal the damage done will soon be disastrous. It is true that men often have an instinct for what is right, and may work to achieve it without understanding the motive they really have, but the fact remains that any theory put forward for human conduct must be tested by the kind of motive and ideal it presents. We may ask, therefore, what kind of ideal is offered by a philosophy which only looks to happiness in this world, and compare it with the Christian ideal. Any such philosophy, whether purely materialist or in a wide sense pagan, must be examined by this test: can it hold out to mankind the prospect of a happiness which will be worth the effort to gain it, and can it attract men permanently by appealing to their deepest desires?

We must ask ourselves whether conditions in this world can ever be such that the happiness of mankind in future ages is an ideal worth striving for at every cost, and capable of satisfying all that we can desire. Suppose scientific development succeeds to the utmost, yet there will still be death, sickness, bereavement, decay, loss, the *lacrimae rerum*. How far can the antisocial tendencies in human nature be cured, whatever success psychological methods of healing may in time achieve? Man's control over the forces of nature may with equal probability be used for destruction as for construction, and all the efforts for progress may lead to ruin. Is it possible, then, that the prospects of human happiness in this world can ever be such as to justify, by themselves, great self-sacrifice in attempting to gain it?

Why should one generation sacrifice itself for another? In this life it seems impossible that the interests of the individual and of the race should be completely reconciled. Why should one man sacrifice himself for another if this life is all that matters? The race is only made up of individuals, no one of whom is more important than another. There can never be a time in this world when the happiness of all men will completely coincide.

. . . But allowing all this, it yet seems to me as certain as any conclusion arrived at by hedonistic comparison can be, that the utmost development of sympathy, intensive and extensive, which is now possible to any but a very few exceptional persons, would not cause a perfect coincidence between Utilitarian duty and self-interest. . . . Suppose a man finds that a regard for the general good—Utilitarian duty— demands from him a sacrifice, or extreme risk, of life. There are perhaps one or two human beings so dear to him that the remainder of a life saved by sacrificing their happiness to his own would be worthless to him from an egoistic point of view. But it is doubtful whether

many men, "sitting down in a cool hour" to make the estimate, would
affirm even this: and of course that particular portion of the general
happiness, for which one is called to sacrifice one's own, may easily
be the happiness of persons not especially dear to one.[16]

It may be said that it is only exceptionally that heroic self-sacrifice is called for, and that in the ordinary way a man may work
for the progress of the race, and be himself happy in so doing,
and that, although there will always be unhappiness, there will be
sufficient happiness on the whole in degree and extent among individuals, to make a satisfactory motive for effort. There is undoubtedly truth in this, yet it is also beyond doubt that heroic
self-sacrifice is not infrequently required if wrong tendencies in
human affairs are to be resisted. Moreover, as we have seen, even
this moderate ideal for mankind is in a high degree uncertain, and
in the end the race must perish, come what may.

The truth seems to be that man needs a motive more inspiring
altogether than that of a problematical and imperfect happiness
in this world, if he is to be moved over a considerable period to
work for the increasing good of his fellow men. He can so easily
see the limits and uncertainty of natural happiness, and can conceive of an ideal so much higher and more satisfying. It seems
unlikely that attempts to give the impetus of religion to a merely
materialistic outlook can ever be lasting; there is too much discrepancy between the end which this offers us and the emotion of
religion which is out of all proportion to it. In other words, unless
man has the inspiration of the highest ideal, an ideal beyond this
world, he will not make the effort for such happiness as is attain-
able in this world, but will throw a false cloak of idealism round
aims which do not deserve it, and will do harm rather than good.
Progress in this world can be achieved as a by-product if the main
object in view is happiness in the world to come; if it is regarded as
itself the main object then it is an insufficient motive, and in the
end will be neglected. These things shall be added unto us, only if
we seek first the kingdom of God.

So we may contrast the Christian ideal with naturalist and materialist ideals. Christianity offers us as the ultimate goal a happiness in which we shall be united to God, and in which love of

our neighbor will harmonize with our own satisfaction in a new
heaven and a new earth, when the conflicts of human nature will
be healed and the interests of all agree. The ultimate goal is in
the next world, but there is a stimulus for effort towards progress
in this world, since precisely through such effort in this life—
charity to our neighbor—the ultimate end is attained. There is
rational ground for self-sacrifice when this is necessary, simply
because it will lead to the end for which it is suffered, either in this
world or the next.

This is the Christian ideal, and it rests ultimately on belief in the
Trinity, since this is the ideal towards which our eyes are directed.
In God there are three distinct Persons in one Nature, and, the
unity in Nature being perfect, there is no limitation of being. Christian perfection is an image of this. Christians are united with Christ
and their fellow men and so with God in a union which is supernatural. As perfection increases, though each remains a distinct individual, limitation arising from this distinction is progressively reduced. No effort towards this end is wasted; it will be successful
in the life to come to the fullest extent, and even in the temporal
order every effort is worthwhile, since an image of the eternal must
always be worth achieving, in however small a measure and for
however short a time.

If this line of thought is sound, the doctrine of the Trinity is no
detached and unreal piece of knowledge, but can form the strongest
inspiration for religion, and the most powerful incentive, if brought
home to men's minds, for effort towards human happiness in this
world.

NOTES

1. *De Libero Arbitrio*, III, 69.
2. I–II, Q.IV, art. 2, c.
3. II–II, Q. XVII, art. 6, ad 3.
4. II–II, Q. XXIII, art. 1, c.
5. II–II, Q. XXIV, art. 2, c.
6. II–II, Q. II, art. 8, c.
7. III, Q. XXIII, art. 2, c.
8. II–II, Q. II, art. 8, ad. 3.
9. III, Q. XXIII, art. 2, ad 3.
10. I, Q. XXVII, art. 3, c.
11. III, Q. XXIII, art. 1, c.

12. III, Q. XXIII, art. 1, ad 2.
13. III, Q. XXIII, art. 3, c.
14. I–II, Q. CXII, art. 1, c.
15. Ch. 5, § 2, p. 133.
16. Sidgwick, *The Methods of Ethics*, 6th ed., pp. 499–500.

THE UNKNOWN GOD

HANS URS VON BALTHASAR

1. The hiddenness of God in our time

NOT only the Christian God, but the God of natural religion is hardly ever mentioned by modern men. The men of the Enlightenment used his name so frequently as to be almost irreverent. Whenever it happens to occur in a modern newspaper or a speech it sounds mostly false and empty. Human respect may be one reason, but also a shyness to call God at all by his old, well-known name. It is as if everybody knew him and were familiar with him, as if he were a being to be treated as one among others, admittedly a Supreme Being distinguished by his position at the summit of beings, but only a *primus inter pares*.

Time and again a generation seemed to be pious and God-fearing if it left in the world gaps which, it was alleged, could be occupied only by God. Yet these would always close, and yet another opportunity was lost for pointing to God and touching him with one's hands. More and more honors and privileges that men had reserved for the First Cause fell to secondary causes. And thus ever more things that seemed to be "known" of God had to be referred to the world. This is the essence of the whole historical process described in the first part, the conquest of the open or hidden religious cosmologism by anthropologism. Even while modern science was carrying all before it, the defenders of the idea of *Deus sive natura,* attempted a cosmological countermovement, and ventured to make God visible and accessible by man. The Idealists even went so far as to attempt to build up the inner being and consciousness of God from nature and the human spirit. Compared with this outrageous irreverence, Goethe was a man of reverence; yet he, too, saw in nature the "sacredly public mystery" of God, and recognized the essence by its colored reflexion, "for it is the eternally One that reveals itself in manifold ways." The modern heirs of German Idealism have lost Goethe's ingenuous accents and moved away from the natural center to the borders of sectarianism. The Goethe of Rudolf Steiner is certainly not Goethe, and the cosmological Eros of Ludwig Klages is not that of his great poems. The "becoming God" that appears sporadically in Rilke's poems is a miserable spectre; and Kerényi's literary heaven of the gods has only the name in common with the classical original.

The world is not God. This much is clear today, to the theist as well as to the atheist. Nor is the world open to God in such a way that he would have to intervene in it at every moment to keep it going. We do not add to the greatness of the Creator if the Prime Mover is called in wherever we notice a gap in the secondary causes. Christian apologetics has probably by now learned from its past mistakes; its history, especially at the end of the nineteenth century, resembles a chain of well-meaning misunderstandings followed by enforced retreats. Today we see clearly that we cannot fight science with Scripture, because the aim of God's revelation in the Bible is not to teach men science. But how dearly had this understanding to be paid for! Perhaps something similar is happening now with the temporary difficulties of the modern science of the world. Surely Christians should help to solve and integrate them instead of constantly finding occasion to postulate an immediate intervention of the Creator, who, they think, shows himself in this way. It seems that the world is an expanding system, which therefore could be traced back to the moment of its origin. Surely a proof of God's creative action, cry the apologists. Perhaps. But perhaps St. Thomas Aquinas was more profoundly right in his view that the beginning of the world cannot be proved by mere reason. The material world contains elements of indetermination. This, it is alleged, is a proof a fortiori for the freedom of the spirit, as if these were not two quite different phenomena. The discussion of the view that life cannot be derived from matter continues; but this could only be assumed if matter did not contain the principles of

life from the beginning. It is the same with the discussion of the
development of mind from life below mind. This would indeed be
unacceptable only if the idea governing the development of life
were not from the beginning the idea of man. In all these cases the
purely evolutionist view would always be only one side of the
truth. The great leaps of nature from one stage of being to another
may be facts; yet this does not prove at all that their explanation requires a supernatural cause.

If contemporary men are here instinctively mistrustful and
cautious, they cannot be blamed if they are also more reserved than
former generations with regard to the Christian accounts of miracles. The Middle Ages, especially at the end, had a real mania for
miracles. But the seventeenth century was the same, as is proved
by its hagiography, and the Romantics, too, in their own way, mixing up miracles with their cosmological occultism. What a Görres,
a Brentano and most of their like-minded contemporaries have produced in this field seems truly frightening to us. Yet even nineteenth-century France had quite a naïve attitude to miracles; we
may think of Léon Bloy's story of Mélanie and of so many strange
happenings at places of pilgrimage which ultimately remain
shrouded in an obscurity that cannot now be penetrated. Things
that are completely clear to a small circle within the sphere of the
grace received need not be equally so for everyone else. The investigations of the limits within which occult and parapsychological
factors operate within the created world are only in their infancy.
The material will be immensely enlarged by Oriental, especially
Indian, data. Many a judgment that at first seemed assured would
better be received with reserve. Christian apologetics itself has
rightly modified its views on the Scriptural miracles. The full force
of argument, especially as regards the miracles of Jesus, is now
seen to consist in their connection with the phenomenon of Jesus
himself. They are not isolated magical feats, but emphasize just
this and no other word, this doctrine, this witness, this existence.
Jesus himself always points to this connection. The miracles draw
men's attention to his words and existence; the "works" are meant
to facilitate this access, and, since the words of Jesus are worthy
of credence, his miracles must be so, too. The progress that leads
from them to faith is proved legitimate—from the point of view of

faith. The same holds good for the Old Testament prophecies.
They, too, are not to be taken as bare philological statements, but
must be seen in their historical setting; they point forward to Christ
as the Messias and find their fulfilment in him.

All these apparent retreats are not signs of scepticism or rationalism, but are caused by the legitimate caution of religious
reason, to which it has become increasingly clear that the First
Cause is transcendent.

God is not a piece of the world, but its presupposition. He is not an
objective piece of knowledge beside other objects, but the infinity
that is always presented in advance to the movement of knowledge, and
within which the latter pursues its courses which will always remain
finite. God is not the concluding hypothesis that follows from the
preliminary sketch of a perfected conception of the world, but the only
thesis that is posited with every one of the hypotheses from which we
build up our concept of the world. . . . The world has become an
entity rounded off in itself, which is neither actually open at certain
points where it merges into God, nor undergoes at certain observable
points the causal impact (*ursächlichen Stoss*) of God (if we disregard for the moment the supernatural dispensation of salvation); but
it points to God as its presupposition only as a whole, and even so not
very obviously. Today man realizes that this is so, having gradually
acquired a scientific concept of the world that is just as profane as the
world itself, which is not God. . . . We are experiencing today that we
can make no image of God that is not carved from the wood of this
world. The educated man of our time has the duty, painful though
fruitful, to accept this experience. He is not to suppress it by a facile,
anthropomorphic "belief in God," but interpret it correctly, realizing
that, in fact, it has nothing in common with atheism.[1]

Nevertheless, the non-Christian can hardly interpret the signs of
the times other than in terms of atheism. This is clear not only
from its organized mass appearance, but also from the reasons we
have explained. Political and materialistic atheism is, in a more
profound view, only the popular historical consequence of a historical necessity. At one time, God's nearness had been felt in nature,
in the whole visible cosmos which on its borders merged almost
without break into the invisible sphere of the divine. This is no
longer so, either emotionally or intellectually.

Men are frightened at the absence of God from the world, they feel they can no longer realize the Divine, they are terrified at God's silence, at his withdrawal into his own inaccessibility. The world becomes profane and devoid of meaning, its laws are impersonally objective, even where it is no more a question of nature but of man. This experience which men think they must interpret theoretically as atheism, is yet a genuine experience of the most profound existence . . ., with which popular Christian thought and speech will not have finished for a long time. But it is fundamentally only the experience that God does not belong to the concept of the world; . . . it means that God is growing in the mind of mankind. We experience anew and most radically what we, and the Vatican Council, have always known theoretically, but have said somewhat unthinkingly: that God is ineffably above all else that exists and can be conceived.[2]

The sentence with which the Council begins[3] is the foundation of all its later statements on natural theology. Surely it is not surprising that this first sentence should become more topical than ever at a time when the cosmological conception of the world is changing into a predominantly anthropological one. As we shall see, it has never been unknown to Christian theology. All truths have their particular hour; and this truth has its hour today. Christian theology and spirituality will perhaps be terrified to realize that they have not been quite prepared for this. The reason is that this great insight into the divine Being, which so completely filled the heart and mind of the Fathers and the medieval mystics, has not remained equally alive in the last centuries. Seen from this point of view, the frightening phenomenon of modern atheism may, among other things, be a forcible measure of Providence to bring back mankind, and especially Christendom, to a more adequate idea of God. The anti-Christian virulence of this atheism cannot be answered by a corresponding "anti" of the Christians. The Christian answer must know how to hold up the blind, hostile stroke in the depth, and to change it into something that brings light and unity.

2. The Christian idea of the Transcendent God

In late antiquity, when Christianity made its appearance, one can notice a similar disappearance of God into an inaccessible transcendence, though in a lesser degree, and with this difference: that the Neo-Platonists recognized the essence of Divinity in this transcendence. Nevertheless, this religion was of an abstractness and partly of an intellectual eccentricity that have a certain kinship with the modern frigidity of mind.

The Christian answer is by no means confined to stressing God's visibility in his economy of salvation, in his nearness to men in the Incarnation, in the apparitions and voice of the Old, the sacraments and graces of the New, Testament. On the contrary, the Patristic doctrine of God lives by, and gains its depth from, the great breathing space of the negative ("apophatic") theology, which the Fathers regard as the crowning of all human thought about God. In this they are in harmony with the philosophers, though they move in a different spiritual atmosphere. The Cappadocians, for example, reject inexorably the rationalism of the Eunomians, according to which it is possible to form a concept (*katalepsis*) of God, by stressing that God can ultimately be "grasped" only insofar as man knows he fails to grasp him. What he grasps, says Gregory of Nyssa, he also dominates; but the mind can only be dominated by God; it experiences something of the reality of its Master when it abandons its claims to rule. In having to resign itself to not knowing *what* God is, the failing spirit divines *that* he is; and this "Is" can therefore not be added to that of the creatures, but shows itself as the altogether Other and Greater than all in the failing of all images and notions. This is the teaching not only of those Fathers who were influenced by Alexandrine and Platonic thought down to its great representatives, Dionysius and Maximus the Confessor; the same was taught by the realistic Chrysostom, whose homilies show their true character only against this background, and by Novatian, from whom we should like to quote a few sentences by way of example:

The human mind is incapable of thinking adequately about God and his essential attributes, what he is, how great he is and in what manner he exists. Nor can the art of human speech develop an eloquence proportionate to his majesty, for he is greater than the mind itself and cannot be thought as great as he is, so that he should not, when he is being thought, be smaller than the human mind that comprehends him. He is above every word and ineffable, so that, being capable of being expressed, he may not be less than the human assertion which could circumscribe and gather him into itself. Whatever can be thought of him is less than he, and whatever can be predicated of him is smaller if compared with him. For we may, indeed, feel him a little in silence, but we cannot express in words what he is himself. If you call him Light, you name a creature rather than himself, you have not expressed him. If you call him Force, you describe his power rather than himself. If you call him Majesty, you express his honor rather than him. Why go into detail? I will say it once and for all: Whatever you say about him, you have explained only something that belongs to him, one manifestation of him, not himself. Unless our intellect might grasp in one unique way what God is—but even that: how could we do it? How could we comprehend it? How might we understand it?—namely by imagining that he is that which cannot be understood or even thought in its intrinsic greatness. . . . God is that which has the property that nothing can be compared with him.[4]

The great "articulation" is between theology (God in himself, exalted above all) and economy (God for us, in his grace condescending from his infinite superiority). But the economy or *syncatabasis* (concession by grace, descending below oneself by way of adaptation) can only be measured in its full character of being a grace if, at every moment of it and in all its manifestations, it always remains clear who it is that condescends and adapts himself, who is making such concessions to the creature as to deign to meet it and be known by it. Thus a true "economy" is possible only if it is constantly balanced by "theology." The Father sends the Son, and the visibility of the Son must point to the invisibility of the Father with all the available means, positive or negative. Hence, within the economy, nothing must be isolated from the background of the ineffable that can only be adored though understanding fails; nothing is to be taken, worked up and rationalized by itself in order to be opened towards infinity, and only then, in a second stage, to ascend from the "literal" to the "spiritual" sense. Nothing can be understood of the humanity of the Son if it is not from the beginning experienced, believed and adored as the humanity of the Son of the *Father*. In no word of Christ and of the Bible can there first be stated an immanent content valid in itself, which would then, afterwards, be opened into the depth of the divine meaning.

Because the Fathers, especially those influenced by Origen, attach such importance to the resurrection and ascension of the Son, their Christology does not become a one-sided theology of glory, but simply a real *theology*. For in this everything depends on the angle that opens from the finite to the infinite, on the gesture of adoration before the mystery which is accomplished ever new in the theological act.

The Fathers worked on this golden background. They had the feeling for the dialectic of that which is always greater. Just because the angels are so near to God, says Chrysostom, they understand better the divine incomprehensibility. And he who knows about God's incomprehensibility knows more than the man who does know about it.[5] We have the same emphasis in Augustine, and again in the Middle Ages in Abelard, Eckhart and Nicholas of Cusa. St. Thomas Aquinas wrote frequently to the same effect. A late work such as the *Commentary on Boethius* is the exact echo of the teaching of the Fathers. He also knew that it is impossible to have an idea, properly so called, of Being, even though everything is known only in its light.

But what has become of this emphasis in recent times? It is there in Ignatius, in the *Ascent of Mount Carmel* of John of the Cross, and in Erich Przywara. But has it still the same effect as formerly? Does it shape the life of Christians, does it influence the sermons of preachers or the thought of theologians? Or has this golden background been damaged and broken, left unrepaired? Are not most people content to worship undialectically God's appearances in the world, to stop short at the visible Son, at his Mother, at the Sacraments, without vitally realizing the dynamisms which this whole world of appearances receives from the invisible Father and impel it towards him? Surely St. John would not have loved the Lord if in him, who could be seen, heard and touched, there had not appeared the Word of Life, reposing in the bosom of him whom no one has ever seen? And would St. Paul have surrendered himself to him, if he had not been the epiphany of him "who only hath immortality and inhabiteth light inaccessible; whom no man hath seen, nor can see"? (1 Tim. 6:16.) Are we the disciples of these men? Or have we not rather, since the Counter-Reformation, clung increasingly to the visible? Perhaps we did so thinking this had to be defended against the spiritualists, and thus, as Henri de Lubac has rightly pointed out, we have begun in these last decades to abuse the conception of the Incarnation for the sake of our earthly interests and conveniences. We settle down in the visible, excusing ourselves with the earthly mission of Christians, with the modern mind that is turned towards the world, and with the Greek infiltrations in early Christian thought. We have been incapable of sacrificing the world to God. A simple Buddhist advances much farther in this respect. Surely it is time for God to show us the aspect of his infinity, his "altogether-otherness."

Only those Christians who are most deeply aware of this utter transcendence of God will be able to interpret to modern atheists their own experience of existence with some hope of success. But they ought not to treat the doctrine of the incomprehensibility of God like an object once possessed but long forgotten in a cupboard, which is now unearthed and dusted for this particular purpose of talking with, say, Jaspers or Buber or Heidegger. Modern man has had the frightful misfortune that God in nature has died for him. Where religion once flowered like a blooming meadow, there is nothing left now but dry clay. Perhaps it is better so; perhaps that religion was like the Pontine Marshes that had to be drained. Nevertheless, the effect remains crushing. The Christian is not allowed to avoid this experience. He share it as a human being; it may even apply to those presentations of his own religion that were themselves an impoverished cosmological form of the truth of Jesus Christ. The resurrection from this tomb is not brought about by reforms of the Church, but by a change in the mentality of the individual, returning to the origins of his religion. The Church as a whole remembers this every year at the stripping of the altars on Good Friday. Jesus was no enthusiast of creation; he approached his goal, steadfastly setting his face (Luke 9:51); this was his hour, the sacrifice of his life in the darkness of the Cross. Even all the St. Peter's Basilicas and Vatican Museums can do nothing else but glorify the memory of this hour.

This is not to say that the natural experience of contemporary humanity must from the start be interpreted in view of the Passion. This will be one of the concluding aspects, but by no means the only one. Before any Christological interpretation of the time,

God's majesty must stand out as the unchangeable background on which the diverse mysteries of Christ are outlined. This must not be a strange God, but one who appears even freer to us, and who, in his freedom, may not only be farther from, but also nearer to us. For he is free to pour out the overwhelming riches of his love. The meaning of our time is that God should be exalted higher above contemporary man who himself occupies a higher position than before, and that man thus exalted should in his turn fall down more humbly before this infinitely exalted Lord. Christians must be more intensely on fire with the love of God; they will have to be so if possible more absolutely, more silently, with less dramatic gestures and forms of devotion, which might still be tolerated in the Baroque period, but become impossible in the nineteenth century. They will have to efface themselves, disappearing in the uniform mass, and by doing so gain in sincerity and intensely humble objectivity. Some at least should be able to do this. Only if this absolute experience has once more become the constant background will it also be differentiated for us in a meaningful economy, taking on the various aspects of the spiritual poverty of the Crib, the hidden years of work, the hurried nomad life of the public activities, and the dread and night of the Cross.

All this and much else can become the inner form of the Christian experience of our time. Joy will not be lacking; nevertheless, the essential joy will be the background of the Resurrection from which all the forms of stripping and detachment are dispensed as gifts of the Holy Ghost which the Son sends from the Father. Everything depends on this poverty towards God and in God, poverty of God in us, as the unknown follower of Tauler described it so impressively in his book on the divine poverty. Then it rests with God whether this "poverty in spirit" is to be experienced as felt or as unfelt "bliss," whether man feels himself incredibly enriched by God's infinity or robbed of all finite things without being aware of having gained God. The quality of God's divinity transcending everything in the world cannot be determined by "nearness" or "distance." The nearness of God who is nearer to man than man is to himself is as overwhelming as his distance, which cannot be bridged, and the aspect of consuming loneliness, which Mechthild and Eckhart called the desert of God.

All those who throughout the epochs of Christian history have had to revitalize the Gospel, came from this background, which gave to the biblical episodes their strangely consuming and burning quality; everything in the Old as well as in the New Testament is flame and tempest, the gentle things even more than the rest. It is quite incomprehensible how a sceptical biblical science could miss this fundamental theme, and thus be mistaken in its judgments from the very start. Surely men, even believers, could never invent such a background, which is diametrically opposed to all the laws of human religious imagination. It is a pity that both orthodox Protestant and Catholic biblical scholars often speak as if the human, historical and philological content of Scripture formed a closed world, and that the divine or "spiritual sense" begins only beyond it. The saints realized how the infinite shines directly through the fearful intensity of the prophets, of Jesus, of Paul and of John; how the human word and gesture are but a thin film before it, while through the mask of the human face those burning eyes are flashing which the apocalyptic seer beheld in bodily vision. How clearly could Augustine, Francis, Ignatius see the Father in the Son! "Smelling and tasting the infinite perfume and the infinite sweetness of the Godhead."

While regretting the absence of great figures in our time, we must not forget the army of those nameless ones who suffer in silence, who have offered, and are still offering, a burnt sacrifice that is generally overlooked, in war and deportation, in camps and torture, victims of the totalitarian powers, externally undistinguished from their unbelieving or weakly believing brethren. From prayers without number, spoken more with the life than with the lips, a figure may yet arise, if God wills it, which will unmistakably point to him. But does this potential of suffering become evident in the forms of contemporary Christendom, in which unbelievers in their distress could read the credible witness of the ever greater God? Has the present moment been grasped and understood, which is always the same for believers and unbelievers? For, if its meaning be veiled to unbelievers, it ought to be understood and made known to the uncomprehending world by Christians. If it is true that God is growing in souls, surely he ought first of all to grow in Christians. When man, having emerged from the world-nature, looks round bewildered in the colder, more lonely space that he forms, indeed that he is, the dignity of his loneliness ought to be interpreted to this puzzled, seemingly forlorn creature. For the most lonely, unique God can only be met in a loneliness worthy of him, communicated from his very Being, the Alone to the alone. This means that the individual of the species leaves the calyx of nature in order to be the individual man before the unique God, whether in solitary private prayer or in the public worship of the assembled Church.

NOTES

1. Karl Rahner, "Wissenschaft als Konfession?" *Wort und Wahrheit,* IX (November 1954), 811–813.
2. *Ibid.,* 812.
3. Denzinger, 1782.
4. *Liber de Trinitate,* Migne, PL 3, 889–891.
5. *Peri akatalepton,* Migne, PG 59, 721, 742.

Hope

HOPE is an audacious virtue. What it amounts to, for the Christian, is the anticipation or expectation of an indissoluble union with God, a joyous permanence only vaguely and clumsily touched upon here below, even in our ecstasies and exaltations. The Christian who argues thus to himself is not necessarily a wildly graced mystic, or a lofty visionary; he may just be an ordinary Christian being bold, daring, reckless almost, as his religion certifies him to be. For that extraordinary leap into eternity is the rock-bottom assumption of Christianity. When at baptism one has been made a member of the mystical body of Christ by the most lavish of gifts and the most exquisite of mercies, one has already begun one's ascension. How, instructed with such a beginning, could one be less than bold?

The audaciousness of Christian hope is not, for all its concentration on personal salvation, a virtue of the inner self alone. It demands much. It is not satisfied with single cases, though each one, in hope, has its large eloquence. But the fullness of hope is the fullness of the mystical body, touching all as Father Mersch makes so clear—all, no matter who they are or where they are, in or out of the Church. For the fullness of hope is the fullness of consciousness to which a Christian must aspire, believing, as he does, that everything that is participates in goodness as its principle of being—everything.

This is not left-over codicil of a distant scholasticism. It is the wellspring of a living faith, of an active hope. Upon its abundance Christians feast today as they did a thousand years ago and will again in a thousand years. It is the constancy which makes change welcome. Not a frivolous change, of course; not change for change's *sake. But the kind of change in which liturgical forms find their deepest and most satisfying effect, constantly enlarging to meet the needs of the faithful until those needs require a shrinking of sorts, a return to essentials, a clearing away of once useful but not always usable accretions.* "At all times," *Father Jungmann sums up,* "the purpose of the liturgy has been to bring the faithful together, so that they might stand before God as the Church, as the people of God. But the liturgy has also intended more than this: it has aimed to lead the faithful to a* conscious Christian faith."

A conscious Christian faith regularly throws up rich speculations about the possibilities of restoring all things in Christ—to use St. Pius X's consecrated phrase. That is the inexorable fiat of Christian hope and its majestic promise. Towards its fulfillment, Christian thinkers come bearing gifts—the arts (Père Régamey), the intellect (Pedro Lain Entralgo), the world within (Jean Rimaud). They come to show us the reserves of the human person, as the philosopher Gabriel Marcel does. They come to remind us that even in the worst of times, even in the last of times, Christians have something to hold out—at least to each other—which will make it possible to hold on.

Romano Guardini's meditation on the end of the world may seem a gloomy one upon which to end an examination of the virtue of hope. In point of fact, it is not. There is everywhere in this essay, the concluding section of his book called The End of the Modern World, *the great bold force of hope. But it is hope that grows out of an eschatological view of things, a theology that looks with serenity towards death, not only each man's passing, but the passing of all men. There is no gloom for a Christian in that view, for he knows that the last things bring the best things and that there is no other way to them. And he always looks towards those things, however unmystical he may be, however little a visionary. For to the extent that he is a Christian, he has hope and his hope is audacious.*

THE MYSTICAL BODY AND CONTEMPORARY HUMANITY

EMILE MERSCH, S.J.

Deus qui solus novit congruentem suis temporibus generi humano exhibere medicinam.

St. Augustine, *De Sermone Domini in Monte*, I, I, P.L., XXXIV, 1231

In our days two tendencies assert themselves more and more in humanity.

On one hand, the individualist tendency, the desire for an autonomous life.

On the other, the tendency which we shall call "collectivist": preoccupation with a life solidly framed in the collective life of humanity.

I

First, individualism.

In a certain sense it is essential to man: in this sense, that man, being a person and an end in himself, demands the right to direct himself and to act only for reasons which he has understood and which he has, in this way, given to himself.

But in our epoch, individualism has become acute. It could not be otherwise. Every day the press brings to each individual most of the data—at least we readily believe it does—on the most diverse problems; it discusses them before the general public, and, as a matter of course, considers each reader a judge. A strong head is needed to resist this daily intoxication of being set up as an arbiter of the nations.

Besides, each one knows that governments fear opinion, and that opinion is himself—at least, that is what he has been led to believe, and there is some truth in it—each one also is an elector; he knows that the masters of the hour have canvassed for his votes and will canvass for them again: they have pleaded with him and will do so again; so he accustoms himself to considering them as at all times amenable to him. In a number of countries besides, public order is based on the play of parties, that is to say, on the recognized right of each one to constitute himself judge of the leaders.

To this must be added the critical spirit which the positive sciences and the historical sciences have developed, the conclusion which each one has reached, that it is in the crowd, among the "each ones" that the great leaders of men have formed and asserted themselves.

So the thought takes root more and more firmly in the minds of men that, in humanity, the individual is everything.

On the other hand, meanwhile, more and more clearly also, the individual realizes that in humanity and even for the best interests of the human individual, it is the group, it is humanity which is everything.

Assuredly, this dependence of the individual in relation to the totality has existed at all times. Always the human individual has been the termination of an entire genealogy: he has always been made by his two ascendants, and each of these by two others, and so on: the root from which he draws all his sap buries itself through ramifications which redouble without ceasing into an immense throng, the same approximately for all, into innumerable humanity. Always the maintenance of his life has been made possible by exchanges; always the formation of his mentality and of his character has been, in large part, the work of his environment. Always, finally, he has been a man only by being a man among other men, that is to say, he has been what he is, in what is most essential to him, only by being the very same which the others are.

Only, today, this dependence of each man on all men has become closer and more visible. It appears even in the details of life: everyone knows, without being astonished at it any more, that he eats the fish of Newfoundland, the apples of Canada, the bananas of the Antilles, the macaroni of Italy, and the dried raisins of California; that he drinks Brazilian coffee, that he smokes American tobacco, that he has a Swiss watch, and that his brief case contains Congolian, Chinese or Egyptian securities. For his nourishment, for his heating, for all the economic order by which he lives, it is the entire universe which has co-operated by a medley of exchanges, of co-operations, of relations. Let the crop be bad in Canada, and the baker, faced with that fact, will raise the price of his bread; let Australia, to favor its own glassworks, close its ports to foreign products, and he will be out of work; let a panic occur on the New York Exchange, and the franc which he has in his pocket will find its value questioned; let Japan enter into a struggle with Russia, and his children will be called to arms.

More and more also, it seems, even in the midst of inevitable rivalries, the different classes of society are aware of their solidarity, or at least everything is calculated to make them aware of it. More and more the nations recognize, without daring to act accordingly, that what causes depression in one causes it in all.

More and more, too, intellectual labor is becoming collective: one no longer attempts anything serious without consulting the literature of the world, and researches begun in Tokyo are continued in Austria and in Germany.

So, everywhere, every day, man realizes that he is caught in a net whose controlling strands are spread over all the universe, and these strands are of steel and stretched to the breaking point.

They encompass even his interior, even his manner of thinking. His thoughts, often without his suspecting it, are shaped in function of the entire universe and by the entire universe.

In the first place there are the daily papers. They are a true school, a school for children and for adults, a day and an evening school. There is no escape in reading almost nothing except the sport pages and the local news. You will constantly encounter dispatches from the entire universe; the matches themselves, and the races, and the Olympic games, and the records, are they not international? So, little by little, men live in communication with the entire human race; so, little by little, the soul becomes fully human.

Evidently we are not much stirred by the recital of distant events: we are almost cold to the story of a lynching in the United States, or of executions in Moscow or in Mexico. But that is because we are not yet formed: the press has not given the details; especially, we have not yet, by radio, by television, heard and seen the victims. But so, one day, we may arrive at seeing and at hearing. . . .

But, we are making a beginning, and the radio, in this matter, is from now on an unprecedented lesson. It is not a toy, that little set of waxed walnut, so simple that a child can start it going; it is a revelation! A nothing, a contact, the turn of a screw, and behold, we hear Berlin, and then Madrid, and then London, and then Moscow, and then Vienna, and then the signals which ships are exchanging on the sea. We might say that the nations, questioned in turn, and by the first comer, reply; we might say that we are everywhere, that we implant ourselves, through some long root, among all peoples; or rather that "everyplace" is here, in the very place where we are listening, and that all the peoples are there, in the little clear-toned box. And, even when we cease to lend an ear, the great silent voices continue to re-echo about the globe; through the night they cross and reply to one another, they mingle and multiply; it is the entire earth which awakens and converses with itself, and all men, when they wish, can hear it. And these voices are human; in them each man can find himself and, at these distant songs, at these fanfares, at these melodies, can feel his soul tremble, for everywhere it is the same human soul which is revealed.

Truly, no man is alone. And what will happen on the day when some universal language will be spread abroad and when, from one end to the other of the world, we shall hear ourselves appealed to, when some distant orator will make his reflections, his enthusiasms, his indignations enter into us, when we shall feel ourselves, throughout all the earth, thinking together and willing together?

At certain moments each individual has been able to have some experience of it. All Catholics remember, for example, the days of last October, when they heard, with the entire universe, the ceremonies at Buenos Aires and the voice of the Pope speaking to all the earth.

At these moments the radio broadcast makes every man experience the collective soul, it forms the sentiment of belonging to the group, of attachment to humanity. What will happen when the experience becomes more universal and more common, and when, besides, the transmission of images will permit us to see what we are still limited to hearing?

In the meantime, the simple radio is diffused more and more widely, and the children themselves pay no more attention to it. Little by little it shapes souls, it teaches every man that he has everywhere other selves, who think and desire as he does, and that, greater than he, overflowing him and penetrating him, humanity exists and even that it is humanity which exists the most here below.

This collectivism—the preceding pages define the term sufficiently—and the individualism which we discussed earlier, are two leavens, and terribly powerful leavens, which ferment in the breast of humanity. Their action in the secret places of men's minds must be intense. So, in our day, within itself, in its concept of man and of the union between men, humanity must change, and change vastly, and change quickly.

But this mentality is what is expressed in society, in the State. Society is indeed imposed on man by God Himself, but it is imposed on him through the medium of his nature, and hence in dependence on the accidental modifications and on the general development which necessarily occur in it.

It is therefore incontestable that at the present hour some accidental, but profound, changes are imminent in the institutions and in the structure of the State. They are imminent because they are already realized and in process of being more fully realized in what the form of the State can only express and make incarnate, that is to say, in the mentality of men.

That is not a prophecy; it is an estimate. Besides, is not the unrest visible enough; are not changes, radical changes at times, occurring frequently, almost everywhere; is there not more talk than ever before of reforming the régime?

All these signs are not necessarily precursors of cataclysm: they are certainly messengers of modification.

To say that the unrest comes only from the fact that we have broken the ancient frames of life, and that the flood will end of itself when the torrent re-enters its bed, is a pleasantry. What has occurred and what must occur, is profound in a different way: humanity has lived, humanity has grown, humanity has become more strongly humanity, both in the individual and in the group of men. Hence, as it has changed in itself, it must necessarily effect a similar change in externals, in its methods of organization and of public presentation.

What can this change be? That is for humanity to make clear; because it is humanity which is worked upon by the forces which are going to produce it. Isolated reflection can scarcely guess at some of its outlines; it cannot see details or definite features.

Will it be an increase of regionalism and of particularism, giving to each part of the country the exact physiognomy which belongs to it, and this with an increase of the central powers and of the amplitude of the groupings; will it be an ensemble of international organizations, professional as well as cultural, and strongly constituted, paralleled by a loosening of the internal bonds of each State; will it be, in States more solidly constructed, relations, even close relations, of certain provinces with provinces of other States, economic, intellectual, and even political relations; will it be all this at once, or will it be something altogether different? No one knows.

But if the imminent halting-places are not yet clearly in sight, what is sure is that we are at a curve in the road and it is a sharp curve.

And the question arises, not from the point of view of the facts, but from that of principles: how shall we make the turn?

II

The question is a hard one.

If what is working on humanity is two opposed forces, what can lie ahead except a catastrophe? What is needed is not reflection but flight. But where can we be safe?

No, some will perhaps say, and it is the first answer—the question is not hard: there is not even a question. These very forces, because they are opposed, neutralize each other. So with two locomotives which are placed in contact head to head: it would be useless for them to get up full steam; they would succeed only in holding each other reciprocally immobile.

Yes, certainly, if they don't both blow up. If poor humanity, so in struggle with itself, is not shattered to pieces, at best it will, and by dolorous efforts, reduce itself to impotence.

A second reply would consist in saying that one of the tendencies must win over the other; let it be, for example, the "collectivist" tendency.

Such is, with differing modalities, the doctrine of the totalitarian State, of the State which rules everything and directs everything, which pretends, alone, to form youth to its image and to its use, which pretends to be the norm of all rights and the last end of all efforts.

Certainly, the ancient social frames are no longer rigorously adapted to actual humanity, and we have said above that, among men, the concept of collective unity has asserted itself more vigorously, and that consequently, this same concept should express itself more definitely in institutions also.

But, precisely, the question is to know how. If we must, for this purpose, absolutely subordinate the human individual to the ensemble of men, we involve ourselves in a contradiction. For Society holds all its reality and all its value from the men who compose it: when we dispute the sacred character of men, we deny that there is anything sacred in Society either. So certain diseases destroy themselves by destroying the patient. Menaced in his most inalienable rights, annihilated as father of a family, as a free economic and social force, the citizen ends by being suffocated, and the city is no longer anything but a cemetery.

Of the narrowness of the political concepts which reduce everything to terms of the State and which, as a result, lose sight of humanity and then of the true dignity of men (understanding here the man who is the citizen of such a State) we shall say nothing at this time. It is not essential to the "collectivist" idea.

A third response would be the one which, in an absolute manner, would lift up individualism above collectivism.

It is as unacceptable as the preceding.

For each man every other man is as respectable as himself. For him to call in question their unrivalled worth, is, by the same act, to make his very own uncertain: he has no human ego except through being what they are. It is from them that he receives what is best in himself; in placing them purely and simply below him, it is himself whom, in his own interior, he turns upside down.

What is to be done then? What indeed, if to unite the two opposed tendencies is to invite catastrophe, and if to choose only one of them is to offer ourselves to the blows, and the mortal blows, of the other? What is to be done? Introduce here the classical distinction between individual and person? Yes, without doubt that would be good. But another solution, or rather, the same one appears, but under another form and with wider applications.

The difficulty comes from the antagonism between these two tendencies. To make it disappear, it suffices to show that this antagonism does not exist. And that is the fact. These two tendencies of opposite direction are the expression of one only and the same internal principle, as, in a tree, the force which sinks the roots in the earth and the force which lifts the crest to the skies, are two manifestations of the same vital force.

This unique principle is the very nature of man. Man, by nature, is social at the same time that he is individual; he is then directed, from the very interior of himself, towards the exterior.

Hence, to develop himself, he must at the same time increase in interiority with relation to himself and in interiority with relation to others. To be entirely master of himself, since he is man, it is imperative that humanity be master of itself, and hence that the union between men be close. On the other hand, in order that this humanity may be master of itself, each man must be, as totally as possible, his own master, and hence his personality, his liberty, must be as complete as possible.

All this is based on the very nature of man, on some truths which the Scholastics express marvelously, but which could be meditated upon at length, for they have wider applications than at first appears, and they shatter some narrow frames. The form, they say, is, of itself, the same for all men. This form, in its concrete realization, is proper to each one, but at the same time, as form, it has, though imperfectly, its own act and its own existence in each man. *Actus, in quo genere est irreceptus, in eo est illimitatus.*

But this concordance, which exists in the nature of man, has been rendered more complete still by the supernatural.

That is what these pages wish to show especially.

The supernatural has rendered it more complete, through what is most essential in it, through the union which it gives to each man with all the others in Christ.

This doctrine of the whole Christ, we have said in another place,[1] sums up all Theology, as Christ recapitulates in Himself all the human race. The present pages would like to show how it also says the last word in the matter of the evolution which is evident in humanity. But this word is much more magnificent than any which man would have been able to find: it is a word which comes from heaven; it is the Word of God.

Individual life first.

In Christ, it acquires a supernatural depth, a depth so great that, for us, it remains a strict mystery; for, in Christ, it penetrates infinitely deeper than all our natural being.

Ego dixi, dii estis et filii excelsi omnes. In Christ, Who is God and the Son of God, men are divinized and constituted sons of adoption. Between them and the secret of the divine life, there is no longer any separation, and the life which springs from the depths of themselves is one and immanent with a unity which has its principle and its model in the unity of the Trinity itself.

This, evidently, is the absolute interiority. It is this which offers itself to and imposes itself on Christians.

So with the collective life also.

By being one with Christ, all men become one with all the others.

Christ, in consequence, as He is the last seal of God on the reality of humanity, is also the last seal of God on the unity of this humanity. This group unity He seals at the same time in the most august depths of God and in the most interior depths of man, because He seals it in Himself, Who is at once the Word of God and the source of life in the interior of each man.

So humanity which, in the natural order, seeks itself, finds itself in Christ. It finds itself there with the unity which it has in

God *eminenter,* but realized in man. Each man remains distinct certainly: one is not man otherwise; but no one is any longer separate: one is not in Christ otherwise.

Before such unity as this, the wildest proclamations of solidarity are dull. One does not say to men: "You are alike, you are near to one another"; one says to them, or rather God says to them: "You are one only, one only with a divine unity": *Omnes vos unus estis in Christo Jesu* (Gal. 3:28); *unum sicut et nos unum sumus* (John 17).

Contemporary experience can give to each man the thrill of feeling that humanity seems to exist and that it throbs near him. Christianity gives to every Christian the certitude of faith that humanity truly exists, and that it exists within him; because Christ, who is all in each one, is all in all.

Collective life, however, forming only one with the individual life.

As these two lives, in Christ, attain their paroxysm, their union also attains its maximum. Both, in fact, taken in their principle, are exactly the same thing, and the same thing totally one, for this thing is Christ, and Christ is one, exclusively, because He is the Person of the Word.

It is from being a member of Christ that the Christian is divinely deepened in his interior life; it is also from being a member of this same Christ that he is, and to the same extent, divinely rooted in the interior life of all the others. The union with all is then an interior thing, like Christ; and the interiority with oneself, like this same Christ, is Catholic.

Does a man wish to find the entire humanity? Let him enter into himself; within himself it is in His presence that he will find himself, and, in Him, he will find himself—within himself—in the presence of the immense throng which cannot be counted, and which is one in Him.

Does a man wish to find himself? Let him forget himself, let him throw himself entirely into the service of others, and behold! the one who in these others will have received him and who will have received all, will be Christ, and this Christ is the mysterious guest of the most profound places of the soul: in losing himself in Him, he will have found himself.

The doctrine of the Mystical Body is then a doctrine eminently actual.

More and more it impresses itself on the attention, on the study, on the meditation of Christians, but especially noteworthy is the fact that the profane movement of the world, supposing that it is profane, is approaching it.

This observation should be made: the tumults of our epoch, Bolshevism, Nazism, Nationalisms of every sort, are signs of the times: they reveal the forces which are working on humanity, even when they are deviations from these forces. But what they make plain—and with what force!—is that, in our day, more than ever before perhaps, humanity wishes to unite with itself.

And behold, in our day precisely, Christian teaching places in the forefront the doctrine of this union of humanity with itself.

The doctrine is ancient certainly; but the divine truth is full of ever new aspects. "Every scribe instructed in the kingdom of heaven, is like to a man that is a householder, who bringeth forth out of his treasure new things and old." (Matt. 13:52.) It happens that the ancient preaching of the Kingdom, the teaching of Jesus, of Paul and of John, is the revelation, not merely of what God makes known, but also of what the man of the twentieth century is seeking within himself without knowing it.

The meeting is not fortuitous. He who made the revelation is the one who made the heart of man, and He made them for each other. The whole Christ, Who is the résumé of this revelation, is also the center in which God wishes to recapitulate all things. Is it astonishing then, if all this joins up, and if the unfolding of the centuries adapts itself to the history of the Word of life?

The meeting is a lesson. It shows that the teaching of the Church, and, in their way, theological studies, are not responsible merely for religious thought; they have charge also of the destinies of humanity. It shows also that in studying the truth about the Mystical Body, in preaching it, in meditating on it, we follow the directions of the Spirit, we obey the truth, and we serve humanity.

But it shows especially that this doctrine must be lived. The world has need of finding it, not in books, but in souls. The witness which it must have today, the witness which Christ arouses and awaits, the one which will be efficacious, is that of the member of Christ acting as a member of Christ, of the member who wishes to labor and to suffer, with Christ and in Christ, for all the immensity of the Body. To forget oneself, to renounce oneself, in order to belong in Christ, to God and to every man, that is the spectacle which will make manifest to all, in the manner which will strike them, that Christ still lives in His own. Abnegation then, but abnegation which shows itself especially in love and respect for all, in the will to efface oneself in the service of the Church and of humanity, in the giving of oneself to God by the consecration of oneself to all the children of God: it is of seeing this that the world has need.

This need is a petition which God Himself addresses to us: "I was hungry and you gave Me to eat." We can be sure that He answers it by giving generously in our epoch the grace of living as a member of Christ, of living not for oneself, it cannot be repeated often enough, but for Christ, and for the whole Christ. This grace we must receive jealously and correspond with attentively: by allowing it to be lost, we would betray the human race, and Him Who has so loved it.

It has often been said that the Church is the school of respect. It is very true, and the lesson, assuredly, is very necessary for our epoch. But it must be universal respect, a respect which includes all men, and which is thus one of the forms of love.

For it is love which is the authentic mark of Christ, and which ought to be, in the Church, the converting sign. She is, it is her primordial mission, the school of charity. And this lesson for our epoch, is the most necessary of all.

Making plain to men, and that in acts, in devotion, in self-sacrifice, in the giving of self to all, how, in fact, they are all one in Christ, and one with a unity at once divine and human, marvelously human and veritably divine, one with a unity far superior to the unities which they seek by their revolutions, alas, and by their murders—it is this which will convert the world.

Only let the salt not lose its savor! Let Christians who live by this unity, who ought to make it shine before the eyes of men, not hide it under their egoisms of class, of race or of persons, under theories of massacre and of hostilities, of reprisals and of parties. They would be responsible before Him Who died that we might be one, for the loss of their brothers and for the exhaustion of humanity in death.

NOTES

1. *Nouvelle Revue Théologique* t. LXVI, 1934, p. 449.

THE PASTORAL IDEA IN THE HISTORY OF THE LITURGY

*JOSEF A. JUNGMANN, S.J.**

CHRIST the Lord taught His Church how to pray, and delivered over to her the sacraments, the Eucharist above all. It was a precious gift, and has been treasured by the Church with reverence through the centuries. But the Church has not merely preserved and guarded this treasure, she has also developed it and embellished it with rich forms; she has created in the course of centuries what we call the liturgy of the Church.

The liturgy has a long history, a history almost as eventful as the history of the Church herself. This history has in the past few centuries been the object of numerous studies, beginning with the first attempts at the time of the Council of Trent, followed by the folio volumes of the Maurists, and continuing in the learned works of our own century. At first these studies had to content themselves with establishing facts, with clarifying relationships and developments, and with identifying the chief factors in the evolution of the liturgy —factors which were often bound up with external, cultural and political conditions, as well as with the generally

* Professor at the University of Innsbruck, and consultor of the Sacred Congregation of Rites.

prevalent spiritual and intellectual outlook of the respective times. But the more these scholarly researches matured, the more too it became possible to recognize and to trace the effects of the silent forces which had ever been active in the liturgy from within. The liturgy is like a tree, which has grown in the changing climate of world history and which has experienced stormy as well as flourishing times. Its real growth, however, comes from within, from those life forces whence it took its origin. The liturgy is the life of the Church with her face towards God—of that Church which is the fellowship of all who in baptism have been granted membership with Christ, and who gather, Sunday after Sunday, to celebrate the memory of our Lord under the leadership of the priestly office.

The priestly office has at all times recognized that its most noble task is to perform the divine service at the head of the assembled community. But it had a further, special mission at the time when the divine service was still in its period of formation. Then it had to create the external forms of the service and determine their order.

The question therefore arises: What were the determining points of view which governed the creation of these forms? Where can we find the key to the mystery of these highly varied and, to us, often puzzling forms of liturgical texts? Why the alternation of Scripture reading, song and prayer, why this abundance of movements and ceremonies? Why this multiplicity of forms at all?

We find the answer in the concern on the part of ecclesiastical authority for the Church: for the Church as comprising the sum total of the faithful, for the Church as *plebs sancta* who, under the guidance of her pastors, even in this earthly life should offer to God in prayer and sacrifice a worthy service and thus herself be sanctified. This pastoral concern has been decisive in determining the forms of the divine service. It embraces several aspects.

I

The first goal to be striven for and which we find realized in the liturgy is that *the Church has to be brought together* in and through the liturgy. Our Lord instituted the Eucharist as a common meal. Thus we see the faithful of the first generation break bread *per domos,* in small communities from house to house. The communities become larger; churches, basilicas and magnificent cathedrals are built. But always there is the clear understanding that the Church, through which God must be glorified, does not consist in last analysis of the building of stone erected by human hands— imposing as it may be—but first and always of that dwelling which God wished to prepare for Himself *ex vivis et electis lapidibus,* from living and elect stones; and this includes not only His consecrated servants who stand at the altar, but also the totality of the faithful whom they have been called to lead.

And therefore we see the liturgy intent upon establishing this communion of the faithful within the walls of the earthly building, upon making it visible. The people of God had to become visible— and in thousands upon thousands of places it becomes visible and audible. The faithful gather around him who is ordained and has the fullness of authority, and thus their common prayer ascends to God.

Already the most ancient forms of the liturgy testify that there was no intention of having a divine service at which the bishop or priest speaks mysterious formulas for himself alone and at which the faithful need be present merely as silent witnesses. Rather, the bishop or priest pronounces the prayers in their name, loudly and distinctly, and he says them in the plural: *"We* pray, we thank, we offer, we praise and glorify." In fact at the very outset of his prayer he invites their participation: *Gratias agamus,* let us give thanks; *Oremus,* let us pray.

To make this invitation even more urgent, he first of all directs a greeting to the assembly: *Dominus vobiscum,* a greeting that demands an answer: *Et cum spiritu tuo.* Only then does he say the prayer, the prayer of the assembled people of God: *populus tuus, Ecclesia tua, plebs tua sancta.* And after he has completed the prayer, he once again expects the community to voice their assent with the word *Amen.* This *Amen,* to quote St. Augustine, is as it were the signature which the people should write under his prayer: *"Amen dicere subscribere est"* (Serm. Denis 6,3).

From earliest times already, special importance was attached to this *Amen,* particularly to that which occurs at the end of the eucharistic prayer. Justin Martyr, in whose First Apology we find the oldest, and in fact a twofold, account of the Church's eucharistic celebration, speaks only briefly of the bringing of gifts and of the prayer of thanksgiving which the "president" offers to the Father of all; and yet in both accounts he mentions this *Amen*. With obvious pride Justin, a layman, stresses the fact that the *Amen* was to be cried aloud by all the people; and he makes it a point to explain to his pagan readers the meaning of this Hebrew word: viz., "So be it."

In this arrangement of liturgical prayer, which is found not only in the Roman liturgy but in all Christian liturgies as well, we hear the voice of the early Church, the voice of the first generations. We have here the oldest and most venerable tradition of the Church in the sphere of her divine service. For in the *Amen* we to our own day not only hear the language of the apostles and of our Lord Himself, but the greeting and the response show unmistakable characteristics of the idiom of that time. The fact that the early Church wished her divine service to be understood as a concern of the entire community could not have been given clearer expression.

The infant Church soon spreads beyond the land of the Bible, and begins to take her place in the world of Hellenistic culture and among people speaking the Greek language. And she carries her tradition with her: not only the teachings that have been committed to her care, but also the liturgical tradition of which we have just spoken. But she also brings with her the basic principle, that the divine service is to be the concern of the entire community.

Though her divine service retains characteristics of its country of origin, the Church for her prayer and readings does not cling to Aramaic or Hebrew but accepts the language of the new nations: not however the dialects of the various tribes of Asia Minor or of Illyria, but the language of literature and written communication, namely Greek, which was more or less universally understood. And later, in the third century, in Rome itself, when the Christian community expanded beyond the circle of the Greek colony and the local Latin population came to predominate, the Church once again undertakes a change of language: the Greek is translated into the Latin divine service.

Since then, it has been in its Latin form that the liturgy of Rome has evolved, because Latin for more than a thousand years remained for the nations of the West not only the language of literature, but also of communication among the educated classes, and it was the obvious language in all the assemblies and councils of the Church. For that very reason it could also continue to be the language of the liturgy.

If, in this case, the law of constancy made itself felt and Latin became a sacred language, we see on the other hand in Rome itself a surprising flexibility of liturgical forms in operation up to the early middle ages. This very fact is indeed a striking instance of liturgical-pastoral care of souls. For not only did the liturgy accommodate itself to the national character of the people as a whole, but it also took into account the fact that the faithful are at home in this particular city, and even in this particular part of the city.

In the liturgy of the stational churches, for instance, the lessons are often chosen with a view to the respective sanctuary or its surroundings. Thus on Sexagesima the station is *ad Sanctum Paulum;* this serves as an occasion to have the apostle tell his life's story. Another time the station is at SS. Cosmas and Damian, the much frequented pilgrimage church. The epistle alludes to the eagerness of the faithful to go on pilgrimage and with the words of the prophet warns against the presumptuous confidence of saying: *templum Domini, templum Domini.* But also, vice versa, the service itself was on one occasion transferred to a cemetery church, that of St. Eusebius, because one wished to call attention to baptism by reading the scriptural account of the resurrection of the dead.

Of course, this accommodation of the liturgy to national and even local circumstances at the time when the liturgical forms were originating, necessarily resulted in tensions when these forms were transmitted to other places and other nations. For the liturgy could not be constantly created anew; it had to be retained and transmitted at least in its substance. It required, therefore, not only adaptation, but also—so far as possible—that it be reverently adhered to and faithfully reproduced. For liturgy is sacred word; liturgy attempts to avoid disquieting change, since it wants to participate to some extent in God's holy rest and thereby communicate to the faithful something of God's own peace.

In transmitting liturgical forms from country to country, therefore, how much stress was to be laid on adaptation, and how much on adherence to tradition? In how far should the respective national character, the need of the *hic et nunc,* decide the matter? Here various solutions were possible according to the conditions of the times.

One element of the divine service, the sermon, has always accommodated itself to the particular nationality, that is, to the needs of those who are gathered *hic et nunc;* and the Church has fought for this right, even in the case of minorities and small groups. And when sermon and catechesis in the native tongue could not be employed because of adverse political circumstances—as happened for centuries in the case of some of the Catholic peoples of the East—the Church sometimes adopted the national tongues for her entire liturgy, or at least for those parts of the divine service which more closely affect the people. She made use of the new languages, particularly of the Arabic, at least for the readings and for the litanies which the deacon says together with the people.

On other occasions, as in our time, for instance, the adoption of the native tongue has been permitted at least for the administering of the sacraments and for the rites of the Ritual. The ceremonies of marriage or the prayers at a funeral are to be performed in such a way that the participants are able, through the spoken word, to grasp the meaning of this event in the light of the great redemptive truths and, through common prayer, together raise their hearts to God. Even in the Sunday service, at least when the *Missa lecta* is used, there is possible a wide variety of common vernacular prayer and song in close dependence on the forms of the liturgy.

II

At all times the purpose of the liturgy has been to bring the faithful together, so that they might stand before God as the Church, as the people of God. But the liturgy has also intended more than this: it has aimed to lead the faithful to *a conscious Christian faith.*

In the course of its history, the liturgy has developed a rich abundance of forms, especially of prayer, only a modest portion of which are familiar to us today. The Church has never contented herself with merely performing the sacramental actions entrusted to her by her Founder. She has, for instance, not been satisfied with merely pouring water over the head of the baptismal candidate: already in the third century she blessed the water with solemn prayer, and led the catechumen by one ritual step after another to the sacrament of rebirth. She has never been satisfied with transmitting the priestly power by simple imposition of hands: from early times she surrounded this event with meaningful rites and prayers. Nor has she been satisfied with pronouncing the sacred words over bread and wine: reverently, step by step, she leads up to this climax of the sacramental happening.

What is the purpose of this lavish wealth of forms, especially forms of the word? Why this particular structure of prayers, why the development of the great truths of faith in the course of the Church year? In his encyclical *Mediator Dei,* Pope Pius XII explained the well-known axiom, *Lex orandi est lex credendi* by inverting the order of its words into, *Lex credendi est lex orandi.* There can be no doubt that at all times the Church has, in connection with her sacred rites, striven also to give expression to her faith by prayer—in all simplicity before God, but likewise before her own faithful. The spiritual world, to which we as redeemed belong, should come alive whenever the Church gathers in prayer. In this manner the faithful should be led to a conscious Christian faith, and be sustained in it. As the mosaics in the apse of a Roman basilica inspire all who enter with their glorious vision of the heavenly Jerusalem to which we are called, and of the enthroned Christ who is our hope, and of the rivers of paradise which flow from our Lord's cross as streams of life, so too the word of prayer and reading should renew in us a vital awareness of the great truths of faith.

Attention has rightly been called to the fact that the oldest formulations of the principal prayer of the Mass, namely the eucharistic prayer, strikingly correspond to the formulations of the Creed. Sometimes, in fact, the preface has been called by names which could equally well be applied to the Creed: thus it was occasionally called *praedicatio,* or even simply *exomologesis,* "profession" (of faith). Moreover, in this prayed profession of our faith, and especially in its oldest forms, we constantly find emphasized precisely those truths of faith which are most fundamental for the Christian. Liturgical prayer was at the same time a catechism of Christian doctrine: not indeed a catechism with a great many detailed teachings, with fine distinctions and much enumeration, but a catechism in which the cardinal truths of faith, and more especially those which had the character of glad tidings, were summarized in a manner that could not fail to make a profound impression.

The principal prayer of the Mass was from the very outset conceived as a prayer of thanksgiving. We are called upon to give thanks by the words *Gratias agamus!* Since God "has delivered us from the power of darkness, and has transferred us into the kingdom of His beloved Son" (Col. 1:13), we can do nothing else and give Him no other answer except thanks: *semper et ubique gratias agere:* because God's action on our behalf was absolutely and in every way gratuitous. It was sheer grace, superabundant grace. How important it is that knowledge of this truth become to an ever greater degree the basic awareness of the faithful Christian: Christianity is not a burden or an irksome duty, Christianity is supreme grace. The liturgy fosters such conscious Christian faith!

It is characteristic, moreover, of the oldest Christian liturgies as well as of today's Roman liturgy, that nearly every prayer, every oration, every preface, and especially the conclusion of the eucharistic prayer is so constructed that the ascent to God takes place *per Christum Dominum nostrum, per Dominum nostrum Iesum Christum, per Ipsum et cum Ipso*. This, too, is a tradition deriving from the earliest period of the liturgy. Hearing these words over and over again, and answering their *Amen* to them, the faithful were constantly reminded that we can approach the presence of God with confidence only because He Himself has gone before us, because Christ is our head and our Lord, the Risen One, who passed through death and gained eternal life for us.

This constantly recurring theme by itself sufficed to make the faithful realize that their Christian religion is not just a collection of teachings and commandments, but that it is the glad tidings about Christ who desires to lead us home to the heavenly Father: and that essentially it is union with Christ and life with Him.

But this word concerning the One in whom alone we can find salvation, was from the very beginning explained and expanded.

First of all in the readings. And the last of these readings, ever since Christian antiquity, has always been that in which Christ Himself appears, and speaks and acts, namely, the gospel. Hence, to this day, when this reading is announced, a cry is raised saluting the Lord as if present: *Gloria tibi Domine!* These readings were destined for the ears of the faithful; they were directed from the ambo to the congregation, and often were preceded by a special call for attention: *Proschomen,* give heed!

But the word concerning the Savior is further expanded and interpreted in the series of feast days which the Church has been celebrating since earliest times. The great feasts observed in the course of the Church year are, really, all feasts of our Lord: the feast of His birth and His epiphany, the commemoration of His redemptive sufferings and His Easter triumph, His ascension and His sending of the Holy Spirit; and then the feast days of His Mother, of His apostles and of His other witnesses. And, finally, week after week, His memorial day: Sunday, *Dominica:* the day of *Dominus noster,* or, as it was called in Greek, *kyriake,* the day of our *Kyrios:* for it is the day on which He fulfilled the work of salvation by His Easter victory.

Thus when, week by week, and year by year, the person of our Lord and His deeds were presented to the minds of the faithful, they could not but realize what it means to be a Christian. So long as the faithful understood this language and were moved by it, they could not go astray, even if their knowledge of the contents of the faith were otherwise slight, or if they were unacquainted with the finer distinctions being made by theologians. And we can understand how, through centuries, a ministry of souls was possible that knew nothing of any systematic catechesis, in which there was little preaching and that usually by the bishop only, and in which instruction by means of the printed word was not yet possible. Nevertheless Christianity flourished and was vitally alive—because the great truths of Christianity were learned and were a living experience in the liturgy.

If the Church did not cease thus vividly to present the person and deeds of our Lord to the minds of the faithful, she actually was doing only what the Lord Himself had in His last hours commissioned her to do, when He said: "Do this in memory of Me." For these words certainly contain the command to perform the sacramental Mystery; but they also include a command to His Church to enact the Mystery in such a way that His faithful will never forget Him, nor will ever forget what He is for them: their way, their life, their truth. The liturgy leads to conscious Christian faith!

III

But we have to ask ourselves once again: Why this abundance of forms in the liturgy? Why was the Church not content simply with keeping the memory of our Lord alive for the faithful by means of instruction, such as in readings and sermons, or through certain forms of poetry, such as hymns and songs? Why the many different forms of prayer; why the predominance of prayer at all, and even of vocal prayer, when prayer, as everyone knows, should be a matter of the heart, of quiet devotion of spirit? Or why at least was not the Mass, this most holy of Mysteries, developed from the very beginning as a silent celebration, as a series of prayers to be said by the priest, with the faithful following in holy reverence from a distance only? For it took eight centuries before even the innermost core of the Mass, the Canon, due to particular conditions of the Church in France, came to be concealed in such silence.

The answer again can only be, that the liturgy is meant to guide and lead the faithful, and above all, *to lead them to Christian prayer and Sacrifice.*

Wherever there is faith, there too is prayer: prayer as the spontaneous response of the creature to the Creator. But the prayer of the individual is always in danger of confining itself to the narrow horizon of individual interests, and to be satisfied with petitions. Hence the Church has from the outset placed in the forefront of her liturgy the prayers of praise, of thanksgiving, and of adoration. She has kept in mind what our Lord said to the Samaritan woman at Jacob's well: God seeks adorers, adorers who worship Him in spirit and in truth. And where else should He find them if not in His holy Church? As the Lord's prayer begins with the *Sanctificetur,* so too the prayer of the Church's divine service reaches its climax in the threefold *Sanctus,* the *Sanctus* that grows out of the great prayer of thanksgiving. The *Sanctus* is the oldest song of the Mass liturgy, and for nearly a thousand years it was simply taken for granted that the entire congregation join in singing it, in order that *una voce* with the angels of heaven they pay God homage. What a joyous inspiration it must have been for the faithful to realize in whose company they were raising their own voices!

But already in Christian antiquity the *Sanctus* was not the only song. Especially in connection with the readings, and above all the readings of the Mass, where we still have the gradual and alleluia, the people were expected to sing. The "psalmist," frequently a youthful reader with a clear voice, sang the psalm, while the people after each stanza sang their refrain, their alleluia or joyful acclaim, or the verse of the psalm that had been intoned at the beginning. St. Augustine, in his *Enarrationes in psalmos,* shows himself a true pastor, a master of the liturgical care of souls, when with evident pastoral satisfaction he stresses precisely those verses which had been sung by all conjointly: "We have heard the psalm," he says, "and we have encouraged each other by singing with one heart and one voice our answer, 'Come, let us adore' " (Serm. 176,1). Such verses could not but have left an indelible impression on the hearts of the faithful; they became a precious treasury of prayer and of holy joy.

The liturgy is meant to lead the faithful to Christian prayer. But petitions also belong to Christian prayer. On some occasions, in fact, prayers of petition loom very prominently in the liturgy, so much so that certain days even derive their name from them: *Rogationes, Litania.* But also within the regular Sunday Mass, it was customary for centuries after the time of Justin Martyr in the West, and is still general practice in the East, that the readings are followed by prayer: prayer for the general needs of all Christendom, for all stations of life and for the faithful themselves. Usually, this prayer is said alternately, and is concluded by the priest with a collect.

In other instances—and this was from ancient times especially true of the Roman liturgy—there was an initial invitation to pray, followed by a brief period of silent, personal prayer. To stress the need of interior devotion during this period, the people were asked to kneel: *Flectamus genua.* Each one was expected to let the words of the previous reading resound in the quiet of his own heart, or to commend to God some petition, whether personal to himself, or named in the invitation to prayer that had preceded. And they were not to rise until the call was heard: *Levate,* after which the priest began his summarizing oration. This manner of praying has again been restored to us by the Holy Father in his reform of the Easter liturgy. The liturgy is our guide to Christian prayer!

It is our guide to *Christian* prayer. However much the liturgy practices the veneration of saints—even the oldest sacramentaries contain a great number of martyr feasts—it never permits prayer to become so diffuse as to mistake God's friends for God Himself, or to speak as if the heavenly patron could aid us by his own power, or to lose sight of Him whom St. Paul calls the sole Mediator between God and man. Liturgical prayer knows the *Ora pro nobis,* and especially in its hymns uses many a bold phrase in honoring the power of saints. But the petition always returns again to the main current: it prostrates before God's majesty and begs for the granting of the request *intercedentibus Sanctis tuis, Per Dominum nostrum Iesum Christum.*

It is significant, moreover, that for many centuries the law of "orientation" was observed during such prayer. One turned toward the East, toward the direction of the rising sun—and to our own day the majority of our churches are so oriented. For in the rising sun one perceived the image of Him who is the Light of the world and our Advocate with the Father. Even the bodily posture, therefore, of those who prayed made clear through whom they hoped to obtain hearing for their petitions.

The liturgy a guide to Christian prayer? Without any force ever being imposed on the freedom of personal prayer, the faithful necessarily became aware simply by listening to the prayers of the Church, to which they answered their *Amen,* what our relationship to God really is. The view of the Christian cosmos came alive to the mind's eye again and again, and they learned the correct attitude that befits Christian prayer.

A guide to Christian prayer. The most exalted theme concerning which the Church had to instruct her faithful has always been and is the Sacrifice of the New Law. There is something great and wonderful in the fact that, ever since the earliest beginning of the Church, wherever there are Catholic Christians they gather in the houses of God Sunday after Sunday in their thousands and millions in order to assist in the holy Sacrifice.

Perhaps there have always been many among them who merely wished to fulfill their obligation of being present. And no doubt there has existed at times a kind of pastoral care which did not attempt more or demand more from the faithful than that they persevere with due reverence until the end of the sacred Action.

But if we inquire from the liturgy of the Church and study it when its forms were still a part of life, we find that the liturgy itself has always aimed much higher. It always sought to assemble the faithful around the altar as *circumstantes*—obviously not in a geometrical, but in a spiritual sense. It permitted them to bring bread and wine or other gifts to the altar. The faithful were expected to respond to the priest, and in the prayer that he spoke and still speaks, they were described as those who are offering the Sacrifice: *Nos servi tui sed et plebs tua sancta.* And to this prayer of offering, too, they were permitted to pronounce their *Amen.*

Wherever the faithful understood and accepted what the liturgy urged upon them, they necessarily became aware that here they were not simply *hospites et peregrini,* "strangers and pilgrims," that they were not called to be mere witnesses of what Christ performed through the priest at the altar in mysterious prayers and rites. Here was not only the Sacrifice of Christ, but the Sacrifice which Christ wished to celebrate with His Church, the Sacrifice which as High Priest He wished to offer at the head of His priestly people, and into which He wanted to draw all the faithful, together with their work and worries, their struggles and sufferings. It is the Sacrifice by means of which He wished to lead the world to the heavenly Father—until that day appears, when "God shall be all in all" (1 Cor. 15:28).

A holy pride must have filled the hearts of the faithful who thus followed the guidance of the Church's liturgy in offering Sacrifice: and also the joyous certainty that "we have already been admitted into the kingdom of God." This awareness strengthened their faith more than many words of systematic, reasoned instruction could have done: for it was a holy joy, a foretaste of possessing heaven itself.

There is no doubt that the essential success of pastoral care is achieved when souls are saved, when it succeeds in leading men in such a manner that at least in the hour of death they find the right way and thus reach their goal. But it is a higher aim, and one more worthy of the Christian vocation, in fact, it is the true task of the Church, to lead the Christian people so that even here on earth they come together in holy and joyous fellowship to glorify God, and to fulfill what St. Peter describes as the duty of God's people: "That you may declare His virtues, who has called you out of darkness into His marvelous light" (1 Peter 2:9). This is exactly what the liturgy has attempted to do at all times.

The living liturgy, actively participated in, was itself for centuries the most important form of pastoral care. This is true particularly of those centuries in which the liturgy was developed in its essentials. In the later middle ages, the liturgy was indeed celebrated with zeal and much splendor in numerous collegiate and monastic churches, and was also further developed in its various forms. But unfavorable circumstances brought it about that something like a Fog Curtain settled between and separated liturgy and people, through which the faithful could only dimly recognize what was happening at the altar.

But even in those centuries we witness a certain expansion and adaptation of the liturgy—and again in the interests of pastoral care. Because the language of the liturgy had become foreign to the masses of the people, certain dramatic elements were introduced as a substitute. The middle ages knew only the solemn form of Mass with chant and, if possible, with sacred ministers, for the Sunday service of the people. Even this afforded considerable religious stimulation. But the solemnity was further increased. Lights and incense were now not merely carried along for the entrance procession, but the altar itself was ceremoniously censed, once, and a second time, and the censing was further extended to the choir and people. The processional lights began to be placed on the altar. The singing of the gospel became an occasion for a triumphal procession in honor of Christ. The sanctus candle was introduced to announce the nearness of the Mystery. And, finally, a striking climax was created by the elevation of the Host and Chalice at the Consecration.

Nevertheless, the Fog Curtain remained. The most important means of the soul's ascent to God, the word of the liturgy itself, had become inaccessible to the people. The prayers and songs by which the sacred Action is accomplished are perceived only as so many sounds in the ear. The liturgy has become a succession of mysterious words and ceremonies, which must be performed according to a fixed rule, and which one tries to follow with holy reverence—but which themselves finally harden into rigid and unchangeable forms.

Perhaps this rigidity was necessary—as a protection against heretical attacks upon the Sacrifice of the Church. It may also have been necessary to safeguard the sacred heritage for future times, for a time of greater need and of more grave decisions, such as we experience in our own day, when the faithful in an especial manner need that same guidance by the liturgy which was the privileged lot of the Christians of the first centuries.

Today the rigidity is beginning to lessen. Forms which appeared petrified have come to life again. The Church feels that she no longer needs the protection of this inflexibility. Just as the Church under Pius XI, by the Lateran Treaties, surrendered that external protection which, in the more crude times of the middle ages, had seemed so necessary to her as a world power, so now under Pius XII she has begun to loosen the protective armor which till now has encased the sacred forms of her liturgy. The interests of care of souls are again, as of old, becoming the decisive factor—those pastoral interests, in other words, from which the forms of the liturgy had taken their origin in the early days of the Church.

What a wonderful experience it was for many of the faithful in all parts of the world when, during the past Holy Week and on Easter Night, they were able for the first time to understand and

take part in the great liturgical events: when all at once they became aware that "this is *our* divine service!"

The Curtain is beginning to lift. A bright day is dawning. The
Church is gathering, and gaining new strength. With confidence
she faces the future—as the praying people of God.

MODERN FORMS OF CHRISTIAN LIFE AND ART

P. R. RÉGAMEY, O.P.

WHAT will probably characterize the present era in the eyes of the
historian of Christian life is the division of the faithful and their
pastors into three groups. An old segment, thoroughly routinized,
the *bien-pensants,* no doubt constitutes the majority of "practicing"
Catholics. Reacting violently to this group are the genuine elite,
that demand "worth" more and more in all domains of life. We
speak here of a genuine elite to distinguish it from the pretended
elite of authority, of money, of pseudo-culture which really belongs in the first category. Finally, these genuine elite groups have
raised up, among the practicing Catholics, and by conversions
among the masses of the people detached from the Church, Catholic Action movements which are rediscovering in a new way the
essential Christian realities (e.g., Young Christian Workers, Young
Christian Students, The Christian Family Movement, etc.).

The appearance of such an elite was the outstanding phenomenon in the Catholic world at the time of Lacordaire. In the course
of the last thirty or forty years, these groups have been increased,
renewed, and diversified in an astonishing manner. In general we
may say that it is these groups which make possible a renaissance
in the religious arts. However, this renaissance is too remote to
have a field as extensive as that of these movements. The most
vital tendencies of an age act upon art only sporadically and indirectly; their influence becomes general only after considerable

delay. Indeed, these influences are not always recognized in the works which they inspire: in the transition from one type of art to another there is much confusion. Thus Delacroix hated Romantic poetry and was delighted with Voltaire; so too Victor Hugo, an artist of power, had a liking for only mediocre and very placid paintings; similarly Leon Bloy condemned Rouault, his friend. We need not be astonished then at the difficulty which real values have in becoming recognized in present-day art, even by the genuine elite, and at the interest these groups sometimes show in that which grossly betrays their aspirations.

Nevertheless, vigilance, generosity of spirit, and a new interest in the values of sensibility often render the Christian elite responsive to works of quality. Thus public interest, which cannot fail to grow, will henceforth exist for such works. This elite is aware of the decadence of sacred art; it is concerned with its renaissance and is even prepared to undertake its renovation. It is more and more coming to recognize the plastic equivalent of those qualities which it loves and for which it struggles. In any case it is armed against vulgar religious ornamentation, and certain elements of it are even appreciative of genuine religious qualities.

Unfortunately, these elite groups are seldom in a position to direct the choice of artists and works. These directives are still given in the majority of cases according to the tastes of the *bien-pensant* majority. It is thus important in order to appreciate fully the artistic conditions which prevail among Catholic groups, first to reflect on the tendencies of this majority. Then we shall be in a position to determine what effects the present leavening of the elite, and the popular movements, can have on Christian art.

I. The Tendencies of Popular Piety

In a famous text, Paul Claudel declares that the churches built in the middle of the nineteenth century have the "interest of a melancholy and guilty confession."[1] In fact, the arts for a century have forced upon our eyes a picture of what is most deplorable in the Christianity of the time. It is worthy of note that the virtues which animated Christian life during the same period did not have their counterparts in the plastic order; or rather, to make matters worse, the arts translated these virtues, and even heroic sanctity, in a deplorable way. The extreme case of this phenomenon is that of St. Therese of the Child Jesus; her personal bad taste (faithfully transmitted to us by the "Art of Lisieux") does not seem to be a fortuitous accident. The best part of her spirituality, authentic to the point of heroism, became in the domain of poetry, music, and the plastic arts mere sentimentality: her evangelical sweetness became saccharine, her way of spiritual childhood was equated with daintiness. Behold to what extremes the artistic mediocrity reigning in pious groups could go!

But we must agree that certain aspects of religious living were of such a nature as to encourage this mediocrity.

The modern characteristics of Faith

At the root of all these difficulties is this situation: Faith, as we now conceive it and consequently as we now develop it, has not been, for the past two or three centuries, a stimulant for the arts. For rather than stimulating the imagination and the sensibility, it tended to sterilize them.

Faith was no longer presented as a mysterious and sure contact with revealed things, vitally linking us with them. It appeared dangerous to show what light it contained, its need to understand, its mystic potentialities, its impassioned *cogitatio,* and the knowledge certainly obscure but very real, rich, and varied that it can offer of its object. In short, it appeared dangerous to show that Faith is the habit of an awakened intelligence participating in the knowledge God has of Himself. The Christian soul, far from being invited to contemplate the mysteries to render them familiar and living, was suspected of pride and dangerous curiosity when he attempted to do so. Pure and simple obedience to incomprehensible doctrines—thus Faith "humbled reason" and all other human gifts. And this was subject for rejoicing! What art could reflect such a despotic Faith, blind and without content, except an art emptied of inspiration and liberty, and made up of formulae more and more meaningless?

In the earlier ages of the Fathers and of the medieval doctors, the Faith brought about a wisdom perfectly one, whether considered in its objects, from the mystery of divine life to human activity in relation to the cosmos, or whether one regarded it as operating through the powers of the soul. "Anima" contributed thereto as well as "animus"; and "anima" under its aspect of "pneuma" or "spiritus," as well as in its role of "psyche." The most rigorous science had a sort of spiritual sense and a free imagination; the most formal analogy made use of metaphor. Dante was a theologian and St. Thomas a poet. Man became wise. The powers of intuition and of creativity, the awareness of mystery, had their share in everything, in this atmosphere developed by the Word of God and by the Liturgy. Such a wisdom was diffused of itself in chant, poetry, and the other arts. It was already made "sensible." Thus, the arts did not receive their themes as abstract studies, but as stories, directives, and pictures.

It is not a question here of justifying or condemning the passage of this wisdom into mediocre forms of thought and of religious life in Catholic circles of the nineteenth century, no more than we should pass judgment on the other characteristics we are going to point out. We want only to understand, after the manner of a historian, the impact of these realities of life and thought on the arts. It was disastrous. Theology, as it was ordinarily taught, ceased to be a unified wisdom and was broken up into fragmentary, distinct disciplines: dogma, moral, asceticism, and mysticism, each of which had its own method, but none of which received any inspiration from the arts. In fact, dogma was a purely rational discipline centering on the formulae of faith, rather than a contemplation of the mysteries; moral science was a casuistic commentary on the commandments and on Canon Law; asceticism, a set of exercises; and mystical theology seemed too high, too sublime to have meaning for ordinary men. If an artist hoped to be inspired by this, he soon realized otherwise, for this was purely negative in spirit, and therefore could offer him no nourishment.

This sad state of affairs is evident in Claudel's description of the Baroque churches: "And there are saints who, by their face and attitude, indicate for us the ineffable and the invisible, and a completely disordered abundance of adornment; and angels who in a flutter of wings support paintings made indistinct and unrecognizable, and statues seemingly inspired by a breath from elsewhere.

But before this 'elsewhere' the imagination is stifled, intimidated and discouraged. . . ." At least during the Baroque period art was permitted to "consecrate all its resources to the arrangement of the framework," and in this it rejoiced with all its heart. But the nineteenth century lost all its sense of taste. The figurative arts had no other contribution to offer the Church than to translate abstract dogmatic syntheses into compositions, to illustrate pages of the catechisms, to reproduce symbols, and to relate, with the prosaic literalness of episodes viewed only from the exterior, the stories of Sacred History.

Faith was no longer nourished by the Scriptures, and simple Christians sometimes even imagined their reading to be forbidden. Nor was this virtue stimulated by the Liturgy, which was limited to the performance of rites and to the recitation of formulae. Everything tended to apologetics and to the affirmation of dogma, to moral guidance, and to sentimentality. Is there anything in all that which could fire the artistic imagination?

Since for many the Faith induced an inferiority complex, because it was insufficient to preserve them from pagan contamination, and even more incapable of affecting the modern world by recognizing what was its own and baptizing it, it could scarcely have any other effect than to establish a cheap spirit of imitation whose artistic expression could appear only in the creation of art forms systematically different from those which were elaborated by contemporary culture. This was an anachronistic state of mind which demanded that art to be "religious" must be a reflection of the past. In the same way Christians spoke glowingly of their ancient glories, were pleased with historical researches, and built up oversimplified systems according to which Faith necessarily imposed certain forms on philosophy, science, economics, and politics. A monument or a painting was definitely not "Christian" if not executed in a specific style, according to certain out-moded techniques.

Finally, to limit ourselves to the essential, Faith was merely an individual affair. The Church no longer appeared as the people of God, but as an exterior structure of magisterium and discipline. The object of Faith, having become too commonplace, no longer was "fascinating," and therefore had little unifying effect on the members of the Mystical Body. But a Christian art is not possible without a Christianity from which to spring.

On what level could one perceive a common sensibility? It was no longer in the one common soul of a divinized people, eager together for supernatural interests and for a sign expressing the Kingdom of Heaven, and having on all occasions lively, original, creative reactions, which would bear witness that sensibility itself was Christian. A common sensibility only reigned in the sacerdotal unction, the "tone of preaching," and all religious frills. Let us not be surprised then, if there was prosperity for the art called "Sulpician" (if one may call it art).

The ecclesiastical milieu and the faithful who embrace it do not realize how gravely they are still affected by these aberrations of the recent past. Their artistic judgments prove this. They form a world apart, where art is either too timid or on the contrary excessively daring. Artists are considered masters who are merely business men, pretentious or incompetent craftsmen. Yet we mock the great contemporary artists with triumphant self-assurance—when, by chance, we happen to know of their existence, or when they propose some new project.

The abuse of obedience

If Faith itself is often reduced to being merely obedience, which is really only one of its aspects (and not the most important), instead of developing itself as the living sense of supernatural realities —"the substance of things hoped for, the evidence of things that appear not" (Heb. 11:1)—to an even greater degree does obedience invade the whole realm of conduct. Do not many go so far as to extend to every precept of authority "obedience of judgment" which is imposed in rare cases where truth is guaranteed by the privilege of infallibility? When conformism is installed in this way even in the irrepressible source of liberty, it can only debase all activities, and especially art.

It is beyond doubt that for the majority of the *bien-pensants* obedience is, in practice, the principal virtue, which holds the place of all others. It results in a general fear of all initiative and novelty, a progressive degradation of values, and this we know constitutes the poorest environment for the unpredictable work of an artist.

The religious attitude which was extolled was one of passivity. Thus was abandonment to the divine will understood, and in this way did the acceptance of social injustices come about, submission to established powers, and respect for received formulae. This general passivity hinders artistic creativity, which demands vigilance, initiative—poetry.

From the point of view of art, there is a domain where this evil was particularly grave: that of the Liturgy. The state of the sacred arts depends on the value of the Liturgy in its actual celebration; it is like a master art to them. Justly is the modern era an epoch of the most profound Liturgical decadence, and one of the reasons for this is the abuse of obedience. The majority of clerics no longer think of the Liturgical celebration as a means of participating in the mysteries of Christ, but as the paying of a debt. Take the case of a parish High Mass: against the Protestants, the Council of Trent justifies ceremonies saying that they "have for end to make the majesty of such a sacrifice known, and to excite the souls of the faithful by means of these visible signs of religion and piety, to contemplate the sublime things which are hidden in this sacrifice."[2] It would be cruel to read that text in the course of High Mass such as it is celebrated almost everywhere. The clergy purely and simply acquit themselves of their functions. The very idea that the faithful may contemplate the mysteries, and that the ceremonies may effectively aid them, would appear to be quite absurd. As soon as the precept and the rubrics are observed, all is well, and since a Low Mass would suffice, if the non-obligatory chants and ceremonies are added more is being done than is required: so everybody should be happy. Such a frame of mind is diametrically opposed to the development of art. Art is in the order of pure "quality," and in the order of "gratuity." It will find its favorable climate in the Liturgy only insofar as its rites have their full spiritual value, are profoundly understood, and are executed from the soul. If they are merely accomplished "to keep a rule," there is in them no need for artistic embellishment. In a group of empty observances, art must be conventional. It is expected to express a milieu

as false as that from which it arises. Only two arts can be admitted:
the current artisanship which is generally conceded to be inartistic,
and the religious craftsmanship of a more advanced status for which
one applies to an "artist"—a member of the "Institut," if one can
afford him. At length one cannot conceive of worship in any other
sense. This leads to such an artificial, even hypocritical reaction,
that if, by chance a truly inspired work were introduced, one truly
drawn from the soul, a pure and clean work, it would shock all
eyes and appear "unprecedented."

Negative and timorous piety

An abuse of obedience is, of course, very serious because the
law has more interdictions than it has positive prescriptions; in
any case, the law has no power to give life. Reduced to itself, the
letter kills. It is evangelical only on the condition that the Spirit be
there to vivify it. The decisions of authority and of decrees presuppose an intelligence which understands them with relation to
the positive realities which have brought them to be, and on which
they remain constantly dependent—a creative life whose better and
surer accomplishment these decisions of authority are supposed to
assure. Clergy and faithful have gone off in quite a different direction. Their first care is not to submit themselves to the nature of
things and to the organic laws of free initiative and development; as
soon as their life escapes the law, it ceases to be in order, and becomes as good or as bad as the general rule (even though the general rule has more and more deviated from the Church, which has
become a minority in the world). Thus, they soon believe that to
be faithful they must cease to be daring. In this context art is
either anarchic or mediocre.

There is in human nature an inclination to restriction, to a sort
of general erosion, against which the human spirit ought constantly
to react. The Holy Spirit demands that we go beyond this disposition, but modern piety condemns us if we do. The destiny of the
most beautiful terms signifies this in a striking fashion: those beautiful words, formerly positive and so rich in meaning, *prudence,
economy, moderation, measure, discretion,* and even *wisdom,* how

deadening they have become—when they are not frankly negative! As for prudence, there is no cause for wonder if the *bien-pensants* continue to hold it for the first of the cardinal virtues, now that they have vitiated it. It was formerly the discernment of a man so vitally connatural to the highest and most vigorous ideal that in difficult circumstances he found a combination of means to conform himself to this ideal; it was a spontaneous, inventive, and courageous discernment which led a person forward, releasing all the dynamism of the other virtues. Now prudence has become greedy precaution which identifies itself with the obedience of the formalist. The *bien-pensants* are tainted with this evil as much as the most timorous civil functionary, but their case is much more serious, since the objects in question are spiritual, as are their motives and intentions. Everyone knows what a "good young man" is, or a "good Sister," or priest; what a humiliating atmosphere one breathes in certain sacristies, certain rectories, and even in certain apostolic works—a sanctity reduced to a moralism, which consists in not breaking the precepts that demand obedience, chastity, and assistance at Sunday mass. This is what the mediocre everywhere make their standard. Christians have the art they deserve!

We have already ascertained how difficult an art at once vital and Christian must be, not only because of its very nature, but even more because it must find a place in the modern world. But such an audience as we now have makes Christian art impossible. The majority of artists of inferior rank conform to a pattern set by their Christian public: these artists are not at all inclined to be creative. They have in them no real vitality to be restrained from falling into disorder (how fortunate for good order!). But should we not keep in mind that order exists solely for the service of life. Religious architecture (the art of order), the sacred object, the "religious article," thus constitute the privileged place in a lamentable piety.

There will be a superficial attempt among the complacent to bring into the arts a "just measure," "to keep oneself midway between opposite extremes," thus adopting an attitude of compromise. Then there will be a question among the complacent of being right in every case; and the true in every case is objectively determined, it is all of one piece, it is inflexible, it has neither less nor more, it is or it is not, and it is "such or such." And this truth in art is determined by a specific group, which is never uncertain. A very characteristic work, it would seem, is that which was given as a motto to the architects of a great enterprise of church construction: "Neither ancient, nor modern: make it in between." So it is in diocesan regulations about art works, and so it is in everything.

Mortified senses

Finally religious motives aggravate the general perversion of the imagination and the sensibility, and consequently, of the arts. The human ideal for our interior universe is no longer the "political" regime which Aristotle and St. Thomas recommend, where intelligence, will, and sensibility work together according to the needs of the human composite. The Stoic and Cartesian influences, and the authoritarian method by which everything is done, have imposed as the ideal a pure and simple "despotism" of the will and intellect, subduing the imagination as if it were a fool, and the senses as if they were impure. The results are obvious. "A sort of prudery," as Alexander Cingria remarks, "lending to life and art a dangerous attraction, gives to whatever is living and beautiful an appearance of sensuality, of which both art and life are entirely innocent."[3] Hence art to be religious is expected to be anemic.

In concluding, it seems necessary to subscribe to the statement of Claudel, for whom the causes of the decadence of the sacred arts are summed up in one: "It is the divorce, the completion of which was seen in the last century, between the propositions of Faith and the powers of imagination and sensibility which are eminently those of the artist."[4] This emphasis on the "propositions of Faith" is very well placed. For only rational formulae are considered in this revealed gift. No longer do we regard the mysteries which we live through the liturgical and Scriptural activation of Faith. Religion is a matter of convictions, of practices, a system of prescriptions, which are mostly negative. The "powers of sensibility and of imagination" are mortified by this dry and sombre religion, and they are placed on trial by academicism, at the very time when the great contemporary artists outside the Church have refined and exalted these powers to new heights.

II. New Tendencies

It would be historical over-simplification to oppose point by point the tendencies of the old group of "practicing" Catholics to those of the new elite, and of the generous movements which they determine. In particular the return to a full Faith possessing the "substance of things hoped for," still remains rather rare even among the most apostolic Christians. Observers are struck with the pragmatic and subjective character of even the most lively piety, by the slight interest many generous souls show in the mysteries. They do not so much seek to know God Himself, as to observe the qualities of His life in them, or to regulate their conduct towards Him.[5] A more or less explicit agnosticism often affects religious thought and piety. Truly objective, contemplative orientation seems rare, and the disinterested cultivation of religion which this requires is equally rare. Doctrinal formation seems sketchy; or rather—for there is no question here of an exterior change, of notional knowledge—we ought to say that Christians do not appear to "dwell in Heaven" by constant study of the things of God, the meditation it is necessary to make on them, and their frequent contemplation. Certainly one must be deeply impressed when he considers this subject. For certain facts seem symptomatic. Thus, in areas where the supernatural necessarily enters in—for example, the religious state—the reaction is very often of a decidedly natural order, emphasis is placed on the human side of these realities, to the neglect of strictly supernatural aspects. To continue, using the same example, we may note that the value of the vows themselves is poorly comprehended.[6] In the spiritual order an element of naturalism is perceptible,[7] and even more is this carried over into the plastic representation of spiritual realities.

If one considers recent tendencies which are noticeable in the religious arts, he must be struck by an excessive taste for symbolism, and even for esotericism. Such art is sometimes violently tragic; sometimes despondent. Or again, it may sometimes burst forth in whimsical and lyric life. It nearly always expresses the

preferences of a school of spirituality which goes to the extreme in
what it thinks or feels, and which does not care for the piety of the
Church. Or else it takes only what is agreeable to itself, interpreting
this according to its own inclinations and theories, and so failing to
appreciate the elements it has overlooked. There is a danger in em-
phasizing one of the qualities which Christianity integrates, rather
than expressing the total Faith of the Church. Such expression of
the total Faith would, of course, be marked by certain qualities
peculiar to certain temperaments in the order of nature and grace,
but it would remain rich because it would be in touch with all elements of Catholicity, or it would, at least, not contradict them. The
majority of the present tendencies express themselves in works too
obviously partisan and extreme. These works, therefore, lack one
of the prime requisites of an art truly Christian, namely, the note
of universality. In the same way the Christian sense of the people
is not in these works. It is hard enough to make the people understand the language of plastic art which, because of the reign of
academicism, is drawn up without any relation to them; but frequently the very inspiration of modern works is of such a nature
as to disturb them.

Let us hope that the more influential artists of our time, instead
of busying themselves with what impressed them most in the solitude of their studios, and no matter how authentically Christian
their intention and even their source may be, will live more fully the
life of the Church by opening themselves to the influences of the
Scriptures, of the Fathers, and of the Church's doctrinal and
spiritual traditions. Thus these artists will come in time to possess
the fullness and balance of the Christian spirit. Let us hope also that
they will share in the life of the faithful, and that they will cause
the contemporary aspiration of the Church—the incarnation of the
"new man through Christ" in modern man—to be re-echoed
among the masses.

Here again we note that great problem of contemporary religious
art which we have already discussed. If the great truths enumerated
below are to receive plastic expression it is necessary for the artists
to become conscious of the astonishing youth of the Church, of the
new awareness the Church has of its eternal principles, and of the
apostolic force to be found within them. Are the arts going to bear

witness in the eyes of the world to the "truth," the "vitality," and the "purity" of Christ and His Church? This success will be achieved only if artists live with Christ so that His life will purify the very source of their works. This purification will take place if artists will contemplate the truth of Christ in itself and allow themselves to be freed by it from the partisan views which now sometimes blind them. Too frequently they do not appear to live in real communion with Christ or the faithful.[8]

If one considers this body of the faithful in whom the youthful vigor of the Church is now manifest, he must observe that they scarcely constitute a milieu favorable to the art forms which best correspond to their aspirations. Their esthetic sense is generally perverted. A noble enthusiasm sometimes praises too highly the religiosity of works whose poverty of means, of exactness, and of suitability clearly leaves sentimental intentions evident. Sometimes, too, in such works distortions and vulgar, over-simplified color schemes betray a seeking after a novel and forceful style. The pictures one sees in the missals of ardent Catholic Action workers are in every sense of the word, "betrayals" of their ideal. They manifest this ideal in so gross a manner that they thereby contradict it; but who could expect these young people to perceive this? They have never encountered anything except what is plastically "false." The more they concern themselves with the artistic expression of their life of union with God the more they illustrate their esthetic ignorance. Then, too, Christians of magnificent spirit are even more scandalized by plastic works which represent their noble tendencies than are the *bien-pensants*. Such militants, logical and precise in their outlook, would disdain to admire pictures of the churches of German-Switzerland, and would instead eulogize a structure such as St. Pierre de Chaillot.

The religious arts are necessarily subject to all the problems inherent in what we today call a "purposeful" (*engagé*) art, that is one which serves some human cause. The public brings about the triumph of non-artistic values at the expense of those which have a more solid esthetic foundation. This problem would be of little gravity if the customary views prevalent among the public and among most artists—as the result of two centuries of academicism —were not entirely disastrous to art, and attuned to a vulgar sentimentality. One need not be astonished, then, that in our time, art so feebly serves the most impassioned causes—thus it was not a coincidence that at the Exposition of 1937, the two most mediocre exhibits were those of Nazi Germany and Communist Russia.

For some time it will be necessary that they who are most deeply penetrated with the Christian spirit should accept—and more than that encourage—churches, paintings, stained-glass windows, and statues which authentically express what they have most at heart. Till now the principal effect of Christian zeal has been—as a reaction to "Sulpician" mawkishness—an affectation of rigidity, violence, harshness, and a pompous turgidity.

It should be remarked also that the majority of militant Christians and of clergy are too anxious for "efficiency." They want immediate delivery, visible and rapid achievement; they bring this trait especially into art which they regard in a utilitarian fashion with a view to their apostolate. They do not doubt that art is as disinterested as the contemplation whence it ought to proceed and which it arouses and aids; they do not doubt that it is in the order of "quality"; but they demand of it formulae which they can use in their works of zeal.

The solution of these difficulties will not be found until the artist brings out in his own spiritual life—prior, so to speak, to the elaboration of his works—a synthesis between the aspirations of renewed Christianity and the most vital tendencies in art. The works thus conceived will not superficially conform to a pattern, after the fashion of one composing an essay in a foreign language; rather they will respond to the needs of Christians in our times, since they will come from the souls of those who clearly feel these needs. We may hope also that among the authorities in the Church, men will be found who unite in themselves a true sense of art values and an awareness of the great Christian needs of today. They will thus progressively create the atmosphere favorable to such works.

We see now how complex are the needs involved, and how rarely they are satisfied. The task is an immense one. At present the influence of the predominant majority of the clergy is opposed to artistic works of real value, and the plastic expression of the aspirations of militant groups is sometimes worse—from an artistic, and even from a spiritual viewpoint—than the old, grotesque, pietistic art.

Reasons for hope

But if so many factors of civilization and Christian life (and of influences more remote than these), give us cause to look forward not to a renaissance of Christian art, but rather to its decadence, when a complete account is taken, it seems that hope ought to prevail. In fact, the Christian renewal is itself of such depth, diversity, and breadth that its activities ought to find more and more accurate expression in art. That religious domain which is of supreme import among the sacred arts is precisely one of those in which the most marked progress is taking place, and in a manner which is directly and immediately favorable to an artistic renaissance. I speak here of the Liturgy. Let us repeat: the Liturgy is like the "master of art" of all sacred arts, which latter are as Pope Pius XI said—and as Pope Pius XII has recently re-emphasized in his monumental encyclical on the Liturgy—"its most noble servants."

Liturgy was understood by the greater part of its devotees in former ages in a fashion too archaeological or, again, as the meticulous execution of rites. The effect of this state of mind on the arts was to limit their activity to the interpretation of dry and out-dated formulae. The great liturgical movement which passed to France from Switzerland and Germany causes the Liturgy to be understood in a more profound and living fashion. As its orientation is decidedly "pastoral," it obliges the clergy to rethink all important realities with relation to the faithful, and it familiarizes the people themselves with these realities. But because all such realities are the Church's, which it has translated into gesture, song, and poetry, the liturgical movement ought to reconcile closely the world of Faith and the powers of imagination and sensibility whose separation was the great cause of decadence. Liturgy is the link connecting mysticism with activity. We have every reason to hope that it will more and more succeed in restoring all Christians to a sense of "values." Once more pure, living, and true, the Liturgy will in its activity create a favorable environment for the accomplishment of works guided by its spirit. May all tendencies of the Christian renewal converge in a true liturgical renaissance; and thus a renaissance of the sacred arts shall be assured in its source, in its spirit, and in its environment.

NOTES

1. "Their Ugliness," he says, "is the exterior manifestation of all our faults, weakness, indigence, timidity in Faith and sentiment, dryness of heart, disgust for the supernatural, the dominance of conventions and formulae, exaggeration of individualized and disordered devotions, worldly luxury, avarice, haughtiness, peevishness, pharasaism, and bombast." (Letter to Alexandre Cingria, June 19, 1919). Inserted into the preface of the second edition of *La Décadence de l'Art Sacré*, by A. Cingria, Art Catholique, 1930, p. x. (There is an English translation in *Ways and Crossways*.)
2. Sess. XXII, cap. v (Denz., No. 943).
3. A. Cingria, *op. cit.*, p. 43.
4. Preface to Cingria.
5. Cf. the article of Père Paissac, *Supplément de La Vie Spirituelle*, 1947, I; special number of *Jeunesse de l'Eglise*, "L'Athéisme des chrétiens," 1947.
6. Cf. Plé, "Conclusion à l'enquête sur la sainteté," *La Vie Spirituelle*, February, 1946, p. 297.
7. Cf. Plé, "Tendances spirituelles de notre temps," *Vingt-cinq ans de la Vie Spirituelle*, 1944.
8. Cf. the Pastoral letter of His Eminence Cardinal Suhard, *Essor ou Déclin de l'Eglise*, 1947. (There is an English translation.)

TOWARDS A THEORY OF
THE CATHOLIC INTELLECTUAL

PEDRO LAIN ENTRALGO

I DO not think it inopportune to begin this inquiry with some precise concepts relative to the terms "intellectual" and "Catholic intellectual." In the course of the following considerations I shall call *intellectual*, in the strict sense, a man consecrated to the theoretical knowledge of reality. If this knowledge is directed towards reality as such, to its "being," the intellectual is given the name "philosopher"; if its object is the "how" of a definite area of present or past reality, the intellectual is called a "scientist." Therefore, since the philosopher can be a metaphysician or concerned with a particular division of reality, the result is that the activity of the intellectual *stricto sensu,* can take three distinct forms: metaphysics, the philosophy of nature, and any distinct science whether it be Astronomy or Criminal Law.

On the other hand the expression *Catholic intellectual* will be used here in a broad sense: by it I shall understand the critic of reality theoretically considered, who lives and desires to live within the Catholic Church. Consequently it can be applied not only to one who makes intellectually manifest his religious confession, to the "Catholic intellectual," but also to anyone who exercises his intelligence without meaning to declare by this his actual adherence to the body of the Church. I shall give a brief example of this: not only the theologian St. Thomas but also the physicist Branly.

The example chosen suffices to suggest that, depending on the reality to which intelligence is applied, two great divisions of Catholic intellectuals can be and must be made: the intellectuals *in divinis,* who attempt to learn, more or less directly, about the reality of God (theologians, scripturists, etc.); and the intellectuals *in creatis,* whose object is the sphere of the created, in its totality or in one of its divisions, according to its "being" or in regard to its "how." Between these two orders can be found that of the philosophers who aspire to understand the divine reality philosophically (theodicy) or man's relation to it (the philosophy of religion).

Despite the scope which I have proposed to give the expression *Catholic intellectual,* I must point out here and now that my reflections are concerned exclusively with the specific group whom I have just called Catholic intellectuals *in creatis:* philosophers of created reality, considered in its totality or in any of its parts; and those who cultivate the special sciences; mathematicians, physicists, biologists, anthropologists, historians, jurists, sociologists. Just what are these intellectuals *in creatis* when they are Catholics? What can they and what ought they to be? What is their position in the economy of humanity and of creation? This is what we shall try to see.

The Fundamental Difficulty

The Christian—the whole man, without any absolute division of his activity between a "natural life" and another "spiritual" or "supernatural" one—belongs simultaneously and necessarily to two distinct worlds: the *Church,* understood as the mystical body and the way of salvation; and a *World* more or less inclined to Christ, but endowed with its ultimate significance through the work of the Redemption. Thus, in its order, the Christian is called by his vocation to what St. Paul called "worldly wisdom," *sophia tou kósmou.* As a member of the Church his final end is salvation through faith and perseverance. As a man of this world and an intellectual *in creatis* his vocation and his duty consists in understanding the reality he sees in the best way possible: stars, plants, cells, diseases, human actions present or past, measurable relationships. Is the conciliation of these two obligations possible?

St. Paul's reply is apparently negative, and consequently, disturbing. "Must we not say that God has turned our worldly wisdom to folly? When God shewed us his wisdom, the world, with all its wisdom, could not find its way to God; and now God would use a foolish thing, our preaching, to save those who will believe in it" (1 Cor. 1:20–21). In opposition to a "worldly wisdom" convicted by God of real folly, St. Paul raises a "folly of preaching" based on the real and true wisdom; a "wisdom of God, his secret, kept hidden till now; so, before the ages, God had decreed, reserving glory for us" (1 Cor. 2:7). These words of St. Paul are so explicit! Will it be impossible for the Christian to reconcile these two modes of wisdom?

Three vital and exegetical attitudes can be adopted by the Christian who confronts St. Paul's moving text, and there is more than one example of the three in History. Despisers of human reason from Tertullian to the intuitionists, fideists and activists of our time, including Bonald, Lamennais and our Unamuno, have tended to see in St. Paul's words—tacitly or expressly—a clear indication of the little or no value of human knowledge: this knowledge would be sheer vanity with regard to its real and ultimate value, and would mislead us with regard to its historical utility.

There are those who gain life without end,
With reason, without reason or against it,

don Miguel de Unamuno, the great reasoner against the human reason, wrote for them all.

Others have had recourse to the formula of splitting their existence into two halves, consecrating one to the "wisdom of God" (faith, prayer, a pious life) and pledging the other to the cultivation of a "worldly wisdom" lacking any formal reference to Divinity. The definitive judgment on the value of human knowledge is tacitly left relegated to the experience beyond death, when the eyes of the spirit can judge to what extent was "really true" that which in this mortal life seemed "humanly reasonable." No one has known how to express this spiritual attitude so powerfully as Tzanck, the distinguished French scientist: *Il faut laisser l'oratoire à côté du laboratoire,* he has said.

Those who act in this way Pascal had called Cartesians. "I cannot forgive Descartes," he wrote. "In all his philosophy he would have been quite willing to dispense with God. But he had to make Him give a fillip to set the world in motion; beyond this, he has no further need of God." But, in another sense, shouldn't those who divide up their own being properly be called Pascalians? Pascal genially erects a science of the visible world, and then states in the form of a proposition: "It is necessary to write against those who penetrate too deeply into the sciences." Few examples of Pascalian—or Cartesian—religiosity are as obvious as that of Laënnec, the inventor of the stethoscope. Laënnec, a fervent Catholic, who dedicates his life to the exploration of the thorax by auscultation, and at the same time writes, in pious solitude: "When a man is on his deathbed, now only an instant away from the abyss of eternity . . . he recognizes the nothingness of the earth and sees that the world has offered only empty visions to his fancy. . . ."[4] A question rises in the reader's soul: are these truths about the diseases of the thorax discovered by Laënnec nothing, even *ante faciem Dei,* but "empty visions" offered by the world to the vigilant fancy of their discoverer?

It must be said that these two spiritual attitudes of the Christian intellectual have some slight justification, as much from the point

of view of history as from that of truth. Man's lack of confidence in
the exercise of his reason usually appears when the human reason,
raised to an autonomous ruling principle, shows itself incapable
of giving man happiness: as in the time of Tertullian (a crisis of the
Greek world), in that of Bonald (a crisis of the French Revolution
and of the "ideologies"), in that of Kierkegaard (a crisis of idealism) and in that of Unamuno (a crisis of the progressive utopia).
On the other hand, the tactical excision of intellectual activity from
the pious activity of the scientist *in creatis* occurs when the
autonomous exercise of human reason reveals itself capable of both
understanding cosmic nature and controlling it effectively: it is the
time of Laënnec, Pasteur and Branly, learned men and Catholics.
It does not seem accidental that the characteristic men of this
religious orientation have been French and belong to the nineteenth century.

But these two attitudes have some basis for existing not only
from the point of view of history but also from that of truth. It is
certain that the human reason is unable to understand created
reality with absolute fullness; likewise it is undeniable that the
preparation of a bacterial culture, the tracing of a linguistic connection, or the use of electronic bombardments can be conceived
only with difficulty as religious acts. But does this partial reason
grounded in history and truth exclude the existence, perhaps, of a
third attitude towards these weighty words of St. Paul; a more
informed, more satisfactory attitude, capable of including, by addition, the individual and fragmentary reasonableness of the
former two?

Actually we must begin thinking that the discovery and the possession of truth about this world situates the human intelligence
—in some way, by some means—in confrontation with the total,
sustaining truth of God. "Wherever there is scientific and historical
truth, there is God," wrote Menéndez y Pelayo in one of his
greater moments. The being of the world is God's creature; and
since the formal cause of produced being is always, in some manner, a "shining forth" ("relucencia") of the being which produced
it (Zubiri), scientific knowledge of the world can only be an *itinerarium mentis in Deum.* "Worldly wisdom" is foolishness, in St.
Paul's sense, when it attempts to exclude from the human spirit

the ever mysterious "wisdom of God," the *verbum crucis,* but not when it serves as an approach to this or seriously attempts to be its preamble. St. Paul himself tells us this in the famous text, so wonderful and so often quoted: *invisibilia Dei . . . per ea quae facta sunt, intellecta conspiciuntur* (Rom. 1:20). From this it follows that the enterprise of constructing a true knowledge of the world—to know according to art *ea quae facta sunt*—is not only, when born of a vocation, to serve God; in a certain way, it is also to discover a little about God, to take a small human step in the endless and unavoidable struggle to understand Him better.

I state openly that this third attitude is mine. I feel obligated, therefore, to speak plainly about what I understand it to be.

The Specific Difference of
the Catholic Intellectual

The Catholic intellectual strives to understand the being and the truth of created things and sometimes to attain them; this is the proximate genus of his position. But this proximate genus is characterized by a very decided difference, whose essential and descriptive notes it is necessary to point out.

Let us look for them in each one of the phases of intellectual work. This will be integrated, when it is complete, by three successive, personal acts: the discovery of the problem, the intellectual elaboration of the problematic reality, and the possession of the truth resulting from this elaboration. The philosopher, the physicist, the philologist and the historian proceed, *mutatis mutandis,* according to this plan.

I. The discovery of the subject of investigation—the "problem" —constitutes, chronologically and entitively, the "principle" of knowing: *arché sophias,* according to the traditional expression. Now in regard to this "principle" of human knowledge there are two laws in effect, venerable theses, apparently not easy to reconcile with each other. One is Hebraic, and is contained in the Book of Ecclesiasticus: *Initium sapientiae timor Domini* (Ecclus. I:16). The other is Hellenic, and Plato and Aristotle agree in attesting to it: "wonder *(thaumázein)* is the beginning of wisdom."

How interpret so notable a discrepancy? Is it possible to speculate that the Scripture formula refers to a "sapiential" wisdom, eschatological or concerned with salvation, while that of the Greeks refers to a "theoretical" wisdom, consisting in purely intellective knowledge only? In addition, it must be admitted that these two ways of conceiving the "principle of wisdom" are the products of mentalities quite distant from each other: the Indo-European of Hellas and the Semitic of Israel. But one can also think that the two theses are radically in agreement—in so far as they are *human* theses—if one knows how to interpret them with sufficient exactitude and depth.

For example, let us take "wonder." This is a strongly admiring surprise. One who feels it takes fright, rejects, and is seized with admiration at the same time; in such a way that as much aversion as admiration is formed, almost inconspicuously, in the discordant frame of mind which suspends him—in the wonder. In the intimate texture of the feeling we call "surprise" are implied the "alienness" of that which surprises us, its condition of being something strange to us, and a certain "resistance" of its reality to the operation of our intellectual habits; and furthermore, we truly admire only what excels us, what surpasses us. To sum up, we feel wonder in the presence of all those things which are alien to us, resist our understanding and seem to surpass the limit of our personal finitude.

But as a matter of fact the finitude of the human spirit can conceive or suspect the existence of realities strictly and absolutely "super-human" or "trans-human"; superior in power and in being, therefore, to every man, to mankind. When this takes place the disposition of the soul in the encounter with them or with their presumed effects is no longer simple admiration, but a distinct feeling: "veneration." It will be enough then to attribute a personal disposition to this superhuman reality that makes us wonder, for the "wonder" to be felt vividly as *timor Domini* or "fear of God."

Thus it is that wonder constitutes the "principle of wisdom" in a two-fold and very rich sense: to human wisdom it gives its chronological or inceptive origin, for to know truth it must begin by wondering about that which it will then try to know; moreover, its ontological foundation concurs in this, because when it is in profound truth, all human learning rests upon an ultimate, radical wonder about what it knows. Yet on the other hand it is in true wonder that veneration and surprise are mutually and intimately founded: it is, at most, a surprised veneration or a venerating surprise. Pure veneration, without a shadow of surprise, is religious piety, no principle of human knowledge. At its highest pitch this is a point of departure for the state in which the soul finds itself "transcending all knowledge," according to the happy formulation of St. John of the Cross. Pure surprise, without a trace of veneration before the enigma of reality, is found in the opposite extreme; furthermore this attitude of the human spirit is not a principle of true knowledge, but clear evidence of frivolous curiosity or of cynical pride of life: "fornication of the spirit," in the pungent phrase of St. Bonaventure.

The first specifying note of the Catholic intellectual is now evident. His cognitive activity begins with wonder and is based on it: it is the universal rule, and Galileo and Claude Bernard obeyed it no less than Thales of Miletus and Pythagoras. But the Catholic intellectual's wonder before created reality is, essentially, *timor Domini,* because in it he sees and cannot stop seeing the creature of an omnipotent and personal Being or Superbeing. When he examines its unsettled condition, partially intelligible and fully tractable, created reality always appears to the Catholic intellectual —to put it in the almost extravagant manner of Rudolf Otto— with a certain character of the "numinous," although now it is only a reflection or "showing forth" ("relucente") of its principle.

II. The same thing cannot be said regarding the second phase of intellectual activity: the methodical elaboration of the reality which has been shown to be wonderful and problematic.

There are different particular acts in this elaboration. The following, I think, can be isolated: the transforming of wonder into a concrete scientific problem; the finding of a "working hypothesis" (Weissmann) or *"a priori* idea" (Cl. Bernard) for the resolution of the scientific problem presented; the testing of this working hypothesis as much by way of pure reasoning as through observation and experimentation and also comprehensive reading, according to the kind of knowledge pursued; and, finally, a "single scientific truth" for the conclusion, when the job of checking has reached a favorable end.

Now in the fulfillment of this long series of intellectual operations

—and mechanical, if the science is experimental—nothing essential ought to distinguish the Catholic intellectual from any other. Each must pay exclusive attention to the demands of truth, to the particular demands of the problematic reality studied, to the correct principles of human thinking and to the capacities of one's own intelligence. The "Laënnec attitude"—remember what was said before—finds its partial justification here. To be convinced of this, it is enough to imagine in detail any of the philosophic or scientific investigations of an intellectual *in creatis.*

III. But there is no genuine intellectual life without the act that truly crowns and defines it: the personal possession of the discovered truth, whether oneself or someone else has discovered it. A man who does not come to possess as a thing of his own a sequence of scientific truths, large or small, is not, strictly speaking, an "intellectual"; he is, at most, a "knowledge-miner," a man who extracts and manipulates truths as the miner does the pieces of the seam on which he works. We must admit that one of the most serious defects of contemporary intellectual life consists in this "use of ideas without understanding them" (Zubiri).

Nevertheless in this definite act of possessing the truth there can be distinguished two spiritual operations which integrate it: a decision about the consistency and the range of the truth achieved, and an idea about its meaning.

Regarding the first, the Catholic intellectual—and this is another of the notes which specifies him—ought to free himself from a common illusion: the attribution of a total and absolute value to the scientific truth, as if this gets at the very basis of reality. Whoever discovers a truth, or whoever personally takes possession of what another has discovered, not only possesses it but also is possessed by it. This dominion of the truth over its possessor—strengthened, sometimes, by the necessity for belief natural to the human soul—can be tyrannical; and when this happens, not infrequently the intellectual has a propensity to see *his human truth* as an immediate part or as an immediate partial expression of the *absolute truth.* Before the mental eyes of Newton, the Newtonian idea of space came to be *sensorium Dei;* before Galileo's, his conception of the natural law became "God's customary activity."

Confronted by those who despise human reason, it seems necessary to assert that science is a certain knowledge of reality. Man's intelligence has no tendency to error when it is operating by itself alone, nor must it necessarily remain limited to mere convention. But in maintaining that a particular scientific truth *can be profoundly certain,* it is not licit to conclude that this truth *must be absolutely certain.* Therefore the double caution with which the Catholic intellectual ought to hold the scientific truth. In addition to the unavoidable "historical caution"—unavoidable, because today's scientific truth can be left quite changed by tomorrow's discoveries—there is necessary a "metaphysical caution," for the full meaning of human knowledge can be gained only through a metaphysical conception of reality. We shall not be long in seeing what this means.

For another thing, the personal possession of scientific truth carries with it an idea regarding its meaning, both for the man who possesses it and for man *in genere.* I think that this "meaning" can only be the presentation, the offering, included when pure possessive fruition prevails in the thought dominant in the soul of the intellectual. Thus the very structure of human existence demands this. But the presentation to whom? An offering to whom? Very diverse answers can be given. The Catholic vision of man's reality and of reality in general requires nevertheless that this "who" be God one and triune as its final end. The Christian meaning of the possession of philosophic or scientific truth is, in a definite way, an *oblatio veritatis Deo.* This is an intellectual act which well deserves separate consideration.

The Oblation of Truth

Someone has said that it is not the mission of the Church to acquire human knowledge, but to offer to God what men achieve. This is a great and luminous truth. But if there is anyone who has not achieved knowledge, be the method of achieving it distinguished or common, can he offer knowledge to God? To no one is it given to offer anything but what is his own. Thus it is that the offering of scientific knowledge can be authentic and efficacious only when the one who offers has created knowledge for himself, or when he has known how to recreate in himself and by himself the knowledge which others created. Whoever does not live in the knowledge will be capable, at most, of "agreeing with it," of "offering it" in some manner.

The offering—it remains to say—can be of what is near or of what is far off. P. Teilhard de Chardin, for example, endeavors to offer to God his own discoveries; St. Thomas, recreating in his spirit the philosophy of Aristotle, knew how to offer God remote creations. It does not matter much, then, that the truth has been born in minds far removed from Catholicism, and even from Christianity. The Jesuits who publish *The Light of the East* in Calcutta understand this well. But it is not that which matters here, but the internal structure of the *oblatio veritatis*.

In the offering of truth there should be distinguished its three principal constitutive moments: the truth which is offered, the act of offering it, and the end of the offering. Or, in other words: the *veritas offerenda,* the *actus oblationis* and the *terminus oblationis.* It is necessary to consider these one by one.

In regard to the *veritas offerenda,* the essential condition can be indicated by an expressive redundancy: it is "truly truth" to the extent to which man can determine it. Two criteria, one intellectual and the other pragmatic, permit the statement of a particular scientific conclusion as "provisionally true." The intellectual criterion concerns the evidence for this presumed truth: that within the historical situation in which it is formulated it be clearly demonstrated to the intellect in an unquestionable, rigorous and comprehensive manner. The pragmatic criterion has to do with its efficacy: that it be effective in man's relation with reality, that it enable him to order and control it. The act of offering can be undertaken if these conditions are fulfilled.

The *actus oblationis* can be made outwardly or interiorly; and even elaborately, at times. To be real and effective, it is enough that its fulfillment be within the one who makes the offering; but undoubtedly its outward expression gives it added historical merit and effectiveness. If St. Thomas was under no necessity to write the *Summa* in order to offer God his personal recreation of Hellenic philosophy, he had to do it to check Averroism. Yet not everything valued by man manages to achieve audible or visible expression. To what acts of offering would God and a soul alone be witnesses?

Whether external or internal, the act of oblation of scientific truth must consist essentially in an "ordination towards" or "reference to." Thus inexorable fact requires that this truth cannot reach the very basis of created reality, the cause or principle which makes it what it "is." I spoke above of a "metaphysical caution" in the possession of truth. This caution is strictly necessary in virtue of the "hiatus" that exists unavoidably between our scientific knowledge of reality and the real constitution of its source. And it follows that the internal configuration of the *actus oblationis* cannot be sufficiently exact without a definite metaphysics. Which one? We shall be satisfied to say: one which of its very nature demands the constitution of the human mind itself and the aggregate of *all* the scientific truths about reality in general and concerning the particular area of reality being studied at the time. A metaphysics, in short, "postulated" by our total knowledge of the created world.

But it is not possible to study the act of the offering of truth fully without a clear idea of the *terminus oblationis*. The immediate ends of the offering can be quite varied: humanity, our country, someone we love. Nevertheless, its final end ought to be Divinity, the one and triune God. This is the real problem. How is a scientific truth "referred to" or "ordered towards" Divinity?

Only one answer seems possible: such reference can be made in so far as Divinity itself has been manifested to man *sub specie veritatis*. To put it another way: when God has revealed Himself to the believer through a *depositum fidei* susceptible of being expressed and defined in a body of "dogmas." Strictly speaking, the divine reality underlying the aggregate of the propositions of faith is the *terminus ad quem* of the oblation of truth. The *verbum mentis* to which human knowledge is reduced requires, so that it can be referred to the Divinity, that this, which St. Paul called the *verbum crucis,* must be done.

And now we can envisage the total structure of the "metaphysical hiatus" between the knowledge of science and the basis of reality. This hiatus ought to be bridged by a two-fold metaphysical construction: that which reality itself seems to demand, and that which fits into the requirements of theology, in as much as it is the rational exposition of dogma. Thus the act of oblation requires of the scientist the adequate intellectual management of a metaphysics "postulated" by reality and of another "urged" (*"solicitada"*) from theology. The formal cause of the *oblatio veritatis* consists in the ever unsettled articulation of this two-sided metaphysics.

This is a task—it is almost needless to say—that demands the intellectual powers of more than one man. At least three are needed: the scientist, the philosopher and the theologian. Only the fortunate concurrence of these three intellectual approaches in the same person can bestow on the offering of truth, an undertaking at once titanic and humble, its individual structure and contour. Nevertheless this will be very exceptional. What we call *team work* today ought also to be the rule for the ever more specifically defining activity of the Catholic intelligence.

I have just mentioned the humility, the radical humility, of the *oblatio veritatis*. The offering ought to be humble in two senses. The first is obvious: it concerns the intention of the one who makes the offering, who attempts to reduce "his" particular truth to a mere preface to "the" absolute truth; in this, humility is synonymous with honor. The second is less obvious: it concerns the internal constitution of the oblative act; and is delineated as much in the unavoidable existence of this metaphysical hiatus between scientific truth and dogma as in the necessarily problematic character of the articulation between the metaphysics postulated by reality and the metaphysics suggested by theology. Clear-headed attention to this hiatus, as I said, is "caution";[1] and the humble acceptance of its existence together with the loyal acknowledgement of the overwhelming qualitative difference between its two most different ends—the human mind and the reality of God— changes caution into "reverence." This caution and this reverence —through intellectual zeal or in the enthusiasm of offering—have not always been properly preserved. I ask myself, for example, whether in the evolutionist theories of not a few contemporary Catholic thinkers—theories otherwise so rich in suggestions—there is not too immediate a contact between the presumed scientific truth from which they start (the evolution of the universe), and the dogmatic truth towards which they tend (Catholic Christology). Do we not notice in these efforts the lack of a sufficiently elaborated "metaphysical hiatus"? But this has not been the only example of "confused enthusiasm," if you will permit the expression, in the history of Christian thought.

I would like to emphasize the essential difference between what has customarily been called "concordism" and what I call the "oblation of scientific truth." At best, "concordism" between scientific truth and dogmatic truth is a formula for getting along together. It is an attempt to point out or to demonstrate the lack of contradiction between human science and faith; and in the majority of cases, the harmony possible between them. In short, in accordance with its program, concordism asserts that scientific truth and Catholic belief can coexist without harm to each other, both in the body social and in the soul of the intellectual who believes. Quite different from this static and defensive attitude of concordism, the "oblation of truth" is the attestation of a dynamic spiritual disposition which gets right at the point. Looked at as the intricate intellectual possession of scientific truth, the oblation constitutes an *itinerarium mentis in Deum;* seen as the assent to dogmatic truth by the one who offers, its meaning is the assumption of human and contingent knowledge in the divine and absolute truth. The necessary "metaphysical hiatus" between the former and the latter prevents their mutual confusion and makes of the offering a difficult, complex, daring and always unsettled intellectual engagement. Only thus can *ea quae facta sunt* lead us towards God by the path of knowledge.

But it should not be thought that the *oblatio veritatis* is exclusively an activity for the Catholic intellectual. Spread by Christianity, it is sometimes proclaimed by men clearly remote from the area delimited by the concept "Catholic intellectual." For example, Ramón y Cajal wrote, "The nobility of the scholar . . . consists in being the minister of progress, the priest of truth and the confidant of the Creator. . . . To him alone has it been given to penetrate the marvelous work of Creation in order to return more pleasing and more acceptable homage to the Absolute: to study his extraordinary works in order to know, admire and reverence him, in them and by them." The idea of an offering of scientific truth to God shines unmistakably in the soul of our great scholar.

For the Catholic intellectual, specifically, his proper object is the trinitarian conception of God, to whom he makes his oblation. Man now offers his truth to the truth of God one and triune. But to discover the internal consistency of this *oblatio veritatis christiana* it is best to turn to St. Paul, our great source of spiritual light.

In that marvelous proclamation of the Christian spirit which is the eighth chapter of the Epistle to the Romans, St. Paul announces and defines what ought to be the orbit of created reality for the Christian. It is worth repeating his words: "If creation is full of expectancy, that is because it is waiting for the sons of God to be made known. Created nature has been condemned to frustration; not for some deliberate fault of its own, but for the sake of him who so condemned it, with a hope to look forward to; namely, that nature in its turn will be set free from the tyranny of corruption, to share in the glorious freedom of God's sons. The whole of nature, as we know, groans in a common travail all the while" (Rom. 8:19–22).

The teaching contained in this text of St. Paul can be explained in three propositions: 1. Up to now the whole creation finds itself in a state of servitude to corruption, due to man. 2. This state keeps it in "impatient hope" (*apokaradokia, exspectatio*), in universal lamentation (*synstenázei, ingemiscit*)and as though in labor pains (*synodínei, parturit*). 3. Creation's "delay" and its "hope" (*eph'elpídi, in spe*) has as its final end the state of "glorious liberty" which must be brought about through the work of men, the sons of God.

Omnis creatura ingemiscit et parturit usque adhuc. What are these words of St. Paul's? Only a metaphor? I believe very firmly that this *gemitus creaturae* should not be interpreted only in a metaphorical sense, but also in a metaphysical sense. This metaphysical understanding of the thought of St. Paul is shown to be possible, I think, by two excellent ideas of Xavier Zubiri, my teacher. Above all, the conception of the reality of finite beings as a "pre-tension," after the model which the constitution of living being offers our intelligence. Comparing created being with infinite and creative being, and in line with the theological thought of the Greek Fathers, Zubiri writes: "In dealing with finite beings . . ., the activity of the act has more of the character of actuality than of action; the virtual, more of the character of potency; and the primary unity of being, more of the character of tendency, of pre-tension." And on another page: "Being is a species of primary and radical active operation by which things are something which *is being realized,* rather than *realities.*"

Creatures, then, are nuclei of active operation in a state of pre-tension. In pre-tension to what? What does its entitive activity "pretend"? Ontologically, the plenitude of its own being. Anthropologically, an offering of "pressures" and "resources" for the existence of man who coexists with them. "On one hand, pressures and resources, on the other an offering," says Zubiri, "these are two dimensions of the same structure. Because things are not given, but *offered,* what is offered to us in them is: either the forcefulness of actuality (pressure), or that which permits actuality (resources)."

But this "pre-tended" ontological plentitude and this actual or virtual constitutive "state of oblation" ought at the same time to be understood theologically. St. Paul points out the way. The *gemitus creaturae* to which his text alludes and the *exspectatio* in which all creation exists are, in the final analysis, nothing but a revealed witness to the ontological constitution of the real world. This suffers a radical, metaphysical deficiency, which affects the internal dynamics of its totality and of each one of its particular beings. "To be" in this world is to be moving actively, in one way or another, towards the final possible perfection which St. Paul called the "liberty of glory" (*eleutheria tes dóxes*); a perfection which man can achieve by himself, and which the non-human world must attain indirectly, through the "sons of God."

Let us leave for the moment that which is relative in man's role in this universal exaltation, and consider only the definitive perfection of creatures. In what does such perfection consist? What can this "glorious liberty" be, of which St. Paul speaks? The answer is given by the Pauline idea of the Redemption. Among others, one decisive text is the famous passage from the Epistle to the Ephesians: "So rich is God's grace . . . to make known to us the hidden purpose of his will. It was his loving design, centered in Christ, to give history its fulfillment by resuming everything in him, all that is in heaven, all that is on earth, summed up in

him" (Eph. I: 9–10). The thought of St. Paul is unmistakable.
Through the work of the Incarnation, not only man but every
creature has gained the good fortune of a complete ontological
ordering, which the apostle calls *anakephalaiosis,* "enrolling" or
"summary"—"anacefaleosis," as our very Spanish Unamuno
used to say—a state in which the person of Christ enrolls and sums
all things up in himself.

Now then, this work of resumption, just as the Redemption
itself, must be fulfilled in this world in a temporal and historical
manner. Prepared by God from all eternity, completed and revealed physically by the Incarnation of the Word, it continues to
fulfil itself in time until the consummation of the world. The history
of the universe and of humanity, considered eschatologically, is the
process in time of the entire creation towards its resumption in
Christ.

And if the "enrollment" ("anacefaleosis") is really taking place,
in what way is it happening? What is the actual historical mechanism, if one can so put it, of the resumption of things in Christ?
One must admit that the entire universe is itself moving naturally
towards it: it is the Christian vision of evolution. But it is also
possible to think—whether evolutionist theses are completely certain or not—that the resumption of non-human creatures follows
upon man's. This was touched implicitly in asserting the Christian
conception of the dynamic relations between the macrocosm and
the microcosm. *Lex divinitatis haec est,* the Pseudo-Areopagite
wrote, *ut infima media reducantur ad summa.* In other words:
that the cosmic creature be raised towards God through man.
Making theological use of the ontological thought of Zubiri, it
could be said that man can "offer" things to God because things
are "offered" to him; or better, because reality "is" of its very self
an offering, an oblation.

And with this we arrive at the real kernel of the question: the
way in which man cooperates in this resumption of things in
Christ. The answer does not seem to be a recondite one. Man
raises the creatures of the cosmos towards Divinity in so far as
he humanizes them in the course of his four-fold biological, technical, artistic and intellectual action. Biologically, man "assimi-

lates" the cosmos, converting into his own human nature something that before was quite remote from that: chemical elements, mechanical movements, radiations, elemental particles. Technically, man "manipulates" the cosmic reality, ordering its spontaneous activity in the world of his specific and personal existence. Artistically, man humanly and ideally "recreates" the reality of things about him and his own distinctive reality. Intellectually, finally, man "comprehends" the entity of the universe, in so far as he makes this intellectual comprehension of his own spiritual habitual state. Assimilation, manipulation, recreation and comprehension, therefore, are the four cardinal forms of the "humanization" of the cosmos. As the person of the Word assumed human nature in Christ, so in its own measure and in its own way the person of man assumes the nature of the cosmos in its concrete reality. The individual life of each man and the historical life of all humanity comes to be, among other things, a huge process of the "humanization" of the universe. It will suffice that man, converted into a "son of God," properly offer the one and triune Divinity the act and the result of his biological, technical, recreating and intellectual operation—one of the modes of human sanctity formally and historically consists in this—for his collaboration in the work of "enrollment" ("anacefaleosis") to be real and effective. *Infima per media reducuntur ad summa,* said the Pseudo-Areopagite. Any human act by a man in the state of grace is also, in some measure or other, a real step towards the full resumption of creatures in Christ.

The ultimate meaning of the *oblatio veritatis* shines clearly now without a cloud, and the significance of the Catholic intellectual in the economy of creation is evident. Let us put it in the form of a positive statement: *the Catholic intellectual is one who cooperates in the work of the Redemption; a cooperator veritatis,* in the profound sense which St. John intended to give this expression (3 John: 8). Every one who knows how to make a truth evident becomes this, involuntarily and indirectly; and in a more direct and voluntary way, whoever also desires and knows how to offer it to the one and triune God.

The meaning of this cooperation is two-fold. As one who

struggles in the work of "humanizing" reality intellectively and as one who offers the truth, his own or another's, which is the result of this humanizing work, the Catholic intellectual participates in an active way in the metaphysical and soteriological process of resumption. Because of this effort of his, at the same time noetic and oblative, things gain the state of "glorious liberty" which St. Paul first declared would be theirs. It could be said that this is the prospective activity or prospect for the future of the Catholic intellectual.

But it also has its bearings on the present. As a member of a human community, he lights up the souls of those needy for knowledge, shows to all the dignity and the humility which is involved in the labor of being a man, and shows the learned, whether they be docile or intractable to the call of Christ, the most profound and noble dimension of his true role in Universal History. Above all, to him can be converted and applied the great words which a Spanish poet spoke to his fellow poets:

> Yes, you . . .;
> The ever questioning, marveled at and alone,
> You, who are men placed at the high point of manliness,
> To return to the others, covered with your blood,
> Ever in a flutter over the eternity which your mind points out;
> Your noble melancholy of banished gods.

While the forces of the flesh make the hearts of men shake with anger or with terror even to the foundations of the planet, this twofold work of resumption and of clarification is the least or the most that the Catholic intellectual can continue to offer to God, to men and even to opaque and mute things.

Translated by JOSEPH L. CAULFIELD

NOTES

1. I speak here of the caution necessary for the scientist and, in general, for the intellectual *in creatis*. But the theologian also needs it to approach the knowledge of created reality intellectually. Unfortunately, there are not a few theologians who speak of this reality with very scanty scientific caution.

PSYCHOLOGISTS VERSUS MORALITY

JEAN RIMAUD, S.J.

OUR childhood morality, taken from the catechism and from theological manuals, was a comparatively simple one. Not easy to practise, but simple. We learned that man's life is ordained to a final end, and we were taught a rule of conduct consistent with a transcendent and consequently universal good and evil. We were told about our obligation to conform to this rule, our liberty to do so, which was the source of our responsibility, and about a personal and autonomous conscience making its claim upon each one of us. Every human act was a free act; every moral act a free and thus responsible act having a relation to the final end. The conditions of responsibility were quite clearly defined: knowledge, consciousness, consent, awareness of what one was about to do and the relation of the proposed act to the moral law: this was to act freely. Theological apprentices undoubtedly experienced some difficulty in unravelling some "cases of conscience," but the majority of their cases were concerned with determining positions in relation to the moral law, the existence of an obligation or its seriousness, and, if it were a question of responsibility, the distribution of responsibility.

Our morality was based on an extremely simple psychology. Clear self-consciousness, a personal moral conscience, liberty, and responsibility were its basic premises. The conditions of a moral act were assumed to be habitually present. Man, acting freely, was supposed to perform moral acts twenty-four hours a day. And the introductory chapter on human acts in treatises of theology was quite unruffled, except that the virtuosi of subtlety found ample scope for their energies in the famous question of indirect volition.

But our calm has now been disturbed by the advances in psychology, a very recent science. And the root of the difficulty is precisely this introductory chapter. Are we really free? There can be no morality without responsibility; and this presupposes liberty. We shed ourselves fairly easily of the physicists' determinism.

Now we find ourselves at grips with the psychologists' determinism. Do we really have a personal conscience? If our conscience is to be anything more than the expression in each one of us of a collective conscience, we must effect a reconciliation between what we describe as personality and our social nature as revealed to us by recent discoveries. For psychology does nothing less than question the very existence of liberty and of the personality. If our concept of a human act does not correspond with reality, then it is only too clear that all our morality crumbles.

Perhaps no other attack on morality has been as dangerous as this one. It calls the conscience into question and tends to destroy the feeling of responsibility. It requires little experience of souls to realize the reception which greets these "ideas in the air." Christians worried about their spiritual life, and even priests, have found occasion to wonder if the conditions of mortal sin are ever present, or if mortal sin exists at all. Let us not hasten to lay the blame for this solely upon the charlatans of popularization who speak at random of psychoanalysis, complexes, the unconscious, psychoses. The discoveries of a psychology with a solid scientific foundation are enough to move men of cool reason and firm moral judgment. We must not confuse Freud, for example, with the clowns of Freudianism.

Now there is one problem which all moralists have a duty to approach directly and with great candor. I wish simply to disentangle its essential notions.

I.

It is a point raised by advances in pathological psychology which struck the first blow at our assurance.

We thought that insanity was comparatively rare, something easily recognized, and as different from mental health as day from night. By definition, lunatics were "madmen" who had lost all control and mastery of themselves and who were therefore irresponsible. All other men were normal, and therefore responsible. We failed to grasp the close link between the organic life and the psychic life, and the very notion of mental illness thus seemed to be a misuse of terms. I have known serious religious who considered "neurasthenia" an imaginary illness and claimed to cure it by an appeal to the will. Our moralists who prided themselves on their knowledge of psychology undoubtedly noted a similarity between passion and madness, but to consider passion as a blind, impersonal and more or less determining force which could even blot out responsibility they regarded as an error of the "romantics."

The study of mental disorders has allowed nothing of this clear distinction between mental health and illness to survive. It has rather shown the continuity between the normal and the abnormal states. "You speak of madmen? . . . But we all are mad. It is a question of degree." These were the words of an eminent practitioner over thirty years ago, when I naively asked him for a definition of madness. A mere witticism? Not at all. It is not easy to trace the lines of demarcation between discouragement, the more or less acute states of depression, and a psychosis of failure; between the instability natural to children and that of a man who is "unstable"; between the lack of objectivity characteristic in jealousy and the deforming delusion of a paranoiac; between a natural bent for inventing and playing at stories, and mythomania; or between uneasy suspicions and the mania of persecution. These are but a few examples from among hundreds. More simply, where does the unhealthy obsession begin? For obsession is nothing but the exaggeration of the motive power of any image from the moment it is not opposed in the consciousness by other images.

An educator accustomed to dealing exclusively with difficult cases might come to consider the normal child an exception. For barring the influence of heredity immediate or remote, or of environment, most laziness, egoism, stealing, and lying, can be explained by a mental aberration or a backwardness in development, uneven growth, instability, a character irregularity, constitutional perversity, or a repressed or deviated sensibility. The doctor becomes a constant and necessary collaborator of the educator. If he wishes to be competent he must have a serious knowledge of general psychology and at least an acquaintance with pathological psychology. Is laziness a fault or an illness? Around 1930, teachers scoffed at this question, but the time for this naive astonishment has passed.

What holds true for children can, in a more or less general way, be applied to adults. Man matures, acquiring inner equilibrium and self-mastery. This is as it should be. But how many normal exteriors conceal more or less serious emotional disorders? In fact certain realms such as sex or anti-social feelings and conduct rarely evidence complete health. In attempting to cure a child it is often found to be impossible without first treating one or the other of his parents, and perhaps both.

We speak of responsibility; but where and what is it? When can one speak of guilt? Formerly, this question was put exclusively to the scrupulous, the only ill ones familiar with our morality. Today we ask the same question everywhere, in cases of laziness or of jealousy, in the dramas of puberty, in marital dissension, and in cases of delinquency. We have linked the notion of responsibility to that of mental health. We know that complete mental health is rare, and is, on the contrary, a precarious and fragile thing. Can we join the author of *Man the Unknown* in attributing this fragility to the abnormal conditions imposed upon us by our civilization with its proud disdain of nature and her laws? But then we are concerned with the men of this civilization.

There is another disturbing chapter in pathological psychology. This one deals with the disorders of the personality. As young students we found the book in which Morton Prince studied the case of Miss Beauchamps and her four personalities as exciting as a novel. We were not in the least aware of the moral problems he raised. It was a "case," a curiosity, like the man in pursuit of his lost body. But since then we have learned that such cases, involving at least a simple doubling of the personality, were not so exceptional. I myself was one day visited by Napoleon, under the guise of a pharmacist's assistant. But above all psychologists have made us recognize the resemblance between cases which are quite obviously pathological and the normal existence in each one of us of many "egos." There is in each one of us the ego of the child, the student, the playmate; the ego of the father, the husband, the professional man, etc.

But all of this seems to have no disquieting effect on us. Mental health can no longer be assumed to be the habitual condition of most men; those afflicted, whether in a serious or minor way, are legion. But then, they are the afflicted. For the rest of us responsibility remains complete, and personality intact. Every defect is not an illness, no more than every bad thought is an obsession or every vicious habit the effect of determinism, or every hasty or regrettable decision the result of an irresistible impulse. Our success in rehabilitating lazy people, liars and thieves precisely by laying stress on their conscience certainly offers sufficient proof of this. Let us not be taken in by these psychiatrists. We know their professional tendencies only too well.

The psychologists pursue us in this retreat. "What is consciousness? What are we?"

Less than fifty years ago manuals of psychology defined psychology as the "science of states of consciousness." For philosophers who refused to allow themselves any metaphysical affirmations, consciousness meant man's awareness of the ensemble of feelings and acts which constitute his "ego." For others the same word designated sometimes this knowledge itself, and sometimes the ego as subject of its states or acts, that is, as a spirit subsisting apart from its thought. But both admitted that clear and distinct consciousness, despite degrees of lucidity, extended to all of our psychic life. Psychological consciousness was thus a firm basis for moral conscience. Knowledge entailed self-mastery. A courageous man might easily follow Socrates' counsel: Know thyself. Some of our retreat masters were not afraid to make the encouraging promise often seen on scales in our railroad stations: The man who weighs himself often, knows himself well. He who knows himself well, conducts himself well.

But alas! this illusion has vanished. The journey into the psychic life has been like an expedition in cave exploration. We have discovered that the simple consciousness comes from a subconscious which is in turn part of an unconscious. Our ego has three layers. It is something like the world revealed by the geological maps which show us the insignificant duration of the Quaternary period, which is simultaneous with the historical epoch, in its relation to preceding epochs. Simple consciousness is but a frothy fringe crowning the waves of a subconscious and unconscious. To know one's self is the most difficult and perhaps the most impossible of tasks. But how can self-possession be attained without self-knowledge?

The same thing holds for the subconscious, for we sometimes reach it through a simple passing of spontaneous consciousness to reflex consciousness.

At other times it can be divined and perceived by its influence or by disorders arising from some deficiency. We can also descend into it by an examination of dreams or by prying into the secrets of conscience with narco-analysis. But the unconscious? Shadows conceal the deep levels of our "ego," the humus which germinates our tendencies. And we understand today that these tendencies are the fundamental fact of psychic life. But we have no control over the surging forth and the first orientation of our tendencies. Sometimes a ray of light is cast upon them. The psychiatrist discovers that some adolescent's paralyzing timidity stems from an early childhood dream. An examination into heredity enables us to explain certain behavior. But in all this there is no place for liberty. That freedom which psychoanalytical exploration occasionally restores to us is very restricted; the grooves have already been formed.

And therefore the conclusion common among psychologists: The explanation of conduct is to be found in our unconscious tendencies from which it springs. Man is determined by them without knowing it and sometimes with the illusory conviction that he is free from them.

Our liberty rebels. Then, like the orator contradicted at a meeting who feels himself dominated and tries to brush off his adversary with a witticism, an argument *ad hominem,* or by plunging into some eccentricity, we muster an attack and denounce the outrages of Freudianism. We find in the Oedipus complex which they are most certainly abusing, a source of amusement. We protest against this mania of complexes. And, more seriously, we question the idea that all of our tendencies can be reduced to a libido which is the sexual appetite. And then what? Let the pioneers of psychic exploration draw even more fantastic maps, what in their errors and outrages gives us the right to reject the truths, unsuspected yesterday, which science has now attained? We can no longer go back to the psychology of simple consciousness. Every philosophy of liberty which ignores the unconscious play of tendencies is pure illusion.

During this time, other psychologists, the specialists of social psychology, menace our certainty of possessing a personal conscience.

Yesterday, our concept of the relationship between man and society very much resembled a chessboard on which each of the diverse pieces, though remaining rigorously itself, was part of a group. Society was a blend of individuals. Auguste Comte had told us that the individual did not exist, but we had seen in his axiom only the condemnation of social individualism. Personal individuality remained beyond dispute.

When psychologists began to speak of a plurality of "egos," we convinced ourselves that they were talking about something more apparent than real, a plurality of roles played by the same person. But they were saying something very different. There was, for example, a distinction between this child and his role as a son, a brother, a student, or a playmate. We doubtlessly noticed that the personality can be deformed by the role played, but to speak of deformation was to return to an assumption of this distinction. In saying that man is a social being, we simply meant that he must live with other men, that egoism or savagery is poor conduct, and that life in common is a law of our nature.

Studies of opinion and of environmental influence have forced us to reconsider the dependence and independence of the mind. We know that opinion springs up spontaneously, that it imposes upon us and is very difficult to resist. We know it exerts formidable pressure on sensibilities, minds, and consciences. Most men's judgments, even when they flatter themsleves on their independence of thought, are dictated by opinion. Where is freedom of thought with the modern means of propaganda? Environment, on the other hand, acts through opinion, its collective mind. We can no longer doubt the truth that man is fashioned by his environment. Our conformist civilization even succeeds sometimes in considering independence of judgment an abnormal and regrettable breach of solidarity. Those who are concerned with delinquent children are not always giving way to an indulgent compassion in so frequently holding the environment responsible for their conduct. But despite all this, we are convinced that the personality is fragile and that true independence, that of moral judgment, is a privilege of the strong. The personality suffers no encroachment once one has a character.

We are cut off from still another path of retreat. To be social necessarily means to belong to a community, for such is our nature. We do not exist as individuals. Individuality is an abstraction. We do not merely play roles; we *are* those roles. The filial relationship, for example, is not reduced to one of origin and dependence. It is by our entire selves that we are the children of these specific parents, and not simply of any man and woman. To be a son is a part (perhaps the most radical part) of our personality. In the case of a natural community such as the family, it is evidently true that our membership in this community is not a situation, but a first condition, a fact of our profound being, of all that we are. Of other communities, such as the school, we might believe that our relations there are enhanced by our personality which nevertheless remains exterior to these relations. This is an error which only rigorous analysis can remove. Let us take stock of our whole social "ego": son, brother, husband, friend, Frenchman, Parisian, of this neighborhood, of this apartment building, middle class, worker or farmer, man of this generation, and of this epoch. . . . Where can we flee, where can we isolate ourselves so that breaking all these ties, and transcending all these roles, we might find ourselves in the solitude of our personality? When alone before God I pray, it is with all that I am that I speak to Him. And I am, to the depths of this recollection and this silence, son, brother, husband. . . . It is vain to seek the personality in abstraction from all our social relationships. It is in being social, and concretely so, that we are personal. But then, what is the personality?

If we look into these truths, for they are truths, then the problem of the personal conscience becomes something new. It is no longer sufficient to preach independence of character and judgment. The child who reads a confession written more or less under his mother's dictation is not making a personal confession. But what confession is he making when he confesses without allowing his faults to be dictated to him or without having made too much preparation for their confession? His sins are the sins of a son, a brother, a student, a playmate, a parishioner. What relation does a personal conscience have to all these community consciences? While it is

certain that the sociologists exaggerate who would see in the individual conscience nothing but the expression of a collective conscience, we still ask, what is a personal conscience?

Psychologists versus morality. Do our readers still see a paradox
in the title of our essay? Personality and liberty once destroyed,
responsibility is but a word; and morality no longer exists. Now
everything in contemporary psychology, which marks an unquestionable progress over that of our childhood, does not seem erroneous or absurd. We are gradually discovering the man we did
not know. Moralists and educators should not be disturbed, much
less frightened. But they must not close their eyes. Whether in
morals or in politics, the ostrich attitude is worthless. We have the
urgent task of proposing to men a morality in accordance with what
man is, and which will be concretely valid, which they cannot reject as an illusory rule of conduct for a man who does not exist.

There is no question here of adapting morality, in the sense
in which this is imprudently understood and discussed by some, that
is by compromising with its demands, taking some and leaving
some, or entering into a path of concession, the end of which no
one ever knows. It is simply a question of going back to this preliminary treatise on human acts which serves as the philosophical
basis for moral theology, and solidifying this base. We should now
like to indicate rapidly, but with precision, some of the principal
psychological problems which the science of morals must solve in
order to do this.

II.

The first is the relationship of our liberty to psychic determinism, the activity of one, the rigidity of the other.

Many people have been slow to admit the existence of laws in
psychology, as though this might threaten the spirituality of the
soul. The soul was obstinately represented as lodged in the body,
undoubtedly linked to it, but somewhat as a neighbor. It was repeated after St. Thomas that the soul is the form of the body; the
intimate union between organic and psychic life was cause for
scandal. But the laws of psychology are like those of physics and

chemistry; far from enslaving us to nature, knowledge of them gives us mastery over it, and at the same time teaches us the limits of our power.

Our liberty is conditioned. We are free within the order defined by these laws. We cannot consciously prevent images from entering and acting upon our subconscious, nor is it within our power to strip an image of its motivating force, command an association of ideas, or always avoid an obsession. That spontaneous sympathies and antipathies determine some first reactions and attitudes it is beyond our power to prevent; the most decided efforts, for example, will not enable a certain child to work in a given environment. We are sexed, and this sex from our very earliest years modifies all our affectivity; it is a fact. Our deepest impulses move, and move us first, without our knowledge.

We are aware of this. But we would prefer to have this determinism exist only in the recesses of our subconscious and unconscious. We imagine that we hold a discretionary power over images, feelings and acts as soon as they belong to clear consciousness. But this is not at all the case. Though consciousness may be a condition for liberty, it does not of itself imply liberty. As a natural consequence of this confusion between consciousness and liberty, we charge the soul with false responsibilities. I have in mind many adolescents who exhaust themselves in an impossible struggle against what they call "bad thoughts" and who should be concerned, when extremely tormented by them, with distinguishing culpable from non-culpable pleasures.

On the other hand it is true that we often have a genuine control over sense impulses when they flow from the depths into the clear consciousness; sometimes we can capture them, sublimating or directing their vitality.

And so we see a double series of disconcerting though equally certain facts: a determinism which continues to act in the awakened conscience, and a power to utilize subconscious and unconscious forces when they become conscious.

Moralists should join the psychologists in studying this play of determinism and liberty in order to refute both those who exaggerate infraconscious determinism and those who claim we are free as soon as we are awakened and fully conscious. For we cannot give a valid answer to the former who suppress responsibility if we compromise ourselves with the latter who misunderstand it.

Now we must first of all free ourselves from this compromise. I recently reopened a few manuals of moral theology which were considered quite authoritative thirty years ago, some of which are still in use today. I re-read the pages on human acts, the will, ignorance, concupiscence and fear. In this metaphysical being, this disincarnate spirit, this abstract subject of morality, how can we recognize the man we have come to know by experience? If such a being existed he might well first of all be held responsible; and, if he were not, he would be an exception. This was indeed the opinion, fortified by this psychology and morality, of certain teachers I met in the schools. For them a child's least word or gesture was willed freely, charged with meaning and naturally culpable. Our moralists, in spite of appearances, were less sure of themselves. Intrepid and arbitrary professors, they had often dealt with souls, and caught between this experience and their pseudo-psychology, they got along by an empirical casuistry, at the risk of seeming obliging when they were becoming just.

To put it correctly, the problem of liberty must be put concretely, and in terms of the man revealed to us by experience. Then it is no longer a question of knowing when man is not fully responsible, but when he is. Our treatises, unfortunately, ignored the unconscious psychic life. Yet there lies the difficulty. But then this problem of liberty, the first in importance, cannot be the first we must approach.

What relation does the clear consciousness have with its underlying psychic life?

On this subject we are constantly confronted with contradictory opinions. For some the clear consciousness merely makes explicit what was implicit though actually present in the unconscious. For others conscious and unconscious psychic phenomena are of different natures. As an example, let us consider the classic case of a child jealous of his younger brother who, by his birth, seems to deprive him of some of his parents' affection. In such a case the first group I mentioned would hold that this jealousy was already existent in the child's unconscious mind before coming to the clear consciousness. The second school would hold that the conscious jealousy was not in the unconscious but that it was the movement of a mis-orientated affectivity, which might just as well have resulted in an increased love for the parents without any touch of rivalry or disturbing demands. These two opinions are erroneous only insofar as they are systematic and claim to be mutually exclusive. In reality, there is sometimes identity, sometimes a simple analogy, sometimes transformation of the psychic phenomena which pass from the unconscious to the conscious.

But as soon as we systematize, admitting only one kind of channel from the unconscious to the conscious psychic life, we are almost fatally brought to one of two errors. Either one makes the unconscious ego the real ego, which the conscious ego must recognize, and absorb, in order to avoid illusion; and then not much is left of liberty; or one holds the conscious ego as the only true one, which prevents our understanding it by cutting its roots, and at the same time overemphasizes responsibility. The example of the Oedipus complex is enlightening here. Some would have it that the son's rivalry with the father is really a sexual rivalry, whether consciousness admits it or not. Others are led to disregard the influence of sex in filial affection. The first group always suspects the clear consciousness of being an illusion and claims that the knowledge of self which results in self-possession is an impossible task without the aid of a psychoanalyst. The latter in turn condemns it to the illusion of a false self-sufficiency or independence, making it bear the entire burden of an unconscious which is not included in free judgment. Let us go back to our example. If, in his crisis of opposition to his father, this six- or seven-year-old child must be considered a rival lover without this being admitted by his consciousness, then all his judgments of his own conduct are invincible errors, but nonetheless errors. But on the other hand if what is partly a mere sentimental conflict should be taken for a proud revolt then he still deludes himself.

In truth the ego is at the same time the subject of both the unconscious psychic phenomena and the conscious phenomena. There is a continuity and a reciprocal causality between the two lives, just as there is a constant link between the organic and the psychic. To build a theory of the moral conscience, as our professors of theology did, on the simple consciousness alone, is to give it a foundation which is too narrow. The true debate on liberty is whether the conscious ego is necessarily the product and the always incomplete and illusion-free expression of the unconscious, or whether we have, and to what extent we can build, given our unconscious, a conscious ego for which we will be responsible.

In opposition to the philosophies of the unconscious we hold that the lucidity of consciousness is a perfection, that it is a condition which is not sufficent but nevertheless necessary for liberty, and even that without this firm hold on a consciousness of oneself we do not truly exist as persons. What is a spirit which is not present to itself? But this firm consciousness should be as completely as possible an integration of our entire ego, raising from the shadows into the light all that we can gather, either to accept it as it is, to take some of it and leave the rest, or to capture its impulses, utilizing their strength or orientating them at will, transmuting them, sublimating them. For the moral conscience should be coextensive with psychological consciousness. And therefore if the knowledge of subconscious determinisms frees us from false responsibilities, we are nevertheless presented with another responsibility, greater and more precise, that of extending moral discipline as deeply as possible under the clear consciousness to our profoundly subconscious life. In the seventeenth century, the great spirits of the Lallemant school foresaw this when they insisted so much more on the purification of impulses than on meditation on present sins. And to go back to an example already given, we would not insist on an adolescent not having any "bad thoughts," but we would teach him that he is responsible for the images that he allows into his subconscious mind through glances, conversation, shows, reading.

Quickly and from every consideration we are brought to the conclusion that theology cannot be content with clear consciousness as the object of the moral conscience because this is to ask at the same time too much and too little of liberty.

The study of the subconscious and unconscious psychic structure seems mandatory for the moralist for still another reason. One of the questions considered at the very beginning of the treatise on human acts was concupiscence. Now psychology is closer to the dogmatic conception of concupiscence than is the Aristotelian notion.

Our moralists held to the latter rather than to the former. In our manuals concupiscence was a conscious movement, appetite or desire. The struggle against it took place in the clear consciousness. One can understand then how it might be said to be either antecedent or consequent, for this conscious desire for evil appeared sometimes before and sometimes after reading some interesting book or performing some imprudent act. It was either spontaneous or provoked. The conclusion was foisted upon either an increased or diminished responsibility. There was, then, no problem. The adolescent who gluts himself with pornographic illustrations is evidently responsible for the disturbing attraction exerted by these images, while this is not the case with a young person who subjects his senses and his imagination to a strong discipline but nevertheless feels the sting of the needle in an unsought meeting.

But dogma invites us to see in concupiscence something very different from sudden stings or caresses—we are presented with the notion of a permanent inclination to sin, an interior disorder of fallen nature. The moral notion and the dogmatic conception were far from close. The plunge into the depths of the unconscious psychic structure, the exploration of complexes, the knowledge we have today of the activity of impulses, of the disguises of the sexual appetite or of the desire for power, help us understand what this interior disorder is and how radical must be its purification, even in its psychic origins. In the light of a wide-awake conscience sin advances with face bared or only thinly veiled, and reason takes pleasure in measuring it with assurance; an act of the will is enough. But the danger comes from within and from below, from the pressure of the *élan vital* which is composed of multiple entangled and anarchical impulses which push forth, beating a path for themselves, and which have already set us in motion before we have had time to become aware of their impurity or their direction.

We are thus brought back to those patients of whom we spoke at the beginning. For they can be divided into two classes. One is the exclusive concern of the doctor. In the others, and they are numerous, the interior disorder of concupiscence is one of the causes of their illness; they will be cured only by a purification; their case must be treated by both the moralist and the doctor. This paranoiac is a proud man drained by egoism. That dreamer runs from the responsibilities of life when awake. Through fear of duty this mentally retarded child refuses to grow up. That unstable person is lazy. This mythomaniac, an artful hypocrite. Many delinquent children are sick without therefore being totally excused; they are at the same time delinquent and sick, and often the immoral or amoral environment in which they have grown up, lacking not only in strong discipline but also in affection, explains why they are both. If, as Carrel noted, there has been such an increase in mental illness in our world, moral anarchy is doubtlessly as much to blame as the absurd biological conditions under which men live today.

With the sick the priest is confronted with the problem of deciding which of the cases should be referred to the doctor alone and which need a moral cure as well as medical treatment. Moral theology should prepare them for this delicate task. There must be here some knowledge of pathological psychology, which is in itself unintelligible to anyone not possessing some notion of the unconscious psychic structure. For underneath clear consciousness concupiscence has its origin and pursues its subterranean work, sapping the spiritual life and often mental health. And in a sense somewhat different from what they meant, the romantics were not wrong in saying that passion is allied to madness. Indeed, concupiscence is not primarily a circumstance which aggravates or weakens responsibility; nor is it a mere natural movement towards sensible good. It is an interior disorder, as illness or a wound.

A doctor of souls, the priest needs training for this therapeutic mission. But alas, we know how in *fact* most of the old manuals seemed to forget this, without ever denying it and even admitting it from time to time, for example on the topic of habits and scruples. They were little more than manuals of law for judges of the conscience. But a vigorous reaction to this has already begun.

Moralists are thus aided in posing the major problem of responsibility by a psychology concerned with impulses, conduct, the unconscious, mental disturbances, etc. But social psychology is not as much help to us in studying the relationship in us between personality and social character, and consequently the personal conscience. This is also because most of the research in this new field is chiefly sociological. A Durkheim, for example, is little concerned with the person. For him everything becomes social and personality vanishes.

Nevertheless these investigations have been advantageous because they have made individualism untenable. This becomes quite clear in going over some of the manuals in use until recently: that abstract being called man, of whom it was decided when he was or was not responsible, is a monad exposed to meeting other monads. An individualistic morality is the only one which could be prescribed for such a being. The treatise on Justice was a perfect example of this. For while they still talked about social morality, our masters never went further than a morality of the individual living in society with other individuals.

But this is not the danger. Our entire civilization of masses tends to blot out faces: This explains so many fiery declarations on the sacred rights of the person whenever they are threatened. Now at a time when the discovery of the multiple social ego makes us doubt the existence of the person, distinct in some way from individuals, it is not sufficient simply to affirm or postulate the existence of personality and a personal conscience; we must establish it. This might well be the capital problem on which our entire concept of morality will finally be dependent.

Psychologists can approach this problem in three ways.

The first is through the psychology of the mind. If we possess free and personal thought, then we must have a personal conscience. This is the teaching of St. Thomas for whom the will is free because it is an intellectual appetite which must remove the indetermination of the practical judgment. Psychology agrees with this metaphysics to which it is a stranger. We know today, better than yesterday, that knowledge is active, that the intellect does not receive the truth directly by an act of reflection, but that it constructs it, and that the essential act of the intellect is the judgment, not the concept. Now the psychology of the judgment shows that its originality lies in its always being a singular judgment by which the intellect binds itself and makes a decision, makes an assertion in virtue of truth, while a repeated assertion, a weak and unassimilated assertion, is not a judgment. Not so long ago scientific rationalism held that belief was a problematical and inferior type of knowledge. We are now discovering that what on the surface appears to be the most impersonal thought is, in truth, belief; that all judgment is a result of experience. On the other hand through research into the origin and development of intelligence we have been made aware of the fact that the child's thought process is different from and independent of the adult's, even though it is expressed in the language of concrete collective thought. Following as closely as possible a child's moral and intellectual growth, one becomes aware of the nature of the intellect and how, even though with some difficulty, it frees itself from judgments suggested first of all by the child's environment, then by his associates and by older people. Moreover, studies of opinion have shown us how and to what extent the mind can be prepossessed and subdued, but they also do not fail to show with what resistance this conformist influence is met, which it cannot always repel, and through what efforts a man can maintain freedom of thought.

The second approach is through the psychology of character. Character means firmness and constancy of the will and of the judgment, but also an originality always singular and an integral unity of impulses and faculties. To be master of oneself one must be oneself. This originality can be grasped at its inception through a special study of the relationship between character and heredity. Moreover it is meaningful that the orphan normally has more difficulty in throwing off his heredity and becoming himself than does the child who has been brought up by his parents: this would verify the old and paradoxical assertion of the philosophers: conscience is in conflict with itself. This paradox is confirmed by experimental pedagogy. They are, in fact, the same activities, bodily exercise, intellectual effort, apprenticeship of social discipline, which at the same time assert and particularize character. The psychological study of the age of seven, the age of reason for our elders, is, finally, the most interesting for our moralists. It is the age of the appearance of the autonomous, and therefore of the personal, conscience. Unless he closes his eyes, the psychologist is forced to see that a decisive progress, a decided step forward in growth, is linked to this appearance, and that from then on the mastery of a personal conscience is one of the major elements of character.

The third approach is through the psychology of conjugal love, so much studied a few years years ago by Christians concerned with better understanding and better living of their marriages. This, better than any other approach, leads us to the heart of the problem. For it is the existence of roles which led us to doubt the person. Now love is only realized in a union so intimate that it seems to demand first of all that the man and wife sacrifice their individual egos, through a mutual assimilation which is like a renunciation of one's self. He who refuses this sacrifice will never love. Will the person be absorbed by the role of spouse? No, for it is this very intimate union itself which frees and perfects, in its deepest sense, the personality of the spouses. Love which is only assimilation has not gone the length of its *élan:* it has not, in spite of appearances, gone beyond all egoism. The total mutual gift is the gift of what each one is in the most profound recesses of his being. To give oneself thus is to reveal oneself to the spouse just as one is in the secret of one's personality; and to make oneself thus known is to become known to oneself as to others, and to be in broad daylight, in the abandonment of love, what one is. Only in this way does complete love involve and safeguard the person in the role of spouse. Now in studying the other roles of the social ego in the same way one would easily notice that the same law of love holds true. The gift of oneself is the fulfillment of the personality through the mortification of egoism.

What do psychologists teach us or recall for us in speaking of diseased and unbalanced people of fragile mental health, of disintegrating personalities, of unconscious determinism, of the amoral stirrings of impulses, of the multiplicity of the ego and of the effacement of the person? That man is not himself, one, free, springing from an autonomous conscience, save through a constant effort to become and remain thus. They upset our old and lazy notion of a consciousness totally lucid and free from illusion, of a liberty born adult, of a personality which goes along on its own power. They invite us to substitute for an abstract concept of liberty all that we hold to be true and concrete in the complex idea of self-mastery. The custom-made psychology ingeniously proposed to us by the old treatises on human acts is answered by a morality which would be only a science of mores. The concrete man, in all ages, needs a pedagogy. True morality is this pedagogy.

What should be the attitude of the educator faced with a difficult, lazy and undisciplined child whom the doctor considers a case of character? Should he stir up and stimulate the will, courage, loyalty and ambition to grow up, and, revealing the demands of these qualities one by one, bring him from little efforts crowned with success to more decisive ones? The conscience, like the mind and like character, is formed by exercise combined with teaching. It is no different with men than with children. Liberty, the personality and conscience are all in danger. It is through constant and confident appeal to responsibility, to moral judgment, and to the courage of being oneself that we will be able to rescue man from the mighty weight of a civilization of necessity and conformism. The danger comes from there and not from psychologists.

Why not be frank? Jurist-theologians have for generations made morality a province of Law. So much so, that with the help of the movement towards specialization, spirituality was divided up and almost separated. Knowing man better, knowing that he is free and possesses a personal conscience only if he works on it courageously through self-domination and self-abandonment, moralists are making morality once more an art of living. And let our readers not be dismayed if in debating with the psychologists we have spoken only of the man they know: this man is the fallen and redeemed man; the morality he needs is not the philosophers' ethics, but it is that of the unique Teacher, a divine pedagogy.

One word suffices as a conclusion. Truth has nothing to fear from truth.

Translated by LEON KING *and* GERARD DE VISSANT

PESSIMISM AND THE ESCHATOLOGICAL CONSCIOUSNESS

GABRIEL MARCEL

A FEW months ago I was talking to Max Picard, the author of *L'Homme du Néant,* by the shores of Lake Lugano, and I shall never forget the calm way in which he said, at a turning point in the conversation: "I am convinced that we are at the end of history. It is probable that there are many among us who will witness the apocalyptic event that will bring it to a conclusion." Max Picard, as is well known, is a Catholic. But more recently still I heard a Protestant, Pastor Dallière, express himself in an identical fashion. In both men—and it would be hard to imagine two men of more contrasting temperaments—there was the same certitude of the coming of the *Parousia.* What specially strikes me is that, though one is a Catholic and the other a Protestant, neither is a man of sectarian mind; on the contrary they have both what I would call an exemplary awareness of the ecumenicity, the universal mission, of the Church. It is in relation to this eschatological affirmation of Picard and Daillière that the reflections I wish to present here will be arranged. (Eschatology in Christian theology is the doctrine of the last things, death, judgment, heaven, and hell.)

As a first step, I think it may be useful to face the immediate objection which a belief in the imminent end of what we call the world is likely to arouse among many Christians who are caught up in the life of this century and who are fighting as well as they can against the injustices and miseries of all kinds that today afflict our sight. Is not this eschatological affirmation, they may be inclined to ask, an example of escapist thinking: of the kind of thinking that distracts us from our immediate duties? If in a very short time everything is going to come to an end, shall we not be tempted to think that nothing has any longer any practical importance? Will there not be an irresistible impulse for us to shut ourselves up in a mood of expectancy, perhaps an anguished and feverish mood, perhaps a joyous and serene one, but in any case a mood which by its nature shuts us off from any kind of effective action in the world? From such a point of view the act by which we would abandon ourselves without restraint to a confidence that the Lord will soon come may be regarded as an act of desertion.

It seems to me that this objection, however much apparent force it has, conceals a number of rather serious confusions. It has a close kinship with something which I remember a Swiss Protestant lady, of rather limited intelligence, saying against monks and nuns who have chosen a contemplative life. It was precisely as deserters that she spoke of monks and nuns, accusing them of slipping away from the most urgent human tasks and fleeing to the shelter of a useless existence, an existence protected and shut off from life. If she had gone a very little further, she would have been treating them as mere impostors. Now the absurdity of such an evaluation of the contemplative life does not need to be demonstrated. Yet it has a kind of tangential value in that it does recall to us certain temptations to which we are, after all, exposed, as soon as we begin to take something for a vocation which may after all be only a kind of spirit of indulgence towards ourselves. In the same way, we should always be on our guard against what I should like to call an eschatological quietism, a quietism which is in direct contradiction to the message with which the Church has been entrusted.

But looking at the matter in a much more general way, one cannot disguise from oneself the fact that the very idea of an end of time, of time coming to an end, of an *eschaton,* is profoundly repellent to a certain type of mental attitude, widely diffused among Christians themselves, and of which we ought to try to get a distinct notion. It will be readily admitted that this idea does smack of a certain obscurantist pessimism, which is one of our legacies from the Middle Ages, and which is always in danger of coming to the surface again on the occasion of one of these passing crises or calamities which mankind so often undergoes. From this point of view people will be inclined to assimilate eschatological affirmations to those dark and sinister and more or less delirious ideas which seize the imagination when it is under the influence of some disease or some kind of intoxication. In taking up this attitude, of course, one postulates the existence of a contrast between the normal and healthy condition which allows man to form a true and relatively encouraging picture of his condition and destiny, and a pathological state which favors the development of such "dark daydreams." And I was certainly very struck, at a meeting which the Bergson Society held to discuss the general subject of techniques, with the way in which such a respected philosopher as Edouard Le Roy sturdily refused to admit that there was anything in the present situation of humanity that had not already been met with on many other occasions. If one were to believe him, sound common sense compels us to believe that, once again, mankind will get to its feet again after recovering from its present grave sickness.

For my own part, I do not hesitate to say that it seems to me essential to take up the contrary position to Le Roy's. His position consists, at bottom, of proclaiming more or less explicitly that there is nothing to do but "make a fresh start" and "avoid crying over spilt milk." I choose these expressions, with their almost aggressive air of platitude, because they express very vividly what one may call the dogmatism of the man who has "made up his mind." But it is important to notice that such a man and such a mind draw their calm certainties from a world that appears to them as normally constituted, though capable, of course, of being progressively guided towards a condition more conformable with the demands of a reasonable being. Here I can bear witness from my personal experience: this world, normally constituted, though capable of being improved in many of its aspects, was the world in which we lived at the end of the last century and the earliest years of this one. Now, it is not enough to say that that particular world is in ruins; we are perfectly well aware that it was not smashed to bits by accident, but that it carried within its own depths the principle of its destruction; and on this particular topic it would certainly be rash to deny *all* validity to the Marxian analysis. But an observation of this sort which brings *the depths* into view deals a mortal blow to the knowledge of himself which the man who has made up his mind, the man of settled opinions and attitudes, imagines he possesses; in the light of what we have lived through, his claim to self-awareness appears merely presumptuous. *In the light of what we have lived through,* I say, for it is just here that we enter a domain in which phrases about "not crying over spilt milk," "starting again as if nothing had happened," and so on, seem mere scandalous nonsense. For we have not merely gone through a harrowing experience, like somebody who has been the victim of an accident or has had a grave illness. We have been instructed by our harrowing experience. Something has been revealed to us, or at least ought to have been revealed to us; an abyss has opened under our feet. I am tempted to bring in the image of a volcanic eruption which reveals a central fire, whose existence was unsuspected, but which was there all the same, and is still there.

But it may be asked whether any kind of historicism, and particularly Marxist historicism, does not tend to have the very effect of blocking up our abyss-like awareness of this central fire—of this demoniac power, that is fundamentally to say—of which we ought to try to take account, it may be suggested, by using the methods of a generalized psychoanalysis and referring to the "collective imagination" or other entities of that sort. Here again we are in the presence of the man of settled mind who is now granting himself a certificate of immunity from various kinds of delirium and aberration whose origins he will attempt to describe. This is the claim, the postulate, that underlies all scientific, literary, and philosophic conferences: "Those of us who are gathered here, all of us reasonable beings and generally thought masters of our subject, have come together to discuss. . . ." Obviously, at some levels of discourse, this claim cannot be criticized: urologists and heart-specialists have a real interest in meeting occasionally to exchange observations on localized and determinate pathological conditions, for which there are suitable special treatments. But the case is altered when such conferences deal with evils from which none among us can really regard himself as immune. In such cases, the attitude underlying such conferences, to the degree in which it implies an illusion about ourselves, a lie, appears more and more factitious and fundamentally open to condemnation. Let us notice, however, that it is just when such evils are extending their scope and striking deeper, that such desperate and fundamentally self-contradictory efforts tend fatally to multiply; and the too glaring and obvious failure which such conferences meet with can only intensify the despair that first gave birth to them. This is especially true at the political level, insofar as that can any longer really be dissociated from the economic level on the one hand, the moral and religious level on the other. And here we touch obliquely on an idea which seems to me an important one.

Optimistic minds seem today to find some comfort in the fact that a kind of world unity is visibly coming into being before us through the growth of modern techniques. But the real problem is whether a unification of this sort, whose chief expression is the elimination of distance, has a spiritual impact of any positive value; one cannot be at all certain that it has, and there is every reason to fear that international conferences and congresses, with all their sterility and speciousness, correspond precisely to this lying vision of a false unity.

The notion becomes fully clarified, I think, if one reflects even a little on what the nature of a real spiritual unity would be. One may, of course, content oneself with making use of a ready-made idea; if instead one makes the effort to ask oneself what unity is, one discovers that the idea is irreducibly ambiguous, if not in itself, at least in its concrete applications. To say that two entities together make merely a single entity is to say that a sort of coalescence has taken place between them that does not allow us to consider them apart; originally distinct, they now form a whole which is only ideally separable into its two elements. But at this abstract level we can imagine several different cases; either this unification of two elements in a single whole has been brought about by a process of reduction, or not: if it has, then one of our two elements has lost some of its specific characteristics in order to merge with the other; unification is linked to the impoverishment of one element, of the other, or of both. If, on the contrary, there has been no process of reduction, it is theoretically possible that the coalescence has been brought about without either of the two elements being modified in any way. To be honest, I am not sure that this is possible even at the level of physics, and at the biological level it is almost certainly inconceivable; at the spiritual level it is not even imaginable. At that level, in fact, the very notion of coalescence does not seem to apply. It seems at a first glance as if spiritual unification could be brought about only by the creation of a whole which had new qualities and within which each contributing element was, as it were, renewed; yet in postulating such a synthesis we remain in practice well below the level of the unity we are envisaging. Strictly speaking, we could here once more take up Nygren's celebrated contrast, which I mentioned already, between *eros* and *agape,* and say that *eros,* above all when taken in its romantic sense, consists of an aspiration to merge one's being in another's, or perhaps rather to merge with the other in a higher —or undifferentiated—unity. *Agape,* on the contrary, transcends fusion, it can take place only in the world of beings—I would say "in the world of persons," but that the term "persons" since Kant's day has tended to take on too formal and juridical a sense; while the confused "personalist movement" in contemporary philosophy does not seem to me to have restored its value. . . . Thus, would the highest unity not be one created between beings capable of recognizing each other as different, but of loving one another in their very difference? Such a unity lies at the opposite pole from any attempt at reduction: for ultimately every reductive process robs the reduced components of certain specific, differentiating qualities.

But it should be observed that technical progress, in its concrete impact, has just such a reductive effect. It reduces human diversity to similarity: it has brought about an extraordinary levelling of groups and of customs. Yet this levelling, on the other hand, has been balanced by the growth of a spirit of separatist self-assertion—the self-justifying spirit in its most fundamentally hateful aspect: as Werner Schee writes in *Le Dard,* in the world around us today everyone tends to say: "I'm no good, but neither is my neighbor." It is glaringly obvious that such a process by which traditional differences are reduced to a common denominator can only breed resentment in the world. There are various ways in which one could illustrate this. Of course, modern ideologies and the slogans that embody them, Marxism, Fascism, and so on, have these modern technical methods at their disposal. Yet it is just as obvious, and we should ask ourselves why this is so, that an ideology cannot be a source and center of love: in the deepest sense it cannot be a religion, but only a pseudo-religion or a counter-religion. These are the characteristics, in particular, of Communism: even though Communism may profit from a deceptive analogy between its own message and that of the Gospels; and even though it may be from this specious resemblance, of which many ignorant and simple-minded people have been dupes, that Communism derives some of its dynamic thrust. But I think there are a few simple statements that we need not hesitate to make at this point.

Ideology aspires to become propaganda—to become, that is to say, an automatic transmission of formulas electrically charged with a passion which is fundamentally that of hate (and fundamentally, also, hateful) and which can only embody itself on condition of being directed against some group of human beings chosen as scapegoats; the Jews, the Christians, the Freemasons, the *bourgeoisie,* as the case may be. But nothing is more striking to witness than the ease with which one scapegoat can be substituted for another.

Such propaganda has a difficult job when it seeks to influence the individual who possesses a critical sense. It even runs the risk of annoying him and putting him on the defensive. In the masses, on the other hand, it finds its chosen field of impact; and yet even to say that, is to say too little.

What we should say, rather, is that it is propaganda which tends to bring into being the masses as such: by diffusing among the individuals of whom it seeks to make one agglomeration, by passing its electric current through them the illusion that they can attain to a sort of mass-consciousness, and that the mass as such constitutes something more real and more valuable than its members taken separately.

Such propaganda makes use, of course, of the feeling of power which individuals experience when they see themselves gathered in great numbers around a single object. But the analogy with great religious assemblies is as misleading as possible. For in a religious assembly worthy of the name all attention is directed upon a kind of mysterious and transcendent reality. Here, on the contrary, the object of attention is a mere pretext, and fundamentally it is *itself* which the crowd is setting up as an idol. The incredible misunderstanding of some French sociologists of the earlier part of this century consisted, we may note in passing, in interpreting the essential nature of religion itself on the basis of this kind of religious degradation. The monster political rallies which have become so frequent in the last twenty or thirty years have precisely the purpose of encouraging this sort of collective *self-worship,* which, of course, by its very nature cannot recognize itself for what it is; for the skill of the organizers lies precisely in making sure that the pretext for self-worship should never be recognized as a *mere* pretext. In passing, let me say that I think the Churches are guilty of a very rash act when they think they help their cause by means of public manifestations more or less exactly modelled on the kind of rallies of which I have been speaking; for such manifestations let loose uncontrollable forces, and there is every danger that these forces will work against the true faith.

One ought to mention here, once again, the temptation of great numbers. This is certainly one of the most formidable temptations with which modern man is acquainted. It belongs to the same order as the temptation of the prestige of statistics. One may say that at the present time no organized body is really able to keep away from statistics, not even a body whose purposes are entirely spiritual (one thinks, for instance, of parochial and diocesan statistics about numbers of communicants). One cannot repeat too often, I think, or insist too strongly, that it is only on condition that one rejects the fascination of numbers that one can hope to remain at the spiritual level, that is, at the level of truth. But it should be added that, in our world as we find it, everything seems to be working in the most visible and tyrannous way to persuade us to the contrary. An ethics of the lie is in the process of being elaborated which commands the individual to make himself as nothing in the face of that multitude of which he is only an insignificant and ephemeral unit.

This does not imply that we can, and obviously still less that we ought to, attempt to restore that nineteenth-century individualism for which the case has now so completely lapsed. That individualism found extremely various and indeed fundamentally incompatible expressions. In its case, also, there is an illusion to be denounced, as sinister as the illusion of numbers—and indeed, notably in contemporary Germany, it has often sinisterly allied itself with the illusion of numbers: I mean the biological illusion. One might say that everything that strikes us as weak, shaky, and also, of course, as evil in the work of Nietzsche has to do with the prestige which the concept of the biological held for him. If Nietzsche admired Dostoevsky, it was perhaps because his knowledge of Dostoevsky was so superficial? If he had read the great novels, he would either have recognized in Dostoevsky his most formidable antagonist, or he would have been converted, for it is probable that in Dostoevsky's case the temptation of the biological was more firmly surmounted than in that of any other thinker. And at the same time there is in Dostoevsky something which infinitely transcends the kind of individualism we still find in Ibsen, not to speak of Stirner and the anarchists.

Thus we are not trying to give an exalted idea of the individual who defies the masses, and in fact we are not trying to give an exalted idea of anybody. By indirect and sometimes dangerous paths we are seeking to scrutinize what I have called, in the title of this chapter, the eschatalogical consciousness: the consciousness of the last things. Such a consciousness can be defined, above all, negatively: by its categorical refusal to adhere to a philosophy of the masses based on the consideration of techniques, and on the support furnished by the latter to what it would no doubt be rash to call civilization. It can be defined also by an equally determined refusal to ally itself with the optimism of men of settled opinions and attitudes: the optimism which, no doubt without daring to subscribe to the frightening and ambitious theses of Hegel, takes up a half-way position and complacently supposes that, at the price of certain regrettable excesses, history is assuring the achievement of certain moderate demands, certain average ideals, in which demands and ideals the man of settled opinions and attitudes can recognize his own comfortable limitations.

But if we seek to consider this eschatological consciousness from a more positive point of view, we shall find that a tiny number of survivors from wartime extermination camps have evidence whose value can hardly be over-estimated. It is enough to remember that among the horrors of Auschwitz and other camps there were men like Jacques Levy, the parish priest of Point-Aven, Edmond Michelet. But from the point of view which I am tending to adopt, we must face the question of whether such camps can be regarded as in some sense an anticipation, a sinister caricature, of the world to come. The general adoption today over a wider and wider portion of a continent which we thought of as civilized of certain totalitarian methods takes on, seen from this angle, a terribly revealing significance. Would not one essential aspect of the eschatological consciousness consist in recognizing this phenomenon in all its amplitude, in its specific reality, and in seeing clearly that one takes upon oneself the guilt of the liar when one claims to regard the atrocities of other centuries as being on all fours with the horrors we have witnessed ourselves? In these distant centuries, the fundamental principles of a humane social order had not yet been either recognized or proclaimed. Today men systematically infringe principles which they are perfectly well aware of; even more, with an unparalleled impudence, the very men who are trampling these principles underfoot do not cease to invoke them and to lend their own authority to the ideas (democracy, liberty, and so on) of which the system of government they intend to bring into being will ensure the final ruin. I should like to add that, this being so, it is very suitable that the philosopher himself should try, by an effort of religious recollection, to gather again within himself everything that has been thus wasted, flung to the winds, profaned.

But it may be asked whether such a consciousness, with its flavor of evensong and the sense of the coming night, is properly speaking an eschatological consciousness, especially in the philosopher's case? Can the latter subscribe in all sincerity to the idea of a sort of suprahistoric event that will come, in some sense from outside, to put an end to history? There is much that one could say on this matter: quite summarily, I will say here that we are today witnessing a universal turning into problems of processes which, in former centuries, were regarded as carrying on by their own momentum, and at the same time these indefinitely multiplied problems of our own age seem to suggest or imply fewer and fewer solutions. Would it not be reasonable to say that, as soon as reflective thinking begins to attack, in order to disintegrate it, the very unity of lived experience—and by the phrase I mean above all the act of living and of giving life—and as soon as questions asking "Why?" proliferate unduly, it somehow happens that even questions which merely ask "How?" become progressively insoluble? A world in which somebody has been able to suggest the granting of a salary to the mother of a family is obviously a world where the very roots of life are poisoned. It is, of course, from this point of view, also, that the cult of the State appears as a major scourge. There is a mad illusion that forces men to unload on the State the burdens they are no longer capable of carrying themselves, so that the wearied and flagging State becomes a symbol of impotence disguised in the trappings of absolute power. It is as he proceeds along this line of argument that the philosopher, considering impartially what is going on around him, is led to ask himself whether we are not in fact after all coming towards the end of history, and whether the atom bomb is not a real symbol of a tendency driving our race to self-destruction. No doubt it is at quite another level that the idea of the *eschaton,* the end of things, as the Holy Book presents it to us, ought to be brought in. But we may ask ourselves whether the situation which I have tried to evoke in these pages is not, as it were, the sensuous and historic garment in which an event presents itself to us, which it belongs to faith alone, not certainly to grasp, but to have a presentiment of in its positive reality.

No doubt some of my readers will at this point attempt to force me back into my last ditch: and I shall be asked: "Do you personally really in good faith and in all sincerity believe that this apocalyptic event is close at hand?" But I don't think it is possible to answer such a question with a simple yes or no. Because it belongs to my essential nature, as a creature who is imprisoned by the senses and by the world of habits and prejudices in which I am caught up, to be for ever divided, this self of mine that is a prisoner may reply: "No, I don't believe it," and thereupon may abandon itself to mere despair or, with more and more difficulty, may take refuge in some optimistic thought, some "Suppose, after all. . . ." However, something happens here which is of decisive importance: it is that this self of mine which is a prisoner cannot declare in all sincerity that it is I. I have an awareness of not being reducible to this captive self; the self of love and of prayer proclaims itself as something distinct, even though between the self of love and prayer and the captive self there is something more than a mere cohabitation. And it is only this self of love and prayer that can become an

eschatological consciousness. Moreover, even to this self of love
and prayer it is not given to prophesy; it would be passing beyond
the limits set to its condition if it were to prophesy. But the task
that does belong to it is that of preparing for this event: like the
condemned man tidying himself for the last time before going off
to execution. But in reality such a preparation could have nothing
funereal about it. On the contrary, it could not be carried out except in a spirit of joy—that joy of being at the same time one and
divers, which belongs to the essential notion of a Church as such.
Incomprehensible to the captive self, this joy is like the anticipated
response to an appeal of which we may now have only a presentiment but which will become, do not let us doubt it, ever more
distinct and more urgent—the appeal which the men of "settled
views" are condemned never to hear.

THE END OF THE MODERN WORLD

ROMANO GUARDINI

DURING the Middle Ages life was interwoven with religion at every
level and in every ramification. For all men the Christian Faith
represented the generally accepted truth. In some manner everything was stamped by Christianity and the Church: the social order,
legislation, the ethos governing public and private life, the speculations of philosophy, artistic endeavors and the historic climate
within which all ideas moved. Even while including all these things,
we do not begin to indicate the cultural values won for the personality of man through this mingling of the cultural and the religious. Even injustice itself stood measured and condemned by
Christianity. Although the Church had grown up in intimate
union with the State, although Emperor and Pope or Prince and
Bishop were often at odds—accusing and heaping abuse upon one
another—men never questioned the Church herself.[1]

In time, man began to doubt the truth of Christian Revelation, and the doubt deepened as the medieval period drew toward its end. As an absolute standard claiming the right to measure the direction and conduct of human life, Revelation was enduring more and more vigorous attack. The new culture taking shape in Europe bred an outlook which thrust into prominence the increasing opposition to the Church. European man was adopting as self-evident truth the point of view which gave to politics, economics, government, science, art, philosophy and education principles and criteria immanent to themselves. In doing so men planted the seeds of non-Christian, even anti-Christian, ways of life in the soil of Europe. The old insistence that life be ordered by Revelation was taken as an encroachment by the Church, so completely had the new mind seized power over men's imaginations. Even the faithful came to accept this state of affairs, accepting as normal the new order which said that matters of religion belonged in one sphere of life and secular matters in another. The individual man was left adrift to decide to what extent he would live in both of them.

As a consequence an autonomous secular order came into existence, uninfluenced by any direct Christian principles, while a new Christian order grew up by imitating the secular bent toward "autonomy" to a remarkable degree. In a parallel manner, science developed as pure science, economics as pure economics, politics as pure politics; similarly a religious religiosity was developed. Religion increasingly lost direct contact with the realities of life as it emptied itself of the secular and limited itself to "purely religious" doctrine and practice. For many men religion retained significance only in its formal aspects—in dedicating or sanctifying the crucial events of life such as birth or marriage or death.[2]

At many points in our study we have noted how this non-Christian culture commenced its growth at the very outset of the modern age. At first, the attack upon Christianity was directed against the content of Revelation. It was not made against those ethical values, individual or social, which had been perfected under the inspiration of the Faith. At the same time modern culture claimed those very values as its own foundation. Due largely to its changes in historic study, the modern world dedicated itself to the theory that it had discovered and developed ethical values. It is true, indeed, that the modern age did further the intrinsic worth of personality,

of individual freedom, of responsibility and dignity, of man's inherent potentiality for mutual respect and help. These human
values began their development, however, during earliest Christian
times, while the Middle Ages continued their nurture by its cultivation of the interior and religious life. But the modern era suffered the invasion of consciousness by personal autonomy; human
perfection became a cultural acquisition independent of ethics or of
Christianity. This point of view was expressed in many ways by
many groups, pre-eminently in the voicing of "the Rights of Man"
during the French Revolution.

In truth, all human values find their root in Revelation; everything immediately human is related uniquely to Revelation. Man is
related to God through Faith, but Faith is the effect of divine grace
freely given and it draws the substance of all things human into
itself. As a result, a Christian Order of life could come into existence in which "natural" human powers would be freed for full
development, a development impossible outside a Christian Order.
Man might then become conscious of values which, although evident in themselves, only take on visible manifestation under the
aegis of Revelation. Those who maintain that these values and cultural attitudes are simply one with the autonomous development of
human nature misunderstand the essential role of a Christian economy of Revelation, Faith and Grace. In fact the misunderstanding
leads—permit me to speak plainly—to a kind of dishonesty which,
as anyone who takes a clear-eyed view can see, is integral to the
contemporary world itself.

Personality *is* essential to man. This truth becomes clear, however, and can be affirmed only under the guidance of Revelation,
which related man to a living, personal God, which makes him a
son of God, which teaches the ordering of His Providence. When
man fails to ground his personal perfection in Divine Revelation,
he still retains an awareness of the individual as a rounded, digni-
fied and creative human being. He can have no consciousness, however, of the real person who is the absolute ground of each man, an
absolute ground superior to every psychological or cultural advantage or achievement. The knowledge of what it means to be a
person is inextricably bound up with the Faith of Christianity. An
affirmation and a cultivation of the personal can endure for a time

perhaps after Faith has been extinguished, but gradually they too will be lost.

A similar loss reveals itself in contemporary man's feeling that personal values inhere in special talents or social position. Gone is that reverence toward the person qua person, toward his qualitative uniqueness which cannot be conceptualized or repressed for any man even if he has been typed and measured in every other respect. A kindred loss is found in the exercise of human freedom. Instead of allowing for the full development of the existent self, freedom has been restricted to psychological advantage or social privilege; it has ignored man's right to choose, to possess his own act while possessing himself in that act. As well human love has been stifled, resting content with sympathy, a willingness to serve or with social duties, but seldom affirming the "thou" of the other even as it must accept the obligations of an "I." Not one of these attitudes can be viable, unless the Christian concept of the person is vigorously maintained. As soon as the true value of the person is lost, as soon as the Christian faith in the God-man relationship pales, all related attitudes and values begin to disappear.

Modern man's dishonesty was rooted in his refusal to recognize Christianity's affirmation of the God-man relationship. Even as the modern world acclaimed the worth of personality and of an order of personal values, it did away with their guarantor, Christian Revelation. This parallel affirmation and negation can be illustrated in modern history in the case of German classicism. Carried forward by truncated attitudes and values, German classicism was noble, humane and beautiful, but it lacked the final depth of truth. It had denied Revelation although it drew everywhere upon its effects. By the next generation the classical attitude toward man had also begun to fade, not because that generation did not occupy an equally high plane, but because an uprooted personal culture is powerless against the breakthrough of positivism. Thus the process of dissolution gained momentum. Suddenly the "value system" of the last two decades broke into history. In its sweeping contradiction of the whole modern tradition it proved that culture to have been only an apparent culture. That vacuum, however, had been created long before; now it was made evident to all men. With the denial of Christian Revelation genuine personality had disappeared from the human consciousness. With it had gone that realm of attitudes and values which only it can subsume.

The coming era will bring a frightful yet salutary preciseness to these conditions. No Christian can welcome the advent of a radical un-Christianity. Since Revelation is not a subjective experience but simple Truth promulgated by Him Who also made the world, every moment of history which excludes that Revelation is threatened in its most hidden recesses. Yet it is good that modern dishonesty was unmasked. As the benefits of Revelation disappear even more from the coming world, man will truly learn what it means to be cut off from Revelation.

The question of the temper of the religious sensibility of the new age remains before us. Although the content of Revelation is eternal, its historical realization, its incarnation in man, varies with the passage of time. We could offer many implications about the religious temper of the new man, but it is necessary to restrict our meditations.

The rapid advance of a non-Christian ethos, however, will be crucial for the Christian sensibility. As unbelievers deny Revelation more decisively, as they put their denial into more consistent practice, it will become the more evident what it really means to be a Christian. At the same time, the unbeliever will emerge from the fogs of secularism. He will cease to reap benefit from the values and forces developed by the very Revelation he denies. He must learn to exist honestly without Christ and without the God revealed through Him; he will have to learn to experience what this honesty means. Nietzsche has already warned us that the non-Christian of the modern world had no realization of what it truly meant to be without Christ. The last decades have suggested what life without Christ really is. The last decades were only the beginning.

A new paganism differing from that of earlier ages will appear in the new world. Again contemporary man labors under illusory attitudes. In many cases, the non-Christian today cherishes the opinion that he can erase Christianity by seeking a new religious path, by returning to classical antiquity from which he can make a new departure. He is mistaken. No man can retrace history. As a form of historic existence classical antiquity is forever gone. When contemporary man becomes a pagan he does so in a way completely other than that of the pre-Christian. Even at the height of their cultural achievement the religious attitudes of the ancients were youthful and naive. Classical man only lived before that crisis which was the coming of Christ. With the advent of Christ man confronted a decision which placed him on a new level of existence. Sören Kierkegaard made this fact clear, once and for all. With the coming of Christ man's existence took on an earnestness which classical antiquity never knew simply because it had no way of knowing it. This earnestness did not spring from a human maturity; it sprang from the call which each person received from God through Christ. With this call the person opened his eyes, he was awakened for the first time in his life. This the Christian is whether he wills it or not. This earnestness prevailed, springing from the historic realization of the centuries that Christ is Being. It springs from man's common experience, frightful in its clarity, that He "knew what is in man," from the awareness in men of all the ages of that superhuman courage with which He mastered existence. When men deny this awareness we gain an impression that they suffer an immaturity, one common to the anti-Christian faiths of the ancient world.

Just as the renewal of the ancient classic myths against early Christianity was lifeless, so was the attempted rejuvenation of the Nordic myths. Seldom was either of those renewals the camouflage for a drive for power as it was with National Socialism. Nordic paganism had existed prior to the decision man had to make before God's call through Christ, as had classical paganism. On the other hand, which ever way contemporary man decides, he must enter the depths of the person as revealed in Christ, leaving behind the secure but static life of immediate existence with its false rhythms and images.

This exact judgment must be made against all those attempts which would create a new myth through secular affirmation of the true Christian vision. Consider what happened in the later poetry of Rilke for instance. Basic to Rilke's poetry is the will to shed the transcendence of Revelation and to ground existence absolutely on earth. Rilke's desire reveals its utter powerlessness when we note its total lack of harmony with the world now dawning. His attempts to adjust himself to the new world have a moving helpless-

ness in a poem like the "Sonnette an Orpheus," an alienating help-
lessness in the "Elegien." In respect to French existentialism, too,
its negation of an intelligible existence is so violent that it seems to
be an especially despairing kind of Romanticism made possible by
the convulsions of the last decades.

A totally different realism would be needed to maneuver human
attitudes before they could contradict Christian Revelation or build
a fortress out of the world fully independent of Revelation. It remains to be seen to what extent the East can develop this other
realism and to what exigencies man will be subjected as a consequence.

The Faith of Christian men will need to take on a new decisive-
ness. It must strip itself of all secularism, all analogies with the
secular world, all flabbiness and eclectic mixtures. Here, it seems to
me, we have solid reasons for confidence. The Christian has always
found it difficult to come to an understanding of modern attitudes,
but we touch an issue here which needs more exact consideration.
We do not mean that the Middle Ages was an historic epoch fully
Christian in nature, nor do we mean that the modern world was
an age fully un-Christian. Such assertions would resemble those of
Romanticism, which have caused enough confusion. The Middle
Ages were carried forward by forms of sensibility, thought and action which were basically neutral to the question of Faith, insofar
as one can say such a thing at all. Similarly the modern world was
carried by neutral forms. Within the modern era Western man
created as his own an attitude of individual independence, yet that
attitude said nothing about either the moral or the religious use
which he made of his independence.

To be a Christian, however, demands an attitude toward Revelation; this demand can be found in every era of Western history. As
far as this Christian attitude was concerned, Revelation remained
equally near and equally distant for each epoch. Thus the Middle
Ages contained its share of unbelief at every stage of decision;
similarly the modern world demonstrated its share of full Christian
affirmation. The modern Christian differed in character from his
medieval ancestor, since he was forced to incarnate his faith
within an historic situation which espoused individual independence, but he often succeeded as well as did the man of the Middle

Ages. Indeed, the modern Christian faced obstacles which made it difficult for him to accept his age in the simple way that the medieval Christian could accept his. The memory of the revolt made against God by the modern world was too vividly impressed on the modern Christian. He was too aware of the manner in which his age had forced all cultural values to contradict his Faith. He knew too well the dubious and inferior position into which the world had forced that Faith. Besides these indignities there remained that modern dishonesty of which we have spoken, that hypocrisy which denied Christian doctrine and a Christian order of life even as it usurped its human and cultural effects. This dishonesty made the Christian feel insecure in his relation to the modern age. Everywhere within the modern world he found ideas and values whose Christian origin was clear, but which were declared the common property of all. How could he trust a situation like that? But the new age will do away with these ambivalences; the new age will declare that the secularized facets of Christianity are sentimentalities. This declaration will clear the air. The world to come will be filled with animosity and danger, but it will be a world open and clean.[3] This danger within the new world will also have its cleansing effect upon the new Christian attitude, which in a special way must possess both trust and courage.

Men have often said that Christianity is a refuge from the realities of the modern world, and this charge contains a good measure of truth, not only because dogma fixes the thought of a Christian on an objective, timeless order and creates a life which survives the passing of the ages, but also because the Church has preserved a full cultural tradition which would otherwise have died. The world to come will present less basis for objecting to Christianity as a refuge.

The cultural deposit preserved by the Church thus far will not be able to endure against the general decay of tradition. Even when it does endure it will be shaken and threatened on all sides. Dogma in its very nature, however, surmounts the march of time because it is rooted in eternity, and we can surmise that the character and conduct of coming Christian life will reveal itself especially through its old dogmatic roots. Christianity will once again need to prove itself deliberately as a faith which is not self-evident; it will be forced to distinguish itself more sharply from a dominantly non-Christian ethos. At that juncture the theological significance of dogma will begin a fresh advance; similarly will its practical and existential significance increase. I need not say that I imply no "modernization" here, no weakening of the content or of the effectiveness of Christian dogma; rather I emphasize its absoluteness, its unconditional demands and affirmations. These will be accentuated. The absolute experiencing of dogma will, I believe, make men feel more sharply the direction of life and the meaning of existence itself.

In this manner, the Faith will maintain itself against animosity and danger. At the forefront of Christian life, man's obedience to God will assert itself with a new power. Knowing that the very last thing is at stake, that he has reached that extremity which only obedience could meet—not because man might become *heteronom*[4] but because God is Holy and Absolute—man will practice a pure obedience. Christianity will arm itself for an illiberal stand directed unconditionally toward Him Who is Unconditioned. Its illiberalism will differ from every form of violence, however, because it will be an act of freedom, an unconditional obedience to God; nor will it resemble an act of surrender to physical or psychic powers which might command one. No, man's unconditional answer to the call of God assumes within that very act the unconditional quality of the demand which God makes of him and which necessitates maturity of judgment, freedom and choice.

Here too we dare to hope. This trust is not based at all upon an optimism or confidence either in a universal order of reason or in a benevolent principle inherent to nature. It is based in God Who really is, Who alone is efficacious in His Action. It is based in this simple trust: that God is a God Who acts and Who everywhere prevails.

If I am right in my conclusions about the coming world, the Old Testament will take on a new significance. The Old Testament reveals the Living God Who smashes the mythical bonds of the earth, Who casts down the powers and the pagan rulers of life; it shows us the man of faith who is obedient to the acts of God according to the terms of the Covenant. These Old Testament truths will grow in meaning and import. The stronger the demonic powers the more crucial will be that "victory over the world" realized in freedom and through Faith. It will be realized in the harmony between man's freedom freely returned to God from Whose own Creative Freedom it was gained. This will make possible not only effective action but even action itself. It is a strange thing that we should glimpse this holy way, this divine possibility, rising out of the very midst of universal power as it increases day by day.

This free union of the human person with the Absolute through unconditional freedom will enable the faithful to stand firm—God-centered—even though placeless and unprotected. It will enable man to enter into an immediate relationship with God which will cut through all force and danger. It will permit him to remain a vital person within the mounting loneliness of the future, a loneliness experienced in the very midst of the masses and all their organizations.

If we understand the eschatological text of Holy Writ correctly, trust and courage will totally form the character of the last age. The surrounding "Christian" culture and the traditions supported by it will lose their effectiveness. That loss will belong to the danger given by scandal, that danger of which it is said: "it will, if possible, deceive even the elect" (Mt. 24:24).

Loneliness in faith will be terrible. Love will disappear from the face of the public world (Mt. 23:12), but the more precious will that love be which flows from one lonely person to another, involving a courage of the heart born from the immediacy of the love of God as it was made known in Christ. Perhaps man will come to experience this love anew, to taste the sovereignty of its origin, to know its independence of the world, to sense the mystery of its final *why?* Perhaps love will achieve an intimacy and harmony never known to this day. Perhaps it will gain what lies hidden in the key words of the providential message of Jesus: that things are transformed for the man who makes God's Will for His Kingdom his first concern (Mt. 6:33).

These eschatological conditions will show themselves, it seems to me, in the religious temper of the future. With these words I proclaim no facile apocalyptic. No man has the right to say that the End is here, for Christ Himself has declared that only the Father knows the day and the hour (Mt. 24:36). If we speak here of the nearness of the End, we do not mean nearness in the sense of time, but nearness as it pertains to the essence of the End, for in essence man's existence is now nearing an absolute decision. Each and every consequence of that decision bears within it the greatest potentiality and the most extreme danger.

NOTES

1. Here we must make a necessary distinction. The Christian Faith is a bond linking man to the God of Revelation. The perfection of Faith is measured by the clarity with which this bond is seen and by the loyalty with which it is maintained. To experience religion per se is another question, regardless of the vitality with which a man senses his relation to the Divine or of the degree to which it affects his life. During the medieval period man possessed a natural disposition to receive the imprint of the Divine which was markedly high. Religious experience was a reality, strong, deep, and delicately developed. Religious values permeated all things, every facet of life. Poetry and art, government, forms of society and economy, customs, myths and legends—even apart from their content—teach us about the religious character of all existence. In its religious consciousness the Middle Ages was linked intimately with classic antiquity, despite the profound changes which the vitality of the Nordic races had brought to medieval Christendom as the great migrations flowed over Europe. From its outset the medieval capacity for religious experience was different from Christian piety per se; similarly, the European view of reality, of things and events, was different from the content of Revelation. Yet the two spheres of experience were definitely related. Natural religious experience was purified by Revelation, taken into it, receiving thereby new significance. At the same time, the capacity for natural religious experience brought to Christian Faith the elemental stuff and power out of which a world and a way of life were brought into being, through which the content of Revelation was made compatible with terrestrial realities.

2. These developments have their contemporary significance, too, which we note in addressing ourselves to the religious situation of the modern era. And there is also another pertinent consideration: the loss of that openness toward the religious itself of which we have already spoken.

The modern era experienced the increasing penetration of nature by rational and experimental techniques. It came to see politics as the mere play of power for the sake of naked interest; it saw economics develop as a discipline gauged to a logic inherent within utility and welfare. The modern era grasped technology as a gigantic apparatus available for any purpose man might conceive. Art became the mere fashioning of forms out of matter according to strict aesthetic criteria. Pedagogy became an instrument with which the teacher produced the kind of men needed to support the status quo and the accepted culture. To the very extent that the new ideal was actualized, the natural ability to open oneself to religious experience waned. By religious openness, we repeat, we do not mean the Faith and its content of Christian Revelation nor a life determined by them. We mean that immediate interest, rather, in the religious per se which is present in all. We mean a concern for, and an ability to be gripped by, those mysterious currents which run throughout the world and reveal themselves to all peoples at all times. To a considerable extent, however, modern man lost both his belief in the Revelation of Christ and this latter ability to experience his world in a religious way. His world had become a "thing" increasingly profane. This impoverishment of the religious sensibility was to have far-reaching effect.

For example, consider that the tapestry of events making up the life of a man was no longer seen as the working of that Providence of which Jesus spoke. It was not even thought to be the work of that mysterious fate which led the life of classical man. In its varied relations, in its over-all pattern, life was reduced to a mere sequence of empirical causes and effects, which, since intelligible to man, could be guided by him. Emptied of the religious, this outlook is expressed today variously. One example can be taken as typical—the present system of insurance. If we look at the extreme development and spreading of insurance promotion today throughout many lands, it appears as a system stripped of all religious base. It "provides for" all eventualities and renders them harmless merely by charting their frequency and importance.

The crucial events of the life of man—conception, birth, sickness, death—have lost their mystery. They have become biological or social phenomena dealt with more and more by a medical science or by a series of techniques which claim an increasing confidence in their own efficacy. Insofar as the great crises in human life could reveal truths which cannot be mastered by modern techniques, they are "anaesthetized" and thus rendered irrelevant. In this connection, we cannot avoid thinking of those auxiliary techniques for the rational conquest of sickness or death which appear today not only at the horizons of our culture but also at its very center, techniques which would remove lives no longer of service to "life" itself, no longer corresponding to the ends of the state.

The state once possessed a religious significance, a majesty which sprang from its dedication to the divine. All of that withered; today it has disappeared. Then, the modern state was thought to derive its power from the people; for a time efforts were made to transfer the old sense of majesty to the people themselves. Note in this regard, the theories of the Romantics, the theories behind nationalism, behind the earlier democracies. But the "majesty of the people" was soon emptied of any positive content; it came to mean that the "people" were the multitudes who belonged to the state. In some manner, the state came to express their will, but quickly it incarnated the many in the execution of its own measures and only for so long as the state itself was not mastered by a powerful or militant minority. Many things could be said in this connection, but let us be content with indicating that the forms of human existence under the state were derived exclusively from the empirical order.

Is it possible to build a life for man or for society upon exclusively empirical grounds, a life which could endure? Could such a life foster the values and insights necessary to remain truly human? Could it even reach the goals which it seeks?

Is not every order of being sapped of strength when taken in a merely empirical way? For example, the state demands the oath, the most binding of all contracts, in which a man guarantees his avowal with a pledge or obliges himself to an action by referring his declaration expressly and solemnly to God Himself. What happens to the oath when it loses this reference to God? (And we must admit that recent usage tends to strip the oath of divine reference.) It becomes a mere declaration: the man swearing admits that he is aware that he will be imprisoned if he does not tell the truth. This formula makes little sense and cannot be effective.

Every being is more than itself. Every event points beyond a bare formal completion of its own act. All things are related to a reality above and beyond themselves; from this reference alone can they be perfected and carried to fulfilment. Failing their reference to the Other, all things, all orders of reality become empty shells. Stripped of their significance, they can convince no one of their root value. The law of the state is more than a set of rules governing human behavior; behind it exists something untouchable, and when a law is broken it makes its impact on the conscience of man. Social order is more than a warrant against friction, than a guarantee for the free exercise of communal life; behind it stands something which makes an injury against society a crime. This religious dimension of law suffuses the entire moral order. It gives to ethical action, that is action necessary for the very existence of man, its own proper norms, which it executes from without and without pressure. Only the religious element of law guarantees the unity and co-operation of the whole order of human behavior.

No such thing as a merely worldly world exists even when the stubborn will seems to have fashioned a strictly secular order, for it has made an order which cannot function. It has produced an unsuccessful, an unconvincing artifact. The living intuition of man the person, lying beyond and under all rationalistic thought, cannot be convinced by a secular world. His heart cannot feel that such a world pays.

Without religion life becomes like a machine without oil; it runs hot; even if it functions, some part of it is always burning out. One after another its varied parts which ought to fit together exactly are immobilized. Just as the center of action is lost, its cohesion is prevented. Existence has lost its order. Finally, the engine of society breaks down, just as it has been short circuited during the past thirty years by the increasing loss of social contacts. Obsessed with the exercise of his own power, man today frantically hunts for a way out of his own social breakdown. As long as men are unable to control themselves from within, however, they will inevitably be "organized" by force from without. To ensure proper, external function the state steps in and places, that is it forces, its own power upon a new order. But, we ask, is it possible for man as man to continue to exist under the naked use of power itself?

3. What we noted earlier concerning the decline of primitive religious sensibility, of the ability to infuse all things with a sense of the religious, will increase in the new era. A fullness of religious sensibility helps faith, but it can also veil and secularize its content. If this fullness diminishes, faith becomes leaner but purer and stronger. The new Faith will therefore open itself to what is genuinely real; its center of gravity will descend more deeply into the personal; it will affect all things with decision, loyalty and self-conquest.

4. We retain Guardini's usage of the Greek *heteronom*. The English derivative would probably be "heteronomous," meaning: not self-governing or not self-determining, etc. Ed.

Love

THE saints of the twentieth century sing the same songs as did the saints of the thirteenth or the third or any other. In borrowed finery or in homemade material, they hymn the Lord, they confess his ineffable sweetness, his immutable beauty, his tenderness, his wisdom, his joy. Their words are the words of Scripture, of theology, of the spiritual classics. Their words are the words of all who have loved God passionately and said so with their own sweetness and beauty and tenderness and wisdom and joy. What more, then, can contemporary expressions of love add to those of the past except more of the same, gathered from the same noble sources for the same noble end?

Much, much can be added: the temper of the times, the special tone of the times; the accents of individuals, each one different not only in degree but in kind, as persons are different from each other, and always will be, in the infinite variety of creation that makes each birth an event to be celebrated. The love of God, like the love of man, is very much of its time and place. There is, in fact, no more revealing insight to be gained into the character of an era than its language of love, its customs and ceremonies of love, whether the love is of God or of man, for the two are never very far apart.

Ours is a psychologizing time. Ours is a time much concerned with the discoveries and deliberations of science. Thus Freud and Jung and their successors and supplanters have made their way into speculations about the relationship of man and God. Thus atomic physics has had its effect in this literature as in every other. As in earlier days there was fear of possession, so now no good Christian

*will go comfortably to his orisons unless he has first checked the
state of his neuroses and the shape of his fantasy life. As in another
time illustrations of the Providence of God could be drawn from
the concentric spheres of the Ptolemaic universe, now they can be
constructed from the design of the proton, the electron, and the
neutron.*

*Ours is a time of constantly deepening implementation of social
justice. Ours is a time filled with a rhetoric of responsibility, the
responsibility of men for each other at every level of human activity, social, political, economic, psychological, spiritual. And so in
our time the connection between the love of God and the love of
neighbor has been drawn as tight as love could make it. Almost
every piece in this section insists upon that connection, not as something new, of course, but as something old understood with a new
freshness and with a new impetus. That new freshness is in the
definitions of the French Dominican Albert Plé. That new impetus
is in the prescriptions of Dr. Grossouw of the University of Nij-
megen in Holland, where Catholics have given such good example
of the close relationship between the love of God and the love of
neighbor. Where that impetus can lead is suggested by the cur-
riculum of fellowship worked out by Jacques Maritain, uniting men
not only in spite of their differences, but also because of them.
Where the freshness is needed is indicated by Karl Adam in an
essay which still, after more than thirty years, preserves its fire and
its beauty and its appositeness.*

*The appeals of Maritain and Adam are very moving. At almost
every turn one discovers in them the depth of spirituality which is
the special mark of the virtue of love. One may notice that same
spirituality in the understanding of the richness of creation which
was the particular accomplishment of Pierre Teilhard de Chardin
in* The Divine Milieu, *and to it must be added the explication by
Henri de Lubac of what it means to be a Catholic, in an essay
that is perhaps the most profound piece of ecclesiological writing
of our time as well as the most affecting.*

*To explication spiritual writers always add example, for they
have such a fullness of example to choose from in the performances
of the saints. It is the saints—our friends the saints, as Bernanos*

*calls them—that give the beautifully drawn argument of Père
Philippe de la Trinité such plausibility, and especially that most
loving of the modern saints, Thérèse of Lisieux. Père Philippe goes
to St. Thérèse for his deepest insights into divine love. "This love,"
he says, paraphrasing her, "is our hope and our strength. The best
response that we can make to it is to have the confidence to abandon ourselves utterly to it. Loving God means allowing oneself to
be loved by Him as He wills, in His own divine way." The saints
of the twentieth century sing the same songs as did those of the
thirteenth or the third or any other.*

THE VIRTUE OF CHARITY

ALBERT PLÉ, O.P.

CHARITY, *agape,* is love—but not just any sort of love. Philologists
tell us that the word *agape,* rare in classical Greek, is distinguish-
able from *eros* by its elective and supra-passional character, while
theologians tell us that charity is one kind of love: St. Thomas
Aquinas makes a "friendship" of it. But we can use the word
"friendship" only with some reserve, because our vocabulary and
ideas are radically inadequate for the definition of something which,
in God, can have only a distant analogy with what we ordinarily
mean by this word. For that reason St. Thomas says that charity is a
certain friendship, *quaedam amicitia,* thus inviting us to respect the
transcendence of a thing that is divine in its essence and in its
source.

Then, too, what St. Thomas and Aristotle call "friendship" is
something much bigger than what is understood by the word in
English or French. For the theologian, there is friendship when
two or more *persons* love one another *reciprocally,* when each loves
the other *for the other's sake* and wishes him good that has moral
value (*bonum honestum*), when there is *community of life* be-

tween the "friends." In this sense there is friendship not only between two "friends"; it extends, for example, to the members of
matrimonial or political communities.

These two remarks were necessary to prevent any ambiguity
about this notion of friendship, which St. Thomas was the first
to take as the principle for understanding divine *agape*.

Being a sort of friendship, charity belongs to the mystery of
love. Love implies a relationship between one and another. Everything that exists is rich in relationship. Creation is kept in being
by a relation of existence and of ordering to the Creator, and
secondarily to other creatures: these relations have their origin and
fulfil themselves through love. Moreover, the Christian faith
teaches us that divine being includes a relationship within its perfect oneness, that of the divine Persons: the Spirit of love joins
the Father and the Son. It can therefore be said that all being has a
relational aspect, and the philosopher and theologian have to study
the nature of love against this background.

To be created is to be fundamentally related to God; and not to
God alone but to the whole cosmos and, more immediately, to a
number of particular beings, with whom each individual has to
be *en rapport* if he is to be himself and fulfil himself. "What hast
thou which thou hast not received?" asks St Paul (1 Cor. 4:7). To
fulfil ourselves we have to give back to them again the life that we
have received from God, from our parents, from our social and
cosmic surroundings. The relation of origin and contribution is
completed by one of growth and completion: the inner law of the
nature of every being is that it is related to something other than
itself.[1] For beings endowed with understanding, this *ordinatio ad
aliud* is effected through knowledge and love.

For Aristotle and St Thomas, to know is "to become the other
as other." This means that he who knows becomes a little more
himself in becoming the other, by that relational operation that the
Schools call "intentional." Through this relation the other is as it
were "digested" by the understanding, which incorporates it, but
without altering it; the understanding draws the other to itself,
enriching itself from the intelligible content of its object; it forms an
idea of it, but however exact that idea may be it is not the reality
itself.

Another relational activity is "affective," and tends really to unite the subject with its object, not in the idea formed of it but in its extra-mental reality: and this is love. Here it is the other that draws that which loves to itself, there being there a fundamental virtuality—due to likeness or complementary quality—which it awakens, fashions and intensifies. The lover then seeks union with the beloved, and by so doing withdraws from self, moving towards the other, living in the other. Love is "ecstatic": "dicitur amor extasim facere quia quod fervet extra se ebullit et exhalet" (*III Sent.*, xxvii, 1, 1, 4).

To love, then, is a natural necessity for every being. Each one who loves enters into an "ecstatic" relationship with others and fulfils himself: thus the other is his good and his end. This relation to another "completes" and "perfects" him. There are degrees of love, and it is well to emphasize that the more spiritual a love is the more "ecstatic" it is. The more love is at the level of mind and spirit, the more the lover loves the beloved for his own sake as a person: life and happiness is found in *the other's happiness*.

As with the relation of creation, so with that of love: the closer the relationship, the more distinct its terms. The more being a creature receives, the more autonomous it is (a beast of the field is not a person, because it has been given less than a man). The more a being is united with God, the more he is himself, the more distinct he is from every other being; his dependence on God, lovingly recognized and accepted, is the ground of his freedom, his independence, his personality. In the same way the more a person loves another for himself, and reciprocally, that is, the better the mutual relationship, the more they are and become themselves in the uniqueness and autonomy of their persons.

It is at this level that love of "friendship" is found. It can exist only between persons; it is not of the passional order but of the spiritual. That is what theologians mean when they tell us that friendship, and therefore charity, is a love of the will. "Will" does not mean here what several centuries of voluntarism have taught us generally to understand by the word: it means spiritual "appetite," our capacity to love those whom our understanding knows and appreciates.

Charity is a Virtue

Thus does St. Thomas put charity in the field of will and teach that it is a virtue, meaning thereby that it is a *habitus* that we have (*habere*), which we are free to dispose, and which "*habilitates*" us to love in charity with constancy and strength, suitably and joyfully. There again etymology is significant: virtue is love, it is strength (*virtus*), it is dynamism (*dynamis,* say the Greeks), we might say a "muscular function" of the will. The charity which is in God, sanctifying grace, exerts its divine dynamism at the heart of our human dynamism. Something in us is changed, something comes from God and makes us godlike. That is why charity is called an infused virtue.

It is also called a theologic (*théologale*) virtue, not so much on account of its divine origin but essentially with reference to the object it enables us to love: God himself and for himself. And that means that charity makes us love God as he loves himself; it divinizes us by making us share in the very life of God: "Ye, therefore, shall be perfect, even as your heavenly Father is perfect" (Mt. 5:48). Such is the fruit of charity. And as in God the Holy Spirit is the "love-knot" that joins Father and Son, the charity given to us is, by appropriation, the special work of that Spirit. Thus, moulding us to the likeness of the Holy Spirit (*Sum. theol.,* II–II, xxiv, 5, 3), charity enables us to have part in the divine *koinonia* (*cf.* 1 John 1:3–7), the fellowship in love of the divine Persons. This perfect love, divine in its nature and its object, is none the less human, in the sense that it is lived in a man. Divine charity is embodied in a human psychology, and there it is given the nature, conditions and psychological dynamism of a virtue.

The Objects of Charity

Every *habitus* is specified by its object, which makes it what it is and distinguishes it from all others. Accordingly, to know what the virtue of charity is theologically its object must be ascertained with precision.

To love, says Aristotle, is "to wish well to somebody." This shows at once that there are two objects in every friendship: a good and the person in whom I love this good. To these two objects—which are inseparable—correspond two aspects of love: a strong desire for the good and friendship towards the person. The desired good is loved only with reference to a person, or to several persons: this is what makes the will's unity of movement. There is as well a third object: the *ratio* of this love.

An example will make this threefold distinction clear. I am abroad, far away from home, and I run into a fellow-countryman. I am drawn to him at once, I talk with him about home, I look after and befriend him. The *ratio* of this love is the quality we have in common of being Englishmen: we both love England. But in loving my country in him I am clearly loving him, his person. No doubt the good I love in him is essentially his quality as Englishman, but it is also all the other goods which he may have, or lack. If he needs a bed or money, I give it to him.

In the exact language of theologians, the first of these objects of love is called the formal object *quo* (*amatur*) or *propter quod:* in our example it is England. The second object is called the term *cui* or the material object *cui:* the person of my fellow-countryman. The third is called the material object *quod:* the fact that he is English, and also the shelter and help he may need.

The three objects of love thus uncovered by analysis cannot be dissociated; they are one, one not only in regard to the subject who loves them, all together in the same act of loving, but also one as having close relations between themselves. Love is "realist," directed to an actual concrete being: the formal object is not loved somewhere up in the sky of abstract ideas but in a living person. Because I love my native land, I love this Englishman; his being English is one thing with his own self.[2] The material object *quod* is loved, with desire, only by reference to the person loved. Love of friendship binds formal and material objects together so strongly because its end is a person; and the more exalted this love is, the greater is its unity. Friendship is finally directed towards a person loved in himself for his own sake; otherwise it would not be friendship but desire: the person would be loved only as a thing.

Applying this general principle to charity, theologians teach that its formal object *quo* is God, or more exactly the divine goodness, as it is revealed to us and the vision of which will be our blessedness in Heaven. The term *cui* is God himself in the three Persons, and secondarily all those who are or can be divinized by him. The material object *quod* is the divine Good which is or can be in the terms *cui* and also all other goods which can be related to this divine Good. So the material objects *cui* and *quod* are many, but the formal object *quo* one only. This accounts for the specific unity of the virtue of charity and the multiplicity in unity of the persons and goods which it makes us love. A little reflection on these three objects and their mutual relations will show how fruitful this analysis is.

Its formal object *quo* being the divine goodness in itself, as set out above, charity is something other than the creature's natural love for his Creator. For St. Thomas, each created being loves God more than himself, since each being is what he is only inasmuch as he is from God: in loving his own being he loves The Being more than himself, he loves himself by reference to that Being. St. Thomas's illustrations are the arm naturally uplifted to defend the body, and the citizen who sacrifices himself for the common good of his society (*Sum. theol.,* I, lx, 5c). True enough that original sin has intervened to corrupt the natural love of creatures for their Creator, but charity does not come in simply to restore it for us: essentially it is something quite different. Charity enables us to love God, not as Creator, but as God, for his own sake and as he is, in his triune life and divine blessedness. Whence we see why in order to have charity we must have faith.

It may be remarked in passing that the life of charity can develop all its virtualities only in the vision of God face to face. Charity in this world is essentially the same as in Heaven, but there its mode will be different because its object will be fully known and open to our understanding.

Charity, then, enables us to love God in himself, whom here below we know by faith; precisely, since the object of all love is a good, to love the goodness of the divine Being, inasmuch as the possession of it makes us sharers in God's own blessedness. It is not *our* happiness that we love by charity—it is God's.[3]

In the concrete, we love this beatifying goodness of God wherever we find it: in God eminently, but also, secondarily, in all creatures who share this blessedness, or are able to do so.

The divine Persons, angelic persons, human persons are therefore terms *cui* of charity. They are loved "for God" (formal
object *quo*), otherwise it would not be charity; but the destination
of our love is in each one of them, otherwise it would cease to be a
"friendship." Like all friendship, charity makes me really love the
person of my neighbor; more than do human forms of love, charity
penetrates to the hidden depths of that person. In loving him "for
God," I love what is most personal in him—his fundamental relation to God: in him I share in the invitation to love and blessedness
that God extends to him when he calls him by his name.

This enables us to grasp the eminent unity of the formal and material objects *cui* of charity: the more I love God in my brother,
the more I love him "within," in his longing for blessedness which
in the last resort rules his whole life and urges him on to become
himself in his most personal aspect.

That is why one of the preferred terms of charity is oneself.
After God, we have to love ourselves with charity, that is, love
what is divine in us, that which pertains to the promise of God's
blessedness. Friendship is a fellowship, and I can love God and
my neighbor only if I first myself enter into fellowship with that
blessedness which is the formal and specific object of charity. How
can I love God in my neighbor if I do not first love him in myself?
"Thou shalt love thy neighbor as thyself," says the Bible (Lev.
19:17–18; Mark 12:33).

Accordingly, charity is "totalitarian." I cannot exclude a single
one of its terms *cui* from my charity without thereby excluding all
the rest. Either I love God, myself, and all my brethren, known
and unknown, or I love nobody. Certainly an act of love of God is
distinct from an act of love of one's neighbor. But the act of love
of God includes love of the brethren at least implicitly; and
brotherly charity is in essence love of God, or else it is no more
than philanthropy.

Charity's material object *quod* is, in the first place and essentially, blessedness. This is the good that I love with charity in and
for every being who has it or is able to have it.[4] There are other
goods which can be referred to beatitude in one way or another:
there is my body and those of others, which are called to share in
blessedness "by superfluity"; there are all the goods of this world,

in the measure that their use is beneficial in the *via ad beatitudinem*. It is only in this context that clothing the naked is an act of charity; the desired good is ordered to the *divine* blessedness of my shivering brother. So even at this level charity is one in the multiplicity of its objects; but the virtue is one, not only because of the oneness of its formal object but also because of the intrinsic relations of its material objects *cui* and *quod*.

The Mystery of Charity

The above is a summary of the ordinary teaching of theology about the virtue of charity and its objects. I want now to speak of a less usual aspect of the subject. It is less usual because, for the past six hundred years, the sense and meaning of "mystery" have been lost to the general mentality of Christians. So much is this so that in our common speech we no longer have words to express what the Bible, the Fathers and the liturgy mean when they speak of *mysterium* or of *sacramentum*. What do they mean?

"God is light" (1 John 1:5), but "light inaccessible" (1 Tim. 6:16). Could we see this light, were it within our grasp, it would not be transcendent and it would not be God. And so, to make himself visible to mankind, God sends messengers[5] who "witness concerning the light" (John 1:6–9), in such a way that the light "enlighteneth every man" from within, but at the same time from outside, by the sign of their testimony. Seeing this sign, hearing it, touching it, the believer reaches God. When the Hebrews saw the pillar of cloud and heard the prophets and touched the ark of the Covenant, they saw, heard and touched God. By so doing God loses nothing of his inaccessibility and transcendence; on the contrary, he manifests them: he makes himself approachable through and in signs chosen by him that reach us at the level of our sense perceptions.

Jehovah's progressive training of his people reached its summit when the Word was made flesh, when he dwelt amongst us and we saw his glory (*cf.* John 1:14), the glory of the only-begotten Son of the Father, showing us the human countenance of God's very being (*cf.* Heb. 1:3). "In him dwelleth all the fullness of the Godhead corporally" (Col. 2:9).

This sign is what, following the Bible and the Fathers, we call a
"mystery." In this sense, Jesus Christ is the mystery of God by
excellence.[6]

But the sign cannot be separated from what it signifies: "sign"
and "signified" form a unity of a very special kind, and it must be
respected in its specificity. Analysis can, of course, distinguish the
signified from the sign; but they ought to be distinguished only in
order to join them together, whereas six centuries of nominalism
and rationalism have accustomed us to a dissociation, to seeing
the signified here, the sign there. Separation of mystery-signified
from mystery-sign is so firmly established that the Vatican Council
and our theological textbooks and our catechisms all call a mystery
something believed by faith, without expressly stating its relation to
the sign. For example, we say nowadays that the mystery of the
Holy Trinity is the oneness of God in three Persons. For the men
of old—and for St. Thomas (*Sum. theol.*, I–II, i, 8c)—the mystery
of the Holy Trinity is Christ, in whom and through whom the
three divine Persons are revealed and given to us. In the same way,
in the high middle ages, the reality signified and given by the
eucharistic meal was called the "mystical Body,"[7] the sign and the
signified of the mystery being thought of in their unity. Today,
by "mystical Body" we understand the Church, without joining it
with its eucharistic sign. Thus, *quoad nos,* the union of the sacrament with the Church is weakened, and the specifically "mysterious" reality of the eucharist is lost sight of. And so it came about
centuries ago that the eucharistic celebration and communion as it
were stopped short at the Lord's body and blood: it seems to have
been forgotten that the ultimate reality given by the Eucharist is
his mystical Body.

Once again, a mystery is a very special kind of reality, whose
specific purpose is to re-present the inaccessible reality of God, to
make it present and active to us through sensible signs.

A mystery is more than a symbol: its unity of sign and of signified is greater, while in the realm of essences they are more
heterogeneous. God always transcends the signs he gives us, but he
is at the same time really present and active in them. That cannot
be said of a symbol such as a flag, which represents a country but
does not make it present. A mystery can rather be compared with a

human face, which is flesh, and which enables us to know the soul
that gives it life and transcends it. The soul both shows and hides
itself in a smile; in making itself visible and accessible it manifests
its invisibility and inaccessibility.

On this earth the objects of our charity belong to a "mysterious"
order.

We have recalled that all friendship is grounded in a fellowship
of life and being, concretely in a community. The foundation of
charity is the community of divine blessedness: God's grace communicates to us the blessedness of the Triune God in such a way
as to make us members of this community, which St. Thomas calls
"the society of the blessed and of those who seek blessedness"
(*Contra gent.*, III, cxliv).

This blessed society is the Church—God's blessedness is communicated to us in and through the mystical Body of Christ: to enter the Church is to join the society of the blessed. Now the
Church is a mystery: she is even *the* mystery of God. Since our
Lord Jesus Christ rose from the dead we can no longer see him, he
is inaccessible to us; it is only through his mystical Body, the
Church, that he can carry on his work as a mystery. The Church
then in her human aspect, that in her which we can see, hear,
touch, is the sign of divine reality. Sign and signified are one, the
two making *a single "mysterious" reality*. For us (*quoad nos*) it is
not a matter of God on one side and the Church on the other;
there is God through and in the Church; there is the Church, the
mystery of God. God is the object of our faith, our hope and our
charity, God himself, but in and through the mystical Body of
Christ, the mystery of God.

In the economy of salvation God and the mystical Body of
Christ are for us one inseparable mystery. The second stands
among us for the first; it adds nothing to him, it leaves all his
transcendence intact, but it gives us access to him. The mystery
lies in the inaccessibility of God through his accessibility; it is not
the inaccessible in itself but the inaccessible in its accessibility.

We again find this symbolical quality of mystery in the theology
of the sacraments, especially the eucharist. Christ is not crucified
anew each time Mass is celebrated; but the Mass is more than
simply a symbolical representation. The Mass adds nothing to the

Cross; but in every Mass Christ *really* offers himself up, in it he is the one priest and the one victim in action. What happened once and for all on the first Good Friday is there again in every Mass, in the "mysterious" reality of the sacrament. And thus the reality and fruits of the Passion and the Resurrection are accessible to us through and in the Mass, given to us in the particular way that we are here calling "mysterious."[8]

Again we are confronted by a very special mode of being, one wherein not only do sign and signified make one, but wherein the signified is present in its substantial reality under the appearance of a "mysterious" sign. God comes to us, and we meet him in his transcendence through and in the appearances that he invites us to see with the eyes of faith.

This general law of the economy of salvation holds good not only for the object of faith[9] but also for acts of charity.

Since it is divine, the community of blessedness is invisible and inaccessible to us; our theologic virtues attain it in and through the mystery of the Church. My visible incorporation in the Church is the efficacious sign of my incorporation in the divine *koinonia*. The entry of my name in the register of my parish is the efficacious sign of my name written in the unseen Book of Life. I enter the fellowship of divine life through and in what is human and visible in the Church's community of life: at the level of the mystery, these are one and cannot be separated. That is why brotherly love for members of the mystical Body is the living sign and observable criterion of my love for God. The whole society of my brethren and each one of them individually are for me "mysterious" objects of charity. In fact, its formal object and its terms *cui* are given me in this mystery of my brethren and the ecclesial community.[10]

The divine goodness that is revealed to us is the cause of our blessedness: we love it in and through the Church, which is at the same time its reality and its sign. The Church is not simply the foundation of charity, she is also its formal object and its sign, the inaccessible object in its accessibility: its mystery. In the same way, human persons, terms of charity, are loved as mysteries of God, charity's first term (1 John 10). "He that receiveth you, receiveth me" (Mt. 40). That scene at the Last Judgment (Mt. 25:

34–40) has a strong bearing on this "mysterious" aspect of our neighbor.[11]

In the light of all this it can be understood how the sight of Christians who love one another in unity shows people that God loves men, loves them so much that he sent his Son to redeem them (*cf.* John 17:23). When looked at in its "mysterious" aspect, brotherly charity stands out in all its apostolic value as testimony. So too in its eschatological bearing. Brotherly charity is a theophany, an epiphany, a showing forth of the fellowship of blessedness as it already exists in Heaven and will be fulfilled at the Parousia.

The Church and each one of her members is thus the term *cui* of charity, not only because it is God who is loved in them but also because the community and each one of its members is a mystery of God. In loving my brother I love God-and-my-brother in the unity of the Church's mystery.

Can it indeed be said that the Church is the term *cui* of charity? Yes and No. Yes, because it is written that Christ loves the Church with charity (Eph. 5:25), and our charity has the same objects as Christ's. Yes, because the Church can be considered as a "person," and to that extent she can be the term *cui*. No, in the sense that the Church is not a physical person. This yes and no are reconciled when the ecclesial community is considered as the "mysterious" term of charity: the Church is as it were the total "mysterious" term, in the midst of which we find those persons, divine and human, whom we love with charity.[12]

This same "mysterious" aspect of charity is found equally in the material objects *quod*. The ecclesial community, the basis of charity, is the mystery of its formal object: there the divine goodness is found, there it is manifest, there it is active. Considered as the material object *quod,* the common good of the society of the blessed is loved for and in its members only in this mystery.

In short, if it be true that on the level of essences charity has the divine beatifying goodness for formal object, God and our brethren for term *cui,* and blessedness and the goods that can be referred to it for material object *quod,* then we must say that, concretely, these objects are only accessible to us and can only be found in the mystery of the Church, the divine-human community of blessedness. Sign and thing signified are but one in this "mysterious" reality.

NOTES

1. "Ex forma sua unumquodquae ordinatur ad aliud" (*Sum. theol.*, I–II, lxxxv, 4c). The end of every created being is outside itself, not within itself. "It is impossible," says St Thomas, "that man's last end should be his soul or even something in his soul" (I–II, ii, 7c). That something is outside the soul—God.

2. The higher a creature is in the scale of beings the "simpler" it is, its qualities are the more bound up with one another and make one in his person. God's simplicity is such that his essence cannot be really distinguished from his existence. It follows that the nearer a being is to God the closer is the bond and unity of the formal and material objects of the love with which it is loved. (The nationality of the illustration given above has of course been changed by the translator.)

3. So far from being sinful, to love the divine blessedness for our own happiness is an act of virtue, and of a theological virtue—hope. But charity loves God's goodness for itself: wonder looks for no reward.

4. The divine goodness is charity's formal object *quo* in that it is the motive, the *ratio*, the quality, loved for its own sake, in the terms *cui* of charity. It is the material object *quod* in that it is loved (with desire) as a good, the good of the terms *cui*.

5. In Hebrew *malak*, "angel," means "one sent": exactly the same meaning as the Greek *apostolos* and the Latin *missus*, from which we get our word "missionary."

6. *Cf*. Plé, "Pour une mystique des mystères" in *La vie spirituelle*, suppl., November 15, 1952.

7. *Cf*. H. de Lubac, *Corpus mysticum* (1944).

8. *Cf*. Abbot Vonier, *The Key to the Doctrine of the Eucharist* (1930); C. V. Héris, *Le mystère de l'Eucharistie* (1943).

9. If the object of faith be expressed in words, images and concepts, the act of faith is directed to the reality of what these signify. *Cf. Sum. theol.*, II–II, i, 2, 2.

10. *Ecclésial*. This adjective has come into use in France to express belonging to the people of God or the mystical Body of Christ. There is an early use of it in Jacques Maritain's *Nova et Vetera* (1938), p. 264—*Translator's note*.

11. *Cf*. A. Plé, "Le prochain, mystère de Dieu" in *La vie spirituelle*, October 1945, and above, page 53.

12. It seems to us that such a conception of the mystery alone provides for a certain understanding of Christ's presence in the Christian whom we love and help. When the apostle Thomas put his finger in the Lord's scars, his hand touched a body and his spirit, believing, touched God, through the mystery of the body. *Aliud vidit, aliud credidit*. Unless "mystical" be given this "mysterious" significance, it is not clear why the ecclesial body of Christ is called the mystical Body. Efforts have been made to establish a physical unity and identity between Christ and Christians; but this doctrine was condemned in the encyclical letter "*Mediator Dei*," and one looks

for a solution in vain. Father L. Malevez, for instance, writes: "Everything goes to show that this last word (mystical) does nothing but take away the precision of the first (identification). It is as if one should say, It is an identification which, strictly, is not one; but as the idea to be expressed transcends our experience and our concepts, as its profundity, unequalled in nature, is beyond us, it is allowable, when every precaution has been taken, to use an exaggerated expression and to say 'identity'" (*Science religieuse*, 1944, p. 390). "Mystical" means "mysterious" or it means nothing. The Body of Christ *instrumentum conjunctum* of grace is a mystery, the mystery by excellence, and grace and *instrumentum conjunctum* make but one in its unity. It is in this "mysterious" unity that Christ is really met in his suffering member. *Cf.* A. Michel, in *L'ami du clergé*, July 27, 1950.

LOVE YOUR NEIGHBOR AS YOURSELF

W. K. GROSSOUW

JESUS placed the Old Testament dictum, "Love your neighbor as yourself," right in the middle of His own doctrine, giving it an entirely new meaning and completely different dimensions from what it had formerly. We must subject this touchstone of the Gospel to a brief analysis.

The precept of fraternal charity presupposes in the first place that the Christian love himself (*"as yourself"*). Jesus does not dwell on this point since this love of self can normally be taken for granted. Even modern-day preachers seldom emphasize the theme, although one may doubt whether this is right, since *true* love of self is not as common in our social life as is commonly imagined. It must be properly distinguished from a wrong type of self-love, which is selfishness or egoism, the fatal and universal consequence of original sin. This distinction is extremely important, since the war against selfishness must not degenerate into aggressiveness against one's self or even into unconscious aversion for one's self. When Jesus says, "Love thy neighbor as thyself," He implicitly demands self-love. St. Thomas, too, teaches that one can and even ought love one's self with a supernatural love (IIa IIae, qq. 25 and

26). In actual fact, however, real love of self, which is the basis for love of neighbor and love of God, is quite often prominently missing. It presupposes a certain spiritual maturity, of which it is the external expression. It is quite probable that in our present (Western) civilization, with its multiple standards, this maturity is reached with greater difficulty and at a later period in life than in earlier periods of time. Let it be noted in passing that this fact bears serious consequences for the rearing and especially for the religious and moral formation of the young.

It would naturally be incorrect to suppose that religious formation can begin only after the natural development has been completed, because the religious interest is an essential component of human nature. There must therefore be a simultaneous development, a related evolution of the human and the religious experience, but always in such wise that the human formation is just one step ahead of the religious development.[1] The biological and psychological foundation for a more or less premeditated formation must always be present. The great danger consists in what I would like to call "anticipation." Attempts are frequently made to introduce adult religion among people who are not adults, to erect a full-blown moral edifice on an insufficient human foundation. People who are not yet spiritually mature are urged on to the perfection of the Christian life; and moral maturity is too readily computed according to the years of a person's age. The authentic exemplification of Christendom ought to be considered as the florescence of human existence, as the full bloom of nature and grace combined. Once again, this does not mean that the religious formation must wait till the child has grown up; but it does mean that one must administer it prudently, that one choose to rely on the casual pedagogic situation, and preserve some confidence in the nature of man.

The implicit command for self-love is enjoined because we cannot really love our neighbor if we do not love ourselves. In what does this love of self consist? In the first place (and possibly also in the last) in this, that we have squarely met our own selves and have come to know and appreciate ourselves. One must use here such an expression as "to meet oneself squarely," since no one begins with a clean slate. The fruit of the tree of knowledge is both

sweet and bitter and an increase of self-knowledge opens a vista
into an abyss which a child cannot see. To love myself means to
learn how to limit and ground myself; to accept myself lovingly as
a creature, and even as an image of God in my own limited but
inimitable reality. It also means the accepting of my darker sides,
my shadows, even the possibility of the evil which I did not do,
but might have done as well as any other man, and in which I somehow have a mysterious share because of our common nature. Since
we are all "evil," to use Jesus' expression, evil—every human
evil—is my real personal possibility even though it may not now
be an actuality. The point is that I recognize that no evil whatever
which is done by man is entirely strange to me, but constitutes a
real and not merely a theoretical possibility within me. Not to
acknowledge this is, in the last instance, only because of a deceptive pride or repression, because of which I unconsciously refuse
to behold and acknowledge myself in all my potentialities. The
last condition will occur more commonly than the former.

And yet, for the exercise of fraternal charity it is necessary to
understand with the ancient poet that nothing human is foreign
to me. Again, this is not meant in the sense that true self-love
precedes fraternal charity in the order of time. It is precisely
through love of my neighbor that I discover myself and build up
my own personality. A fruitful cooperation of love of self and
love of neighbor is indispensable, otherwise I cannot possibly love
my neighbor "as myself"; otherwise I will regard him as a stranger,
as one who does not concern me.[2] Otherwise the possibility of
hatred has been already established. "If you were of the world,
the world would love what is its own. But because you are not
of the world, but I have chosen you out of the world, therefore
the world hates you" (John 15:19). Aversion and aggressiveness
will frequently arise simply because I do not know or acknowledge
one of the possibilities of my own personality. A person wants to
eliminate or even destroy that "strangeness" which he projects
into others. One hates those whom one knowingly considers as
strange, as not being one's self, whereas in reality they represent
one of our possibilities, and exactly the one we are trying to hide
with shame. This throws light on many of the unbelievable doings
of the War (and even later) and on the ruinous influence of

modern propaganda, which necessarily works with black-white contrasts and feels a need for having or creating scapegoats, so as to foster an aggressiveness which is spawned from fear and aversion. But Christ freely chose to become a scapegoat for us all. "Jesus, that He might sanctify the people by His blood, suffered outside the gate. Let us therefore go forth to Him outside the camp, bearing His reproach" (Heb. 13:12–13). "For our sakes He made Him to be sin who knew nothing of sin" (II Cor. 5:21). Paul urges Christians to bear one another's burdens (Gal. 6:2). What burden is heavier than the sinful and hateful element that exists also within ourselves?

Christ thereupon gave a new meaning to the notion of "neighbor," by removing all limitations. In the Old Testament, as also in contemporary Judaism, the concept was practically limited by kinship in race and local proximity; that is to say, by a sort of concentricity which measures all things from myself as the central point.[3] My neighbors are those who are nearest me, my family, neighbor, tribe, fellow tradesmen, race. And thus it becomes a static, predetermined concept, depending on accidental situations. Jesus deprived the existing notion of neighbor of its original meaning and freed it from all these particularizations. He transferred the central point from man to God and proclaimed the love of one's enemy as the hallmark *par excellence* of His disciples: "You have heard that it was said, 'Thou shalt love thy neighbor, and shalt hate thy enemy.' But I say to you, love your enemies, do good to those who hate you, and pray for those who persecute and calumniate you, so that you may be children of your Father in heaven, who makes His sun to rise on the good and the evil, and sends rain on the just and the unjust. You therefore are to be perfect even as your heavenly Father is perfect" (Mt. 5:43–48). One may also affirm that He Himself, the new Man, has been set by God as the central point of our circle: "Amen I say to you, as long as you did it for one of these, the least of My brethren, you did it for Me" (Mt. 25:40). For the Christian, therefore, every man is his neighbor.

But this universality must be understood in a concrete manner; it cannot be taken abstractly as meaning humanity in general. Christian love of neighbor is not some humanitarian sentiment about humanity based in Stoic fashion on the sharing of a common nature or of universal reason. It is always personal, even individual, and directed toward whoever happens to be "near." Somewhere in the novel, *The Brothers Karamazov*, Dostoyevsky distinguishes between the distant neighbor and the close neighbor. Jesus is concerned with the latter. Everyone can be my neighbor, can become my neighbor in a certain situation; but not all men are so actually. Even the pious man of the Old Testament comprehended this when he wrote: "Man may be merciful to his fellow man, but the Lord's mercy reaches all flesh" (Sir. 18:11). Only God can truly love all men.

What then did Jesus really do with the concept "neighbor"? He made of it a notion that is of itself unlimited and unconditioned, defined only by the concrete situation in which one finds himself. My neighbor is the person with whom I find myself in a circumstance of proximity, that is, anyone with whom I by my love establish a relation of nearness, which in turn engenders a response. It is not determined beforehand who is my neighbor; anyone can become this. It is he, toward whom *in concreto* I have a relation of neighborliness, not the one whom I may casually meet, but him with whom I hold communication. My neighbor is the one, anyone at all, whoever he may be, whom I wish to encounter in the total concrete situation of my being-in-the-world and not because of something which has been added to my human status.

Our Lord teaches us this in an inimitable manner in the parable on the Good Samaritan (Luke 10:25–37), a concrete illustration which is far more telling than all general considerations, and gave the answer to the theoretic question of the lawyer: Who is my neighbor? This question was occasioned by the reference to the two commandments. The response shows anew that the originality of Jesus' preaching consisted especially in His doctrine on love of neighbor. This in turn immediately casts new light on the precept of love of God. Besides the robbed and wounded traveler, there in his passive role, three other personages appear in the parable. They are a priest, a levite, and a Samaritan, of whom the first two were much "closer" to the victim, not only in the Jewish view, but also in that of mankind generally. The Samaritan belonged to the semi-strange, and therefore estranged, people. All three chance on a fortuitous situation (v. 31) in which they bear a special relationship to the unfortunate traveler. Of all three the Master says explicitly that they "saw" him. However, for the priest and levite, both of whom are kinsmen and even belong to the officially pious class, their acquaintance remains a chance meeting. Only with the stranger does it become communication.

It is noteworthy how the text of the Gospel describes with succinct sobriety various phases in Christian charity: awareness, sympathy, a simple but expressive deed. "But a certain Samaritan, as he journeyed, came upon him, and seeing him, was moved with compassion. And he went up to him and bound up his wounds, pouring on oil and wine. And setting him on his own beast, he brought him to an inn and took care of him. And the next day he took out two denarii and gave them to the innkeeper and said, 'Take care of him; and whatever thou spendest, I, on my way back, will repay thee.' " Christian love of neighbor is preeminently practical. The point of the parable may startle us: "Which of these three," Jesus asked the lawyer, "in thy opinion proved himself neighbor to him who fell among the robbers?" And the man naturally answered: "He who took pity on him." And Jesus said to him, "Go and do thou also in like manner." Here we see how dynamic and concrete the notion of neighbor is for Jesus. We may ask: Were not then the priest and the levite neighbors to the traveler? Jesus denies it, because they did not behave like neighbors, like people who wished to be near and let themselves become personally entangled in the situation of another which would somehow or other infringe on their independence. One is truly a neighbor only through love and mercy, through a deliberate availability. In that sense "neighbor" becomes synonymous with Christian.

Love, placed as it is by our Lord as the supreme "law" of the Christian life, does not annul justice nor general ethics, but makes the latter fully possible by incarnating it in the reality of human existence. As the guiding norm of Christian morals it supplants case-study with the situation. It appeals to the person and his responsibility, and consequently gives concrete shape to the objective norms. Charity knows only the real, and only charity can fulfill the meaning of the real. This does not mean that one must disregard abstract norms or the transcendent laws of nature; but it does mean that we must give the norms existence in human reality. There are in the first place the universal objective norms, such as they are found in the Decalogue. Then also there are the (objective) applications of the rules to objective "cases"; e.g., what serious inconvenience is sufficient to excuse someone from the positive law of keeping holy the Sunday? And so on. But casuistry is not sufficient for concrete behavior. Here a determined decision must be made by the personal conscience, enlightened by *Christian* prudence, which in turn takes into account the general norms, and presumably also the examples of casuistry if it is up to it. But as a Christian virtue, prudence is governed especially by faith and the intuition of love, since love is not blind but clairvoyant. Nor does this mean that in certain cases the eternal laws cease to be valid, for the supreme Christian law is charity, and it always remains in force. But it does mean that there are exceptions to casuistry, or rather that casuistry does not cover and cannot cover all cases. The Christian revelation of charity as the supreme law includes the doctrine of personal responsibility, which no one can take away from me, and which I must repeatedly exercise anew in every instance. Whoever elevates charity to the supreme principle, thereby elevates liberty as a principle, and accepts the risk which is inseparably intertwined with authentic human existence.

It may therefore be rightly asked whether charity can be imposed as a *precept;* in what sense may one speak here of law? To feel for someone, as it is commonly understood, can certainly not be imposed or commanded. Does therefore what is commanded bear relationship only to the intellect and will, to an abstract, cold, "supernatural" type of love? In daily life, however, I never love anyone with my will alone; *if* I love, then "*I*" love, with the concrete totality of my person. In the parable of the good Samaritan we are also told that "he was moved with compassion." Love is deeply interested in the being of the other, and shares in it by a disinterested dedication of its own entity to the other. For this reason the emphasis which Jesus places on the precepts of love of God and love of neighbor signifies a breakthrough from the

juridical order and from the abstract-juridical attitude. He commanded what no man could or would dare command.

From this it does not follow that the juridical aspect finds no
place in Christendom, and even less that the command to love
is not in earnest. It means, rather, that the juridical attitude is
really not the Christian one, and that the precept of love of
neighbor is not imposed in the same way as that of keeping holy
the Sunday. It is not imposed on us in the manner of some work
which we must do, nor as some feat we may attempt at will. It
is placed on us as an appeal to the heart (and "heart" is not to
be taken in a romantic or sentimental sense, but as the very ground
of our existence). The commandment of love is an appeal by
God to the creative potentiality of our heart, to our possibility to
express ourselves in the encounter of the other. God speaks to us
personally here; the text says: "You shall love" in the singular.

In its perfect state love therefore undoubtedly presupposes
rational maturity and human liberty (both of which are acquired
piecemeal precisely by the exercise of a still imperfect love). And
even he who possesses such maturity must still frequently be
satisfied with only an honest effort. This means that comparatively
few are capable of a full expression of love. But this again does
not mean that the precept of love is not meaningful to the rest.
Even though I am not able to realize charity fully, as man and
as a Christian I can nonetheless by my deliberate choice elect
charity as my course and my goal, as the condition of existence
which I freely accept as my own. For this reason it can be categor-
ically imposed upon all as a precept by God, and not by man,
since God can rightfully address Himself to me in my inmost
being, and by His grace does so efficiently. Because in my efforts
at exercising charity I constantly meet with my inabilities and my
limitations, I experience myself to be a sinful creature. Even to
grasp this is, speaking as a Christian, supremely salutary. Charity
is at the same time the school of humility. "Loving humility is a
power, the strongest of all, and there is nothing that approaches
its power" (Dostoyevsky). People with *faith,* no matter where
they may be in the world, have always known this.

If a person wants to start with the old division, according to
which life can be considered as a combination of relationships

toward God, toward man, and toward one's self, he can find the
Christian picture of these three relationships in three beautiful
parables of Luke's Gospel. The relationship of man toward the
heavenly Father is delineated, as has already been explained, in
the parable of the prodigal son (15:11–32); that toward our neighbor, in the parable of the good Samaritan (10:25–37). How the
Christian must behave toward himself (and at the same time toward God) is taught us in the brief parable of the Pharisee and
the Publican. "But He spoke this parable also to some who trusted
in themselves as being just and despised others. Two men went
up to the temple to pray, the one a Pharisee and the other a Publican. The Pharisee stood and began to pray thus within himself:
'O God, I thank thee that I am not like the rest of men, robbers,
dishonest, adulterers, or even like this Publican. I fast twice a
week; I pay tithes of all that I possess.' But the Publican, standing
afar off, would not so much as lift up his eyes to heaven, but kept
striking his breast, saying, 'O God, be merciful to me the sinner!'
I tell you this man went back to his home justified rather than
the other" (18:9–14).

A man can truly humiliate himself only before the face of
God, as is done in an exemplary fashion in this parable. He cannot humiliate himself before a fellow man, except and only so far
as the latter represents God, which properly speaking is possible
only in the sacramental order of the Incarnation. This parable is
the human counterpart of the one on the prodigal son, where, as
has already been noted, the behavior of the father, who represents
God, occupies the center of our attention. Here the emphasis is
placed on the behavior of sinful man toward God. Strictly speaking, this parable does not treat of the "relationship toward oneself,"
because a man is not inclined to an autonomous relationship
toward himself; he is essentially directed to something outside
himself, toward another. It shows us again the relationship toward
God wherein man experiences himself to be a sinner; and this
in simple truth without fear or anxiety. In this honest acceptance
of himself he discovers deliverance from his sins and freedom
from the burden of excessive demands which he would impose
on himself because of distorted idealization or idolization of self.
Consequently, he also goes to his home justified, exulting, but

not exalting, with his head erect and lifted up by God. Because
he acknowledged his uncleanness in the sight of God, he is purified, and thus enabled to enter the path of love for another. Love
for one's neighbor cannot exist without humility of a type which
opens us toward our fellow men because we accept our own small-
ness, thereby acquiring a certain innate dignity, and finding favor
with God.

NOTES

1. Development is to be taken here especially in the sense of purposive
formation, such as is generally stressed strongly in our concrete religious
educational program; generally speaking, the indirect system really merits
preference.
2. There seems to be an old Chinese proverb to the effect that: "To
forgive another the fact that he is different is the beginning of wisdom."
3. For details (to which belong the possibility of hatred as well as the
first spark of love for one's enemy) see Ps. 108; Prov. 25:21.

TRUTH AND HUMAN FELLOWSHIP

JACQUES MARITAIN

Si fieri potest, quod ex vobis est, cum
omnibus hominibus pacem habentes.
St. Paul, Rom. 12:18.

I

O LIBERTY, how many crimes are committed in thy name!"
Madame Roland said, mounting the scaffold. O Truth, it may be
said, how often blind violence and oppression have been let loose
in thy name in the course of history! "Zeal for truth," as Father
Victor White puts it, "has too often been a cloak for the most evil
and revolting of human passions."[1]

As a result, some people think that in order to set human existence free from these evil passions, and make men live in peace and

pleasant quiet, the best way is to get rid of any zeal for truth or attachment to truth.

Thus it is that after the violence and cruelty of wars of religion, a period of skepticism usually occurs, as at the time of Montaigne and Charron.

Here we have only the swing of the pendulum moving from one extreme to another. Skepticism, moreover, may happen to hold those who are not skeptical to be barbarous, childish, or subhuman, and it may happen to treat them as badly as the zealot treats the unbeliever. Then skepticism proves to be as intolerant as fanaticism—it becomes the fanaticism of doubt. This is a sign that skepticism is not the answer.

The answer is humility, together with faith in truth.

The problem of truth and human fellowship is important for democratic societies; it seems to me to be particularly important for this country, where men and women coming from a great diversity of national stocks and religious or philosophical creeds have to live together. If each one of them endeavored to impose his own convictions and the truth in which he believes on all his co-citizens, would not living together become impossible? That's obviously right. Well, it is easy, too easy, to go a step further, and to ask: if each one sticks to his own convictions, will not each one endeavor to impose his own convictions on all others? So that, as a result, living together will become impossible if any citizen whatever sticks to his own convictions and believes in a given truth?

Thus it is not unusual to meet people who think that *not to believe in any truth, or not to adhere firmly to any assertion as unshakeably true in itself* is a primary condition required of democratic citizens in order to be tolerant of one another and to live in peace with one another. May I say that these people are in fact the most intolerant people, for if perchance they were to believe in something as unshakeably true, they would feel compelled, by the same stroke, to impose by force and coercion their own belief on their co-citizens. The only remedy they have found to get rid of their abiding tendency to fanaticism is to cut themselves off from truth. That's a suicidal method. And it is a suicidal conception of democracy: not only would a democratic society which lived on universal skepticism condemn itself to death by starvation; but it would also enter a process of self-annihilation, from the very fact that no democratic society can live without a common practical belief in those truths which are freedom, justice, law, and the other tenets of democracy; and that any belief in these things as objectively and unshakeably true, as well as in any other kind of truth, would be brought to naught by the pre-assumed law of universal skepticism.

In the field of political science, the opinion which I am criticizing was made into a theory—the so-called "relativistic justification of democracy"—by Hans Kelsen. It is very significant that in order to establish his philosophy of the temporal order and show that democracy implies ignorance of, or doubt about, any absolute truth, either religious or metaphysical, Kelsen has recourse to Pilate; so that, in refusing to distinguish the just from the unjust, and washing his hands, this dishonest judge thus becomes the lofty precursor of relativistic democracy. Kelsen quotes the dialogue between Jesus and Pilate—St. John, Chapter 18—in which Jesus says: "To this end am I come into the world, that I should bear witness unto the truth," and Pilate answers: "What is truth?" and then delivers Jesus over to the fury of the crowd. Because Pilate did not know what truth is, Kelsen concludes, he therefore called upon the people, and asked them to decide; and thus in a democratic society it is up to the people to decide, and mutual tolerance reigns, because nobody knows what truth is.

The truth of which Kelsen was speaking was religious and metaphysical truth—what they call "absolute truth," as if any truth, insofar as it is true, were not absolute in its own sphere. As Miss Helen Silving puts it,[2] the burden of Kelsen's argument is: "Whoever knows or claims to know absolute truth or absolute justice" —that is to say, *truth* or *justice* simply—"cannot be a democrat, because he cannot and is not expected to admit the possibility of a view different from his own, the *true* view. The metaphysician and the believer are bound to impose their eternal truth on other people, on the ignorant, and on the people without vision. Theirs is the holy crusade of the one who knows against the one who does not know or does not share in God's grace. Only if we are aware of our ignorance of what is the *Good* may we call upon the people to decide."

It is impossible to summarize more accurately a set of more barbarous and erroneous assumptions. If it were true that whoever knows or claims to know truth or justice cannot admit the possibility of a view different from his own, and is bound to impose his true view on other people by violence, then the rational animal would be the most dangerous of beasts. In reality it is through rational means, that is, through persuasion, not through coercion, that the rational animal is bound by his very nature to try to induce his fellow men to share in what he knows or claims to know as true or just. And the metaphysician, because he trusts human reason, and the believer, because he trusts divine grace and knows that "a forced faith is a hypocrisy hateful to God and man," as Cardinal Manning put it, do not use holy war to make their "eternal truth" accessible to other people; they appeal to the inner freedom of other people by offering them either their demonstrations or the testimony of their love. And we do not call upon the people to decide because we are aware of our ignorance of what is the good, but because we know this truth and this good, that the people have a right to self-government.

It is, no doubt, easy to observe that in the history of mankind nothing goes to show that, from primitive times on, religious feeling or religious ideas have been particularly successful in pacifying men; religious differences seem rather to have fed and sharpened their conflicts. On the one hand truth always makes trouble, and those who bear witness to it are always persecuted: "Do not think that I came to send peace upon earth; I came not to send peace, but the sword" (Mt. 10:34). On the other hand—and this is the point we must face—those who know or claim to know truth happen sometimes to persecute others. I don't deny the fact; I say that this fact, like all other facts, needs to be understood. It only means that, given the weakness of our nature, the impact of the highest and most sacred things upon the coarseness of the human heart is liable to make these things, by accident, a prey to its passions, as long as it has not been purified by genuine love. It is nonsense to regard fanaticism as a fruit of religion. Fanaticism is a natural tendency rooted in our basic egotism and will to power.

It seizes upon any noble feeling to live on it. The only remedy for religious fanaticism is the Gospel light and the progress of religious consciousness in faith itself and in that fraternal love which is the fruit of the human soul's union with God. For then man realizes the sacred transcendence of truth and of God. The more he grasps truth, through science, philosophy, or faith, the more he feels what immensity remains to be grasped within this very truth. The more he knows God, either by reason or by faith, the more he understands that our concepts attain (through analogy) but do not circumscribe Him, and that His thoughts are not like our thoughts: for "who hath known the mind of the Lord, or who hath become His counselor?" (Is. 40:13) The more strong and deep faith becomes, the more man kneels down, not before his own alleged ignorance of truth, but before the inscrutable mystery of divine truth, and before the hidden ways in which God goes to meet those who search Him.

To sum up, the real problem has to do with the human subject, endowed as he is with his rights in relation to his fellow men, and afflicted as he is by the vicious inclinations which derive from his will to power. On the one hand, the error of the absolutists who would like to impose truth by coercion comes from the fact that they shift their right feelings about the object from the object to the subject; and they think that just as error has no rights of its own and should be banished from the mind (through the means of the mind), so man when he is in error has no rights of his own and should be banished from human fellowship (through the means of human power).

On the other hand, the error of the theorists who make relativism, ignorance, and doubt a necessary condition for mutual tolerance comes from the fact that they shift their right feelings about the human subject—who must be respected even if he is in error—from the subject to the object; and thus they deprive man and the human intellect of the very act—adherence to the truth—in which consists both man's dignity and reason for living.

They begin, as we have seen apropos of Kelsen, with the supreme truths either of metaphysics or of faith. But science also deals with truth, though in science the discovery of a new truth supplants most often a previous theory which was hitherto considered true. Well, what will happen if human fanaticism takes hold of what it claims to be scientific truth at a given moment? Suffice it to look at the manner in which the Stalinist state imposed on scientists its own physical, biological, linguistic, or economic truth. Now, it is a little different: a certain amount of diversity among scientists is *commanded* in Russia, and the Russian state is endeavoring to *manage* and *control* free discussion itself. Shall we then conclude that in order to escape state-science oppression or management, the only way is to give up science and scientific truth, and to take refuge in ignorance?

It is truth, not ignorance, which makes us humble, and gives us the sense of what remains unknown in our very knowledge. In one sense only is there wisdom in appealing to our ignorance: if we mean the ignorance of those who know, not the ignorance of those who are in the dark.

Be it a question of science, metaphysics, or religion, the man who says: "What is truth?" as Pilate did, is not a tolerant man, but a betrayer of the human race. There is real and genuine tolerance only when a man is firmly and absolutely convinced of a truth, or of what he holds to be a truth, and when he at the same time recognizes the right of those who deny this truth to exist, and to contradict him, and to speak their own mind, not because they are free from truth but because they seek truth in their own way, and because he respects in them human nature and human dignity and those very resources and living springs of the intellect and of conscience which makes them potentially capable of attaining the truth he loves, if some day they happen to see it.

II

A particular application of the problem we are discussing can be found in the philosophical field. Some years ago I was asked whether in my opinion philosophers can cooperate.

I felt rather embarrassed, for on the one hand if philosophy is not search for truth it is nothing, and truth admits of no compromise; on the other hand if philosophers, that is, lovers of wisdom, cannot cooperate, how will any human cooperation be possible? The fact that philosophical discussions seem to consist of deaf men's quarrels is not reassuring for civilization.

My answer was that philosophers do not cooperate, as a rule, because human nature is as weak in them as in any other poor devil of a rational animal, but that they *can* cooperate; and that cooperation between philosophers can only be a conquest of the intellect over itself and the very universe of thought it has created—a difficult conquest indeed, achieved by intellectual rigor and justice on the basis of irreducible and inevitably lasting antagonisms.

A distinction, moreover, seems to me to be relevant in this connection. The question can be considered either from the point of view of *doctrinal exchanges* between systems or from the point of view of the *mutual grasp* which various philosophical systems can have of each other, each being taken as a whole.

From the first point of view, or the point of view of doctrinal exchanges, each system can avail itself of the others for its own sake by dismembering them, and by feeding on and assimilating what it can take from them. That is cooperation indeed, but in quite a peculiar sense—as a lion cooperates with a lamb.

Yet from the second point of view, and in the perspective of the judgment which each system passes on the other, contemplating it as a whole, and as an object situated in an external sphere, and trying to do it justice, a mutual understanding is possible which cannot indeed do away with basic antagonisms, but which may create a kind of real though imperfect cooperation, to the extent that each system succeeds (1) in recognizing for the other, in a certain sense, a right to exist; and (2) in availing itself of the other, no longer by material *intussusception* and by borrowing or digesting parts of the other, but by bringing, thanks to the other, its own specific life and principles to a higher degree of achievement and extension.

It is on this genuine kind of cooperation that I would like to insist for a moment.

If we were able to realize that most often our mutually opposed affirmations do not bear on the same parts or aspects of the real and that they are of greater value than our mutual negations, then we should come nearer the first prerequisite of a genuinely philosophical understanding: that is, we should become better able to transcend and conquer our own system of signs and conceptual language, and to take on for a moment, in a provisional and tentative manner, the thought and approach of the other so as to come back, with this intelligible booty, to our own philosophical conceptualization and to our own system of reference.

Then, we are no longer concerned with analyzing or *sorting* the set of assertions peculiar to various systems in spreading them out, so to speak, on a single surface or level in order to examine what conciliation or exchange of ideas they may mutually allow in their inner structure. But we are concerned with taking into account a third dimension, in order to examine the manner in which each system, considered as a specific whole, can, according to its own frame of reference, do justice to the other in taking a view of it and seeking to penetrate it as an object situated on the outside— in another sphere of thought.

From this standpoint, two considerations would appear all-important: the one is the consideration of the central *intuition* which lies at the core of each great philosophical doctrine; the other is the consideration of the *place* which each system could, according to its own frame of reference, grant the other system as the legitimate place the latter is cut out to occupy in the universe of thought.

Actually, each great philosophical doctrine lives on a central intuition which can be wrongly conceptualized and translated into a system of assertions seriously deficient or erroneous as such, but which, insofar as it is intellectual intuition, truly gets hold of some aspect of the real. And, consequently, each great philosophical doctrine, once it has been grasped in its central intuition and then reinterpreted in the frame of reference of another doctrine (in a manner that it would surely not accept), should be granted from the point of view of this other doctrine some place considered as legitimately occupied, be it in some imaginary universe.

If we try to do justice to the philosophical systems against which we take our most determined stand, we shall seek to discover both that intuition which they involve and that place we must grant them from our own point of view. And then we shall benefit from them, not by borrowing from them or exchanging with them certain particular views and ideas, but by seeing, thanks to them, more profoundly into our own doctrine, by enriching it from within and extending its principles to new fields of inquiry which have been brought more forcefully to our attention, but which we shall make all the more vitally and powerfully informed by these principles.

Thus there is not *toleration* between systems—a system cannot *tolerate* another system, because systems are abstract sets of ideas and have only intellectual existence, where the will to tolerate or not to tolerate has no part—but there can be *justice,* intellectual justice, between philosophical systems.

And between philosophers there can be tolerance and more than tolerance; there can be a kind of cooperation and fellowship, founded on intellectual justice and the philosophical duty of understanding another's thought in a genuine and fair manner. Nay more, there is no intellectual justice without the assistance of intellectual charity. If we do not *love* the thought and intellect of another as intellect and thought, how shall we take pains to discover what truths are conveyed by it while it seems to us defective or misguided, and at the same time to free these truths from the errors which prey upon them and to re-instate them in an entirely true systematization? Thus we love truth more than we do our fellow-philosophers, but we love and respect both.

At this point I should like to observe that even when they are wrong philosophers are a kind of mirror, on the heights of intelligence, of the deepest trends which are obscurely at play in the human mind at each epoch of history; (the greater they are, the more actively and powerfully radiant the mirror is). Now, since we are thinking beings, such mirrors are indispensable to us. After all, it is better for human society to have Hegelian errors with Hegel than to have Hegelian errors without Hegel—I mean hidden and diffuse errors rampant throughout the social body, which are Hegelian in type but anonymous and unrecognizable. A great philosopher who is wrong is like a beacon on the reefs, which says to seamen: steer clear of me; he enables men (at least those who have not been seduced by him) to *identify* the errors from which they suffer, and to become clearly aware of them, and to struggle against them. And this is an essential need of society, insofar as society is not merely animal society but society made up of persons endowed with intelligence and freedom.

And even if philosophers are hopelessly divided among themselves in their search for a superior and all-pervading truth, at least they seek this truth; and their very controversies, constantly renewed, are a sign of the necessity for such a search. These controversies do not witness to the illusory or unattainable character of the object that philosophers are looking for. They witness to the fact that this object is both most difficult and most crucial in importance: is not everything which is crucial in importance crucial also in difficulty? Plato told us that beautiful things are difficult, and that we should not avoid beautiful dangers. Mankind would be in jeopardy, and soon in despair, if it shunned the beautiful dangers of intelligence and reason.

Moreover, many things are questionable and oversimplified in the commonplace insistence on the insuperable disagreements which divide philosophers. These disagreements do indeed exist. But in one sense there is more continuity and stability in philosophy than in science. For a new scientific theory completely changes the very manner in which the former ones posed the question. Whereas philosophical problems remain always the same, in one form or another; nay more, basic philosophical ideas, once they have been discovered, become permanent acquisitions in the philosophical heritage. They are used in various, even opposite, ways: they are still there. And finally, philosophers quarrel so violently because each one has seen some truth which, more often than not, has dazzled his eyes, and which he may conceptualize in an insane manner, but of which his fellow-philosophers must also be aware, each in his own perspective.

III

At first glance it seems particularly shocking, as I observed at the beginning, that men dedicated to wisdom and to the grasping of the highest truths might be not only in mutual disagreement—which is quite normal—but might display, as happens more often than not in actual fact, more mutual intolerance—refusing one another any right intellectually to exist—than even potters, as Aristotle put it, or painters and writers with respect to each other. In reality this is not surprising, for mutual toleration relates essentially to living together in concrete existence; and, as a result, mutual toleration is easier in practical matters than in theoretical ones. When it is a question of rescuing a man from a fire, mutual toleration and cooperation between an atheist and a Christian, or an advocate of determinism and an advocate of free will, will be a matter of course. But when it comes to knowing the truth about the nature of the human will, the cooperation between the advocate of determinism and the advocate of free will will become more difficult. We just saw on what conditions and in overcoming what obstacles such cooperation between philosophers is possible. To tell the truth, philosophers are naturally intolerant, and genuine tolerance among them means a great victory of virtue over nature in their minds. The same can be said, I am afraid, of theologians. This theme was particularly dead to Descartes, who made theologians (non-Cartesian theologians) responsible for all wars in the world. And yet both philosophers and theologians are surely able to overcome the natural bent I just alluded to, and to nurture all the more respect for the man in error as they are more eager to vindicate the truth he disregards or disfigures.

Thus we come to our third point: mutual understanding and cooperation—in uncompromising fidelity to truth as each one sees it—between men of different faiths: I do not mean on the temporal level and for temporal tasks; I mean on the very level of religious life, knowledge, and experience. If it is true that human society must bring together, in the service of the same terrestrial common good, men belonging to different spiritual families, how can the peace of that temporal society be lastingly assured if first in the domain that matters most to the human being—in the spiritual and religious domain itself—relationships of mutual respect and mutual understanding cannot be established?

I prefer the word fellowship to "tolerance" for a number of reasons. In the first place, the word *tolerance* relates not only to the virtue of mutual toleration between human individuals, which I am discussing in this lecture, but also to problems which are extraneous to my present topic. For instance, on the one hand there is the problem of "dogmatic tolerance": Has man a moral obligation to seek religious truth and to cling to it when he sees it? Yes indeed. Has the Church a right to condemn errors opposed to the deposit of divine revelation with which she has been entrusted? Yes indeed. And, on the other hand, there is the problem of "civil tolerance"[3]: Must civil society respect the realm of consciences and refrain from imposing a religious creed by coercion? Again, yes indeed.

In the second place the word *fellowship* connotes something positive—positive and elementary—in human relationships. It conjures up the image of travelling companions, who meet here below by chance and journey through life—however fundamental their differences may be—good humoredly, in cordial solidarity and human agreement, or better to say, friendly and cooperative disagreement. Well then, for the reasons I have just mentioned the problem of good fellowship between the members of the various religious families seems to me to be a cardinal one for our age of civilization.

Let me say immediately that this attempt at rapprochement might easily be misunderstood. I shall therefore begin by clearing the ground of any possible sources of misunderstanding. Such a rapprochement obviously cannot be effectuated at the cost of straining fidelity, or of any yielding in intellectual integrity, or of any lessening of what is due to truth. Nor is there any question whatever either of agreeing upon I know not what common minimum of truth or of subjecting each one's convictions to a common index of doubt. On the contrary, such a coming together is only conceivable if we assume that each gives the maximum of fidelity to the light that is shown to him. Furthermore, it obviously can only be pure, and therefore valid and efficacious, if it is free from any *arrière-pensée* of a temporal nature and from even the shadow of a tendency to subordinate religion to the defense of any earthly interest of acquired advantage.

I am sure that everyone is agreed on these negative conditions I have just enumerated. But as soon as we pass on to positive considerations each one sees the very justification and the very reason for being of this good fellowship between believers of different religious families mirrored in his own particular outlook and in his own world of thought. And these outlooks are irreducibly heterogeneous; these worlds of thought never exactly meet. Until the day of eternity comes, their dimensions can have no common measure. There is no use closing one's eyes to this fact, which simply bears witness to the internal coherence of the systems of

signs, built up in accordance with different principles, on which
human minds depend for their cognitive life. Fundamental notions
such as that of the absolute oneness of God have not the same
meaning for a Jew as for a Christian; nor has the notion of the
divine transcendence and incommunicability the same meaning for
a Christian as for a Moslem; nor the notions of person, of freedom, grace, revelation, incarnation, of nature and the supernatural,
the same meaning for the Orient as for the Occident. And the
"non-violence" of the Indian is not the same as Christian "charity."
No doubt, as I just said apropos of philosophical justice, it is the
privilege of the human intelligence to understand other languages
than the one it itself uses. It is none the less true that if, instead of
being men, we were patterns of Pure Ideas, our nature would be to
devour each other in order to absorb into our own world of thought
whatever other such worlds might hold of truth.

But it happens that we are men, each containing within himself
the ontological mystery of personality and freedom: and it is in this
very mystery of freedom and personality that genuine tolerance or
fellowship takes root. For the basis of good fellowship among men
of different creeds is not of the order of the intellect and of ideas,
but of the heart and of love. It is friendship, natural friendship, but
first and foremost mutual love in God and for God. Love does not
go out to essences nor to qualities nor to ideas, but to persons; and
it is the mystery of persons and of the divine presence within them
which is here in play. This fellowship, then, is not a fellowship of
beliefs but the fellowship of men who believe.

The conviction each of us has, rightly or wrongly, regarding the
limitations, deficiencies, errors of others does not prevent friendship between minds. In such a fraternal dialogue, there must be a
kind of forgiveness and remission, not with regard to ideas—ideas
deserve no forgiveness if they are false—but with regard to the condition of him who travels the road at our side. Every believer knows
very well that all men will be judged—both himself and all others.
But neither he nor another is God, able to pass judgment. And what
each one is before God, neither the one nor the other knows. Here
the "Judge not" of the Gospels applies with its full force. We can
render judgment concerning ideas, truths, or errors; good or bad
actions; character, temperament, and what appears to us of a man's

interior disposition. But we are utterly forbidden to judge the innermost heart, that inaccessible center where the person day after day weaves his own fate and ties the bonds binding him to God. When it comes to that, there is only one thing to do, and that is to trust in God. And that is precisely what love for our neighbor prompts us to do.

I should like to dwell a moment on the inner law and the privileges of this friendship of charity, as regards precisely the relations between believers of different religious denominations (as well as between believers and non-believers). I have already made it sufficiently clear that it is wrong to say that such a friendship *transcends* dogma or *exists in spite of* the dogmas of faith. Such a view is inadmissible for all those who believe that the word of God is as absolute as His unity or His transcendence. A mutual love which would be bought at the price of faith, which would base itself on some form of eclecticism, or which, recalling Lessing's parable of the three rings, would say, "I love him who does not have my faith because, after all, I am not sure that my faith is the true faith, and that it bears the device of the true ring," in so saying would reduce faith to a mere historic inheritance and seal it with the seal of agnosticism and relativity. Such a love, for anyone who believes he has heard the word of God, would amount to putting man above God.

That love which is charity, on the contrary, goes first to God, and then to all men, because the more men are loved in God and for God, the more they are loved themselves and in themselves. Moreover this love is born in faith and remains within faith, while at the same time reaching out to those who have not the same faith. That is the very characteristic of love; wherever our love goes, it carries with it our faith.

Nor does the friendship of charity merely make us recognize the *existence* of others—although as a matter of fact here is something already difficult enough for men, and something which includes everything essential. Not only does it make us recognize that another exists, but it makes us recognize that he exists, not as an accident of the empirical world but as a human being who exists before God, and has the right to exist. While remaining within the faith, the friendship of charity helps us to recognize whatever beliefs other than our own include of truth and of dignity, of human and divine values. It makes us respect them, urges us on ever to seek in them everything that is stamped with the mark of man's original greatness and of the prevenient care and generosity of God. It helps us to come to a mutual understanding of one another. It does not make us go beyond our faith but beyond ourselves. In other words, it helps us to purify our faith of the shell of egotism and subjectivity in which we instinctively tend to enclose it. And it also inevitably carries with it a sort of heart-rending, attached, as is the heart, at once to the truth we love and to the neighbor who is ignorant of that truth. This condition is even associated with what is called the "*ecumenical*" bringing together of divided Christians; how much more is it associated with the labor of bringing into mutual comprehension believers of every denomination.

I distrust any easy and comfortable friendship between believers of all denominations, I mean a friendship which is not accompanied, as it were, by a kind of compunction or soul's sorrow; just as I distrust any universalism which claims to unite in one and the same service of God, and in one and the same transcendental piety—as in some World's Fair Temple—all forms of belief and all forms of worship. The duty of being faithful to the light, and of always following it to the extent that one sees it, is a duty which cannot be evaded. In other words, the problem of conversion, for anyone who feels the spur of God, and to the extent that he is pricked by it, cannot be cast aside, any more than can be cast aside the obligation of the apostolate. And by the same token I also distrust a friendship between believers of the same denomination which is, as it were, easy and comfortable, because in that case charity would be reserved to their fellow-worshippers; there would be a universalism which would limit love to brothers in the same faith, a proselytism which would love another man only in order to convert him and only insofar as he is capable of conversion, a Christianity which would be the Christianity of *good* people as against *bad* people, and which would confuse the order of charity with what a great spiritual writer of the seventeenth century called a police-force order.

The spurious universalism I just alluded to—and which would make all faiths have their stand, window display, and loudspeaker in a World's Fair Temple, on the condition that all of them should confess they are *not sure* that they are conveying the word of God, and that none of them should claim to be the true Faith—is sometimes advocated in the name of Indian wisdom, which teaches a kind of transcendent liberal indifference with respect to any definite creed.

At this point I should like to observe:

First. Such liberal indifference actually applies to non-Indian rather than Indian creeds, and consequently resembles very much an illusory theme of propaganda. Moreover, as a matter of fact, "Right view or right thinking is the first step in the path of the Buddha, and the word *orthodoxy* is precisely its Greek equivalent. In the Pali scriptures there is much that reads like accounts of heresy trials."[4] And finally was not Buddhism, which was born in India, persecuted by Brahmanism and expelled from India?

Second. Indian wisdom, be it Brahmanist or Buddhist, does not teach indifference to any supreme truth; it teaches undifferentiation of supreme truth, and this is a definite metaphysical creed indeed. To be sure, Indian metaphysics is rich with invaluable insights and experiences. Yet it is seriously mistaken, insofar as it teaches that the supreme Truth is sheer undifferentiation, and the Supreme Reality so transcendent that it cannot be known in any expressible manner, even through concepts and words which God himself used to reveal Himself to us. And this boils down, on the one hand, to disregarding the intellect as such, which can grasp through analogy divine things themselves, and, on the other hand, to forbidding God the right to speak. Then all religious forms are embraced and absorbed in a formless religiosity.

Third. The Western or Westernized caricature of Indian metaphysics, which preaches, in the name of one "sophy" or another, indifference to any religious dogma and equivalence between all religious creeds henceforth decidedly relativized, displays itself a most arrogant dogmatism, asking from its believers unconditional surrender of their minds to teachers who are self-appointed prophets. And the kind of mysticism supposedly free from, and superior to, any revealed dogma, which is advocated by this cheap gnosticism, is but spiritual self-complacency or search for powers, which make up for the loss of the sense of truth.

True universalism, as I have insisted all through this lecture, is just the opposite of indifference. The catholicity it implies is not a catholicity of relativism and indistinction, but the catholicity of reason, and first of all the catholicity of the Word of God, which brought salvation to all the human race and to whose mystical body all those who live in grace belong visibly or invisibly.[5] True universalism presupposes the sense of truth and the certainties of faith; it is the universalism of love which uses these very certainties of faith and all the resources of the intellect to understand better, and do full justice to, the other fellow. It is not supra-dogmatic, it is supra-subjective. We find a token of such a universalism of love—not above faith but within faith, not above religious and philosophical truth but within religious and philosophical truth, to the extent to which everyone knows it—in the development of certain discussion groups between Moslems and Christians, for instance, or of certain studies in comparative theology and comparative mysticism. I would like to cite as an example the case of a book written a few years ago by two Thomist authors[6] on Moslem theology which proved to be so illuminating for Moslem as well as for Christian readers that a professor of the Al-Hazar University wished to translate it into Arabic.

As to comparative mysticism, it is genuinely comparative only if it avails itself of all the analytical instruments provided by philosophy and theology. According to the principles of Thomist philosophy and theology, it is a fact that, if divine grace exists and bears fruit in them, men of good will who live in non-Christian climates can experience the same *supernatural* mystical union with God "known as unknown"[7] as Christian contemplatives do: it is so, *not* because mystical experience is independent of faith, but because faith in the Redeemer can exist implicitly, together with the grace of Christ, in men who do not know His name, and this faith can develop into grace-given contemplation, through union of love with God. On the other hand, studies in *natural* mysticism have shown that the disciplines of the Yoga, for instance, normally terminate in a mystical experience which is authentic

in its own sphere but quite different from grace-given contemplation, and has for its object that invaluable reality which is the
Self, in its pure act of existing, immediately attained through the
void created by intellectual concentration. Thus it is that a Christian can do full justice, in the Christian perspective itself, to mystical experiences which take place in non-Christian religious areas;[8]
and he can develop genuine understanding of, and respect for those
who are dedicated to these experiences.

I have given these indications only to illustrate the fact that
genuine human fellowship is not jeopardized—quite the contrary!
—it is fostered by zeal for truth, if only love is there.

NOTES

1. Rev. Father Victor White, O.P., "Religious Tolerance," *The Common-
weal,* September 4, 1953.
2. Helen Silving, "The Conflict of Liberty and Equality," *Iowa Law Re-
view,* Spring 1950.
3. See Charles Journet, *The Church of the Word Incarnate* (London and
New York: Sheed and Ward, 1955), I, 215–216, 283–284.
4. Rev. Father Victor White, *op. cit.*
5. See the chapter "Catholicité" in the remarkable book *Chemins de
l'Inde et Philosophie Chrétienne* by Olivier Lacombe (Paris: Alsatia, 1956).
6. Louis Gardet et M.-M. Anawati, *Introduction à la Théologie Musul-
mane* (Paris: Vrin, 1948).
7. Thomas Aquinas, *Sum. contra Gent.,* III, 49. Cf. Pseudo-Dionysius,
Mystica Theologia, cap. 2.
8. Cf. Louis Gardet, *Expériences mystiques en terres non-chrétiennes*
(Paris: Alsatia, 1953).

LOVE AND BELIEF

KARL ADAM

ONCE upon a time—so the Babylonic Talmud runs—a pagan came
to the Rabbi Shammai and said: "I am willing to become a Jew,
if you can explain to me the entire Jewish law in the time during
which I can stand on one leg." Shammai dismissed him. He

thereupon went to the Rabbi Hillel and made the same request to him. Hillel at once answered: "Do not do to your neighbor whatever you would hate to have done to you. That is the entire law. Everything else is but the commentary to it. Go and learn to do that."

The New Testament tells of a similar incident. A scribe came to Jesus and asked him: "Master which is the great commandment in the law?" Jesus said to him: "Thou shall love the Lord thy God with thy whole heart, and with thy whole soul, and with thy whole mind. This is the greatest and the first commandment. And the second is like to this: Thou shalt love thy neighbor as thyself. On these two commandments dependeth the whole law and the prophets" (Mt. 22:36, *seq*). Jesus thus mentions two commandments, not only one, and he places first the commandment of the love of God; but He too observes that the entire law is comprised in these commandments to love. And in the Sermon on the Mount He even reduces the whole law, like Hillel, to love of one's neighbor: "All things therefore whatsoever you would that men should do to you, do you also to them. For this is the law and the prophets" (Mt. 7:12; Lk. 6:31). This formulation differs from that of Hillel only by the fact that Jesus states the essence of the law not negatively, but positively. The law is fulfilled not merely by not doing evil to one's neighbor, but by doing to him all the good that one would like to see done to oneself. Determined devotion to others, active service to our brother, brotherly love: that is the essence which matters above all. Our Lord emphasizes with great solemnity that it is in this faithful, devoted love to our brothers that we are to see the new, specific feature of his message: "A new commandment I give unto you: That you love one another; as I have loved you, that you also love one another. By this shall all men know that you are my disciples, if you have love for one another" (John 13:34–35).

The essence of Christianity is therefore exhaustively expressed by the word "love." Nor have the disciples of Jesus understood their Master otherwise than in this sense. "Follow after charity," demands St. Paul (1 Cor. 14:1); "Charity is the bond of perfection" (Col. 3:14); "by charity of the spirit serve one another, for"—and here St. Paul repeats the words of Jesus—"all the law

is fulfilled in one word: Thou shalt love thy neighbor as thyself"
(Gal. 5:13–14). St. James calls the commandment to love "the
royal law" (James 2:8). St. Peter says that "charity covereth a
multitude of sins" (1 Peter 4:8). And St. John, the subtle, favorite disciple of our Lord, goes deeper and points out the metaphysical basis of the essence of love, when he writes, (1 John 4:7, 8):
"Dearly beloved, let us love one another: for charity is of God.
And everyone that loveth is born of God and knoweth God. He
that loveth not knoweth not God: for God is charity."

The disciples of the Apostles and the subsequent centuries took
over this gospel of love from the Apostles. The oldest non-biblical
document that we know, the *Didache,* which represents in its teaching of the "two ways" a sort of primitive Christian catechism, opens
with these words: "The way to life is this: first, thou shalt love
God who has created thee; secondly: thou shalt love thy neighbor
as thyself. But whatsoever thou wilt not that be done to thee, do
not thou also to thy neighbor" (1, 2). The same is said by Clement
of Rome, by Ignatius of Antioch, by Polycarp and all the other
Fathers. St. Augustine, the saintly bishop with the glowing heart,
erects his entire theological system on the basis of charity. Illuminated by it, he penetrates into the depth of the Triune God and
finally ventures upon the bold saying: *Ama et fac quidquid vis—*
"Act in charity and you can do whatsoever you will."

If then Christianity is in essence love, is not Christianity something incredibly simple and at the same time marvellously luminous, something which must win all hearts by nothing more than its
sheer inner beauty. Why then the hard, strict duty of faith? Why
the rigid dogmas, the wearying symbols of Councils of the Church?
Why all that immense apparatus of the Church: Pope, bishops,
priests? Why this vast, complicated ecclesiastical administration
and the *Codex Juris Canonici?* Is not the Gospel, this joyous,
simple luminous message of love, made, *pro tanto,* wearisome and
oppressive? Is it not an unbearable burden that is laid thereby upon
man? If it is true that love constitutes the essence of Christianity,
is it not also true that everything outside this sphere of love, all the
external ecclesiastical trappings, all outward dogmatic faith, is
something merely peripheral, secondary, even something that leads,
experience shows, away from the essence of Christianity, something

that hinders, even kills love? Is it not just because of the dogmas that love has suffered the fiercest injuries, that it has been drowned in floods of blood and burnt at the stake? Is it not again today still the rigidity, the dogmatism, the external Church that divides men and nations in their most intimate feelings and makes the gospel of Christian love an object of derision? Ought we not really with Tolstoy and Dostoevsky to condemn and curse the churches and all ecclesiastical creations as anti-Christian, even satanic products, as the creations of the spirit of this world in which there still lives the sinister figure of the grand inquisitor who in the name of faith drags love to the scaffold?

These are serious and difficult questions. They demand an answer. Is it really the case that faith kills love? Or at least that faith hinders and impedes its pure working? What is the relation between faith and love?

It is certainly true: Love is the essence of Christianity. Faith without love is but a "dead faith." Such faith even the devils have (James 2: 18, 19). "If I should have all faith, so that I could remove mountains, and have not charity, I am nothing" (1 Cor. 13: 2). But is it not strange that these same men who as with burning tongues praise charity, will not desist from their faith? With the same emphasis with which they exhort to love, they demand faith. The same sacred lips that announced to us the new commandment of His love, uttered those threatening words: "He that believeth not shall be condemned" (Mark 16:16; see John 3:36). The same St. John who said that charity was born of God, said also: "Whosoever believeth that Jesus is Christ is born of God" (1 John 5:1). And however enthusiastically St. Paul sings the high canticle of love, much more often, much more gravely and insistently he speaks of faith and its hidden wonders. It is the high triumph of the Christian that "by grace he is saved through faith" (Eph. 2: 8). And the later ages learnt from the Apostles. So much was faith at all times recognized as the very foundation of Christianity that the Christians were simply called the "faithful" (*fideles*).

So there is after all a connection between faith and love! Is it perhaps that only he can really love who believes? In that case faith would be the spring of real love, and there would be no love where there is no faith? In other words: faith and love, should we say, stand in a sort of causal relation to each other?

In order to clear up these questions, we must first be clear what Christ and His disciples mean when they speak of love. There is hardly a word that is so handled, so worn, as the word "love." But for Jesus it was wholly unambiguous. When He spoke of love, He was not referring to sentimental moods which come today and go tomorrow, aim only at the satisfaction of a personal, lower or higher appetite and are in the last resort merely relevant and related to the *ego*. In its formal aspect love is for Him an act of the will; as regards its content it is selfless service rendered to the "neighbor." And the "neighbor" means he who here and now is nearest to me, nearer than father and mother, not only he who is a relative or a friend, but every human being who is in need, be he Samaritan or pagan or Jew. The love of the neighbor, according to Jesus, passes beyond all personal, social, national and religious divisions. It seeks man *"per se,"* precisely among the ruins of sin and want. His care, His labor and troubles, His miracles and his vigils are devoted to this man. "He went about doing good" (Acts 10: 38). In this service rendered to the neighbor there is no room for prudent reserve, not even towards the prostitute, no careful weighing and hesitation, but sheer determined venture and high-souled action. "If a man ask thee to go with him a mile, go thou two with him." This devotion is so limitless, so unconditional, so wholly a determination of the will, that it does not recoil before the hardest task, even before the sacrifice of our own life. "I have not come to be served, but to serve and to give my life for many." Jesus has confirmed this commandment of love on the cross.

Jesus then means by love the staking of our entire personality on behalf of our brother in need, be he who he may: service to our fellow-man even to the limit of self-sacrifice. "Greater love has no man but that he should give his life for his friends."

As we see, Jesus places before us an ideal of love, overflowing with energy, illuminated by devotion, saturated with the blood of sacrifice. Never before had any prophet set up before mankind or lived an ideal of love with such impressiveness and energy, of such delicacy and affection, so embracing and exhaustive as Jesus,

the bringer of this new love. It is only through him that mankind
discovered what true love means.

But why does Jesus insist upon so limitless, so severe and even
cruel a love, a love even to death? It is nothing less than this question which brings us to the very heart of the message of love of
Jesus. Is it the charm of a high-minded humanity that captivated
Him? Does He see in man, like Auguste Comte, an "*être suprême,*"
the absolute, ultimate value, to whom everything has to be sacrificed? Nothing could be more mistaken. Jesus was no philanthro-
pist with an enthusiasm for the cult of the merely human. He was
too profound and too whole to feel any enthusiasm for man. He
perceived but too clearly beneath the varnish of the purely human
the all-too-human sides of him. If we look closer, we might even
detect in His attitude to man something like a restrained disgust.
Does He not call even Peter—one of his most intimate disciples,
who has just solemnly acclaimed Him as Messias—a "satan"?
And he uses the expression with an eye to all His disciples who,
he knew, shared Peter's opinion (Mark 8:33). He had selected
as His disciples plain, seemingly straight, unwarped men, the best
He could find. Yet He knew that what linked them to His person
was an egoistical motive, the hope for the twelve thrones of Israel.
He knew moreover that one of the plain simple people who at
the moment were so affectionately attached to Him would deny
Him in the hour of His need, and another would betray Him, and all
of them would run away.

No, no— it was not the merit of humanity that Jesus loved man.
"*Omnis homo mendax*"—he knew that as well as, he knew that
better than, anyone. How petty, how insignificant were the men
of the world that surrounded Him. Narrow-minded, block-headed,
ambitious pharisees, frivolous, cynical Sadducees, the dissolute,
credulous people, swayed by every mood of the moment—those
were the types of men, certainly no better, but also certainly no
worse than others over in Rome or down in Alexandria. Such
men are not the ultimate, highest value whom one loves and sacrifices one's life for. If this sort of humanity were the only consideration, then love would be sheer delusion and self-deception. In that
case, we ought to shake the dust from our feet and preach a quite

different gospel: the gospel of our own *ego,* the gospel of "the Only One and His All."[1]

But then why did Jesus all the same love these men even to the sacrifice of Himself, and why does he demand from His disciples this same love?

It is just where he speaks of the hardest, most difficult love, that for our enemies, that the point becomes clearest: "Pray for them that persecute and calumniate you: that you may be the children of your Father who is in heaven, who maketh his sun to rise upon the good and the bad and raineth upon the just and the unjust . . . Be you therefore perfect as also your heavenly Father is perfect" (Mt. 5:44, *sqq.*). So Jesus finds the determining motive of his love for men not in men, but in God. The human value is not the ultimate, but only the penultimate value; the last, the highest value is God the Father. He alone is the cause and the measure of all things, cause and measure of all valuations, cause and measure of all love. Because this Father loves men—no matter whether they are good or bad—and because we prove ourselves His children precisely by showing that same love, are we to love men. My relation to men has therefore its ultimate roots in a transcendental fact, namely in that fundamental relation of love in which God includes men, all men. Man is a mystery. He is the culmination-point of an eternal love which issues from God; a point in the actuality of the world where, as nowhere else, the love of God burns. That is the reason why man is worth loving: not by reason of what he is in himself or for himself, but by reason of what he is for God; or in the language of theology: not for a natural but for a supernatural reason. I shall never reach man by starting from the earth; I must first reach to heaven to find man through God. The floodstream of the love of man passes through the heart of God. I must first have God, before I can have man. God is the way to man.

Jesus states therewith a fact which is an essential feature of love. We shall realize this fact as soon as we recall once more what "Christian love" is meant to signify. As was said before, its characteristic trait is its complete detachment from all personal, social and national considerations, its selflessness, and, connected therewith, its active tension, its readiness for sacrifice. Wherever this characteristic is lacking, we find merely the bastard of this true love, an apocryphal distortion of it. What we human beings mean when we speak of real love is fulfilled only in such a love of selflessness and energy. Wherever love is egocentric and therefore selfish, it has lost its peculiar nuance, the sweetness of its scent, its special savour. When it finds its satisfaction in mere wishing without proceeding to self-sacrificing action, it is merely stuffy and sentimental, a mere wave of a mood, a flower without fruit, which dies even before being put forth.

What now is the answer to the question: is such a selfless active love, ready thus to realize itself in action, intelligible from the point of view of the actual world? Has it even any sense? If I consider actuality simply in itself, isolated I mean from its supporting, metaphysical basis, detached from God, then there cannot, nay there ought not to be any higher value than my own ego. It is only by reason of my own self that I can posit or affirm extra-personal values. For they are values only so far as I feel them to be values, because of their egocentricity. It may be that outside myself there are still higher values than I; it may be that this or that is better, more perfect than I—but all that is mere supposition, never a certitude, and the fact remains in any case that I am the most certain fact for myself, that my self is my world, my domain, and that everything else can exist for me only inasmuch as it adjusts itself to my world and domain. I alone am my own king and master, my only and highest value, my all.

Seen from this purely logical standpoint, all unselfish, disinterested love is foolishness. For it would be a venture, a leap in the dark. It would even be immoral, for it would signify an abandonment of myself, a denial of my own *ego*.

Yet, on the other hand, the same person who by pure logic ought to reach the conclusion that every selfless, active love should be condemned as foolish and immoral, feels with the evidential directness of an immediate ethical experience that an egocentric, selfish, paralytic love is intolerable and repulsive. That is not what we mean when we speak of genuine love. It lacks precisely what gives genuine love its fascination, what allows us to find rest in it, what satisfies and captivates us. Its very heart, the selflessness of its devotion, has been cut out of its breast.

Are we then to say that an antinomy gapes between the logical and the psychological view of love? How is this antinomy to be reduced? How is it possible for man to love truly unselfishly without being foolish and unfaithful to his own being?

It is possible only by means of a sort of fiction whereby the lover attributes to his beloved a value which outstrips not only his own, but altogether all empirical values of a world of space and time, which transcends them all; a value, accordingly, which belongs in no wise to his own spatial world of values and can be adjusted to it; in short an absolute value, superior to the *ego*. This is the only value before which egocentric desires can and must be silent. It is that to which I am bound to surrender myself, since it is the value in every way superior to all else; it is that alone to which I can and may devote myself with my innermost, freest assent. So in every experience of true love there lies hidden an absolute, or rather the assent to the sphere of the absolute, a secret *credo in Deum*. Psychologists have therefore described this experience of true love as an acosmic, superterrestrial experience: for it is "not of this world." It transcends in its essence all temporal and spatial data of experience. It includes in its essence the positing of an absolute. In other words: there is no true love except a love in God. It may be that one or other, who loves truly, knows nothing of this absolute, of this love in God; he may even be short-sighted enough to imagine that he acts reasonably, when he loves selflessly, without consciously believing in God, as the absolute value. But if this love is true love "in deed and in truth," as St. John expresses it, then his experience of love contains implicitly, at least, whether he knows it or not, the positing of God. God, His absoluteness, His infinite perfection and lovableness, is the secret motive, the secret spring of the energy, the secret native soil of his love. Even some of the favorite phrases of love—like "to adore his beloved"—indicate this fact. The lover can reach his beloved only through God. God alone can carry him over that dead point which lies between the *ego* and the *alter* and cannot be transcended by mere logic. It requires understanding and courage to appreciate this position and to affirm one's faith in the Absolute despite its human wrappings. As Descartes once said: *Je pense, donc je suis,* so here it might be said: "I love, therefore I believe." Thus in every genuine, unselfish, serious love belief in God is contained, even really presupposed. No one has expressed this truth with greater profundity than the Apostle of love, St. John, when he exhorted his disciples: "Dearly beloved, let us love one another: for charity is of God. And everyone that loveth is born of God and knoweth God."

Considered, then, even merely phenomenologically, love points towards faith. For it is only by faith that I can grasp that absolute, which love essentially includes, without which it cannot exist. When this faith in the absolute is artificially removed from the experience of love, the consequence is that love is incapable of reaching beyond the range of an earthy, crude, selfish existence and of rousing the heroism of devotion.

It is therefore symptomatic that monistic ethics, which on principle abstracts from belief in God and from any supernatural foundation, proves incapable of even theoretically maintaining a heroic morality, let alone of realizing it among its followers. Why did people in the distress of the world war call so insistently for those Sisters of Charity who draw all their love from their faith, whose love was a love for God's sake? Why do we find those heroic figures of heroic charity to whom even unbelief pays its tribute of respect, figures like St. Vincent de Paul, like Camillus de Lellis, like Don Bosco or St. Elisabeth, just there, where faith has received its purest and fullest form in dogma, its most active and exhaustive expression in cult and in life—in the Catholic Church? Is there not food for thought in the fact that even those pagan philosophers who (perhaps not uninfluenced by Christian thought, for all their fundamentally monistic attitude) for the first time seriously considered and proclaimed in pagan lands the ideal of a general love of man—for instance, the slave Epictetus—gave a strongly religious tone to their stoical speculation and combined with their profession of universal love of man also the profession of God as the Father of all things? There is only the Indian sage, Guatama Buddha, who seems to contradict this principle of an essential connection of faith with love, so far as he formulated, as many think, a purely atheistic morality, devoid of all faith, and swore in his numerous followers upon this teaching. But apart from the fact that this assertion of the atheistic character of Buddha's ethics has met with scepticism recently, and leaving aside the fact

that this irreligious ethics, even if it was actually preached, remained restricted to a small circle, while the large mass of the
Buddhist faithful relapsed into a wild polytheism, it is worth while
to point out that Buddha's commandment to love, his teaching of
"mettasatta," can in no way be put on the same level as Christian
charity. Kindness to animals and men (*metta*) is one of the chief
commands of the Indian sage, but this kindness is something purely
negative, a mere tolerating and suffering of evil, not active conduct
as in Christian faith. Its object is, as Buddha expresses it, none
other than to "free the soul," i.e. by non-acting on principle, by
willing suffering, to stifle the thirst for life in the soul and to prepare
thereby for Nirvana. Buddha's command to love is thus in the last
resort conceived in terms of egoism. The purely negative, passive
suffering and toleration is simply a means to self-deliverance. It
lacks therefore what is just the characteristic feature of Christian
charity: the selflessness of devotion, its active even vehement element, and its determined practical helpfulness.

We may then say: wherever there is true love, there is faith.
Even in the Old Testament we find faith placed next to love; next
to the command: "Thou shalt love thy neighbor," the other:
"Thou shalt love God with thy whole heart." Even in the Old
Testament there is no morality which was not at the same time
religion, no love without faith. It is true that the inner connection
between faith and love was not sufficiently clearly formulated. The
two commands were quoted side by side, without their overlapping
and mutual dependence being fully seen. A Rabbi one day asked
one of his disciples: "Which path do you see before you, when you
awaken of a morning?" The disciple answered: "The path of the
love of God and that of the love of my neighbor." Thereupon the
Rabbi asked: "And which of these will you take first?" The disciple blushed and could not give the answer. Then the master remarked: "The first path you are to take is that of the love of your
neighbor."

It is clear then that for the Old Testament the two paths are still
distinct. Hence also the question of the Rabbi. For the disciple
of Christ the question has no longer any sense. For him there are
not two paths; there is but the single path of salvation: the love

of God and of his neighbor. They cannot be separated. Where true love of God is found, there also is true love of one's neighbor; wherever there is true faith, there also is true love. Both attitudes are merely different reactions of one and the same fundamental attitude: Love in God.

It was an original feat of Jesus to have set this internal connection of faith and love clearly before us. As elsewhere, so here He fulfilled the Old Testament. In His own Person, the appearance of God among men, the bodily revelation of the supernatural, the mystery of faith and of love at the same time, He revealed by his subtle touch the supernatural basis of all true love on earth, rooted in the faith in the Father. There is only one true love, that which springs from faith. All true love is love in God, love for the sake of the Father.

Even a philosopher like Nietzsche was unable wholly to escape the spell of this revelation. In his work "Beyond Good and Evil" occurs the significant remark: "To love man for God's sake is, up till now, the noblest and remotest sentiment attained to among mankind. That love of man without some sort of sanctifying *arrière-pensée* is merely another foolishness and bestiality, that this propensity to love man has yet to receive from some higher tendency its measure, its refinement, its little pinch of salt and its little grain of spice—whatever man it was who first felt and experienced this, however much his speech may have blundered when it attempted to formulate anything so delicate, he must remain for us for all times sacred and worthy of reverence."

Since the time of Jesus we know that every true love lives and breathes and has its being in faith. Faith alone carries myself, my intellect, my heart out of this terrestrial microcosm, out of the limitations of purely terrestrial points of view and considerations, out of the narrow selfish desires and cares up into those altitudes where infinity opens before me, where something "quite different" shines, Divinity, Sanctity, perfect Purity. Here, in the kingdom of God, is purest reality, the Life of life, the Power of powers, the Spirit of spirits, the Value of all values. True life comes, not from below, but from above, from the Father of light. The strong impulses, the pure mind, those streams of strength that never fail, spring from there. So faith belongs to love in an essential, indissoluble bond: faith creates love, safeguards love, purifies love, strengthens love. For it gives to love that which profane love is lacking, the deep passionate breath of infinity, that characteristic tendency to superhuman greatness, that passion for heroic, incredible, unheard-of things, that foolishness of the Cross, before which all earthly pathos crumbles and breaks into dust.

Let us gather up what we said: true love can be found only where the absolute, the divine, is somehow co-involved: in other words, true love is at the same time love of God. And inasmuch as the reality of God is apprehended through faith, faith cannot be separated from true love.

This is an important conclusion. For it comes to this, that everything necessarily belonging to faith, whatever provides its foundations, its protection and usefulness, consequently the entire means of salvation of the Church, her dogma, her sacraments, her cult, her constitution, must stand in some essential relation to love. For all this serves in the last resort precisely the purpose of bringing home to us that world of God from which true love springs. Faith, in all its utterances, institutions, functions is concerned with God and His saving reality, and therefore ultimately with love, which has its roots in that reality. This applies especially to dogma. Dogma is, after all, nothing else but the glad news of the incarnation of the Word of God, the joyous fact that God's sacred reality has been revealed to us in His Son. Whatever is formulated in the individual articles of faith serves merely the all-round unfolding, the safeguarding and application of this single fundamental truth of the appearance of God upon earth. The sacraments, the cult and the priest serve that same theophany. They bring within our reach the supernatural blessings of the reality of God, manifested in Christ, and illustrate and apply it. The same theophany is served by the Pope and the bishops, by their supreme pastoral measures and decisions. Through them the kingdom of God in us becomes the kingdom of God among us, a visible community of the faithful, protected against error and safeguarded against divisions and decay. In this manner the Church proclaims and bears witness to God as the ultimate spring of all blessings by her entire essence as an institution of the means of salvation. She creates that supernatural world and that range of life saturated with divine power

where true love can alone thrive. Everything about her is related
to that love which overcomes the world, to the preparation and
protection of that heavenly kingdom which is wholly love, "charity
from a pure heart, and a good conscience, and an unfeigned
faith" (1 Tim. 1:5).

But the Church stands not only in so indirect a relation to love.
Rather is she linked with love so intimately that love penetrates
down into the last cells of her organism as an institution for salvation, and makes her in her essence into a wonderful revelation of
love. Everything about her not merely points to love, but is born
of love, steeped in love, breathing love. So dogma is in reality
nothing but the joyous message of that love wherewith God first
loved us, created, saved and sanctified us, the joyous message of
the continuous process of the love wherewith God gave Himself
to men. The sacraments are nothing but the irradiation and continuous working of this divine love in the Church and in the hearts
of the faithful. The papacy and the episcopate have sprung from
the love of the Saviour, an act of love towards his brethren, the
service of a servant, as St. Paul expresses it. And the Church herself, sacred, immaculate, is in her deepest being the mystical Body
of Christ on earth, the manifestation in time and space and the
revelation of His incarnate love, the empirical completion and perfection of that last extreme act of the love of God in which He revealed Himself not only by signs and words, but gave His only Son
so that we might come to the Father.

Wherever we may look in our Church, on all sides everything
points to the one thing needful: "That is the first commandment:
Thou shalt love the Lord thy God with thy whole heart. . . . And
the second is like to this: Thou shalt love thy neighbor as thyself."
The entire ecclesiastical organism is not only in its ultimate purpose, but in its very essence, an urgent call to the love of God and
of our neighbor, the high canticle of love ringing through the
centuries and millennia. And whoever refuses obedience to this
Church, to the Holy Father, to his God-given bishop, sins in the
essence of his rebellious attitude against love. Whether he knows
it or not, whether he wills it or not, he places the axe upon that
very root from which alone love shoots up.

The last, the deepest significance of the Church upon earth is that she is the school of this love. Her being as a means to salvation aims in the last resort at this. Inasmuch as she is the means to salvation, she will have fulfilled this her existence at the moment when according to the inscrutable will of God the sowing of the seeds of that love is completed. When the sign of the Son of Man will appear in the heavens, and the new heaven, the new earth and the new kingdom of the Blessed will appear in their radiance, all the functions of the Church as the means of salvation—dogma, sacraments, bishop and Pope—will drop off like the petals when the fruit ripens. Henceforth only the essential of her will remain and will shine in eternal light: the communion of love. All that which is purely the means of salvation in her is only the *signum praefigurativum, signum prognosticum,* something preparatory, a pointer, that will vanish at the moment when its purpose has been fulfilled. "Prophecies shall be made void, tongues shall cease, knowledge shall be destroyed. . . ." Faith will pass into vision, hope will change into possession. What alone will remain is love and the communion of love, the Church of the Blessed. "For charity never falleth away" (1Cor. 13:8).

And wherever here on earth dogma, the sacraments and the Church fail to lead a soul to this love, these means to salvation have been deprived of their deepest significance. Then they are, as St. Augustine says again and again, mere external forms of piety (*formae pietatis*), lacking in the power of salvation; they are a form without content, a flower without fruit. Theology speaks of a *fides informis,* a "shapeless faith," meaning a faith atrophied and crippled in its essence because it is lacking in love. And the Church never wearies in sermon and catechism, in spiritual exercises and missions to bring home to the faithful the tremendous words of St. Paul which condemn with unparalleled force all that empty, merely external form of churchmanship, that sheer formalism: "If I should have prophecy and should know all mysteries and all knowledge, and if I should have all faith, so that I could remove mountains, and have not charity, I am nothing. And if I should distribute all my goods to feed the poor, and if I should deliver my body to be burned, and have not charity, it profiteth me nothing" (1 Cor. 13:2, 3). It would be merely continuing on the lines of St. Paul to add: mere observance of the dogmas of

the Church, mere obedience to the infallible Pope, mere frequent
communions, participation in Church societies and organizations
—all that will not do it either. Even if you do all these things, but
have no charity, it will profit you nothing. "But charity is patient,
is kind; charity envieth not, dealeth not perversely, is not puffed
up. . . ." If you have not this charity, nothing will profit you.

If thus all and everything aims at this love and finds its ultimate
significance in this love, whence comes that terrible and undeniable
contrast between faith and love which we pointed out at the beginning? What is the reason why common opinion so definitely
refuses to see in the faithful the natural vehicle and messenger of
true love? Why is it that the intimate and essential correlation between faith and love which we have established, is by no means
always visibly present in the individual Christian? And why is it
that in certain periods of history the contrast between faith and
love went so far that faith killed love? Why is it that we even
nowadays suffer under this contrast?

A priori such a contrast is possible and thinkable because
faith and love are not identical, but are only in their essences ordered towards each other. Who could deny that this contrast
actually emerged and still exists? But the fault of this contrast
does not lie with faith or with the Church as the foundation supporting the reality of this faith. We established the fact that whatever is in the Church, her essence and her function is born of the
spirit of love and aims at love. There is nothing in the Church,
neither in her dogmas nor her ritual nor her organization, which
in and by itself, by its mere existence or its special function could
offer a hold or motive for hatred and dispute.

It is then out of the question that the Church herself can provide the basis of this deplorable contrast between faith and love.
This basis must be sought, not in the objective, ecclesiastical factors, but in the subjective, personal factors of the situation. The
fault lies, not in the Church, but in her members. And not
only the lay-folk, but ecclesiastics, even bishops and popes have
been at fault. Sin is possible wherever there is flesh and blood; it
may be that through incompetence or weakness the highest and
only purpose of all ecclesiastical life and functioning, namely this

holy love, may be frustrated. Could the separation of the Eastern
Church have happened, could the cleavage in the Western Church
in the sixteenth century have occurred, if the sacred commandment
of love with a pure heart and unfeigned faith had remained for
all, on both sides, the supreme and immoveable directing line of
thought and action? Every cleavage, every heresy in the Church is
reducible, as St. Augustine points out, to a weakening, a failure of
the spirit of love among the members of Christ. Wherever is true
love, there also is the *unitas caritatis,* the union of love. There may
be differences of opinion and dogmatic disputes, but the union of
love will never be threatened with disruption and a mutilation of the
Body of Christ.

That same lack of love among the members of Christ bears the
responsibility, if a similar contrast between faith and love is so
acutely felt in our present narrow, small lives. Is it not unspeakably
sad that we Catholics are no longer, as formerly, recognized by our
love, that no longer faith and love, but faith alone is our distinguishing mark. Whose fault is it that the old equation, Catholic Christianity = love in faith = faith in love, applies no longer, that it cannot longer be said as it was of the primitive faithful: "See how
they love one another"? Certainly not the fault of the Church, who
never wearies, day by day, to exhort to love and to give love, but
the fault of ourselves alone, her members. Where is the Catholic
who would not have to confess in this respect: *mea culpa, mea
maxima culpa?*

Is it not our own fault to a very large extent that the recruiting
power of our Church, which in the time of primitive Christianity
had been so sweeping and victorious, has failed now for centuries
so uncannily, that the riches of our faith are so largely unknown
and despised, because our faith does not bear that fruit of love
which should be expected of it? Why are we in the works of our
love no proof of the spirit and strength in the victoriousness of the
Catholic faith? Why do we rather take refuge in cheap speech and
in dead books to testify to our faith, whereas the only overwhelming
and effective apologia for the living reality is that of the glowing
heart, of active devoted love? Should we not long ago have con-
quered the whole world for the joyous news of our faith, if not

over wide stretches the words even now applied to us: *refrigescet caritas multorum?* The love of many is cooling! Here destiny lies in wait for us; here our responsibility stares us in the face; here our crisis awaits us and judgment threatens. For are we worthy that our Church should flourish, when our love wilts? Unless the Catholic faith kindles the spirit of love at least in our families, unless our sodalities and parishes are real centers of love—ἀγάπαι, as St. Ignatius of Antioch calls them—unless our public life is touched by the warm breath of our charity, unless every errand-boy and every charwoman is for us our brother and sister, there can be no hope of a renewal, of a deepening and expansion of Catholic life in the world. Here, at this point and no other, the decision will be reached whether Catholicism nowadays is strong enough to overcome the spirit of modern times in its inner being, to reconquer the mind of Western Europe and to carry the Gospel into all the world, as once St. Paul did in a few years, or whether it is first to lapse, according to the intentions of Divine justice and mercy, into a period of stagnation or perhaps even into the hard times of the catacombs, until its faith, purged by sorrow, shall again put forth the fruits of love.

Heavy with questions and cares, in prayer and trust we lift our eyes to him who has planted faith in our hearts and has given it the waters of love. *Veni sancte Spiritus!* Help us, O God! for indeed we know "unless the Lord build the house, they labour in vain that build it; unless the Lord keep the city, he watcheth in vain that keepeth it."

VENI, SANCTE SPIRITUS,

REPLE TUORUM CORDA FIDELIUM

ET TUI AMORIS IN EIS

IGNEM

ACCENDE

AMEN

NOTE

1. *"Der Einzige und sein Eigentum"*: this is the title of the work of the noted solipsist Max Stirner, published 1844, which became notorious later during the period of enthusiasm for Nietzsche (Translator's note).

THE GROWTH OF THE DIVINE MILIEU

PIERRE TEILHARD DE CHARDIN, S.J.

THE Kingdom of God is within us. When Christ appears in the
clouds He will simply be manifesting a metamorphosis that has
been slowly accomplished under His influence in the heart of the
mass of mankind. In order to hasten His coming, let us therefore
concentrate upon a better understanding of the process by which
the Holy Presence is born and grows within us. In order to foster
its progress more intelligently let us observe the birth and growth
of the divine milieu, first in ourselves and then in the world that
begins with us.

A. The coming of the divine milieu.
The taste for being and the diaphany of God

A breeze passes in the night. When did it spring up? Whence
does it come? Whither is it going? No man knows. No one can
compel the spirit, the gaze or the light of God to descend upon him.
On some given day a man suddenly becomes conscious that he is
alive to a particular perception of the divine spread everywhere
about him. Question him. When did this state begin for him? He
cannot tell. All he knows is that a new spirit has crossed his life.

"It began with a particular and unique resonance which swelled
each harmony, with a diffused radiance which haloed each beauty.
. . . All the elements of psychological life were in turn affected;
sensations, feelings, thoughts. Day by day they became more fra-
grant, more colored, more intense by means of an indefinable thing
—the same thing. Then the vague note, and fragrance, and light
began to define themselves. And then, contrary to all expectation
and all probability, I began to feel what was ineffably common to
all things. The unity communicated itself to me by giving me the
gift of grasping it. I had in fact acquired a new sense, *the sense of*
a new quality or *of a new dimension.* Deeper still: a transformation
had taken place for me *in the very perception of being.* Thence-

forward being had become, in some way, tangible and savorous to me; and as it came to dominate all the forms which it assumed, being itself began to draw me and to intoxicate me."

That is what any man might say, more or less explicitly, who has gone any distance in the development of his capacity for self-analysis. Outwardly he could well be a pagan. And should he happen to be a Christian, he would admit that this inward reversal seemed to him to have occurred within the profane and "natural" parts of his soul.

But we must not allow ourselves to be deceived by appearances. We must not let ourselves be disconcerted by the patent errors into which many mystics have fallen in their attempts to place and even to name the universal Smile. As with all power (and the richer, the more so) the sense of the All comes to birth inchoate and troubled. It often happens that, like children opening their eyes for the first time, men do not accurately place the reality which they sense behind things. Their gropings often meet with nothing but a metaphysical phantom or a crude idol. But images and reflections have never proved anything against the reality of objects and of the light. The false trails of pantheism bear witness to our immense need for some revealing word to come from the mouth of Him who is. With that reservation, it remains true that, physiologically, the so-called "natural" taste for being is, in each life, the first dawn of the divine illumination—the first tremor perceived of the world animated by the Incarnation. The sense (*which is not necessarily the feeling*) of the omnipresence of God prolongs, sur-creates and supernaturalizes the identical physiological energy which, in a mutilated or misdirected form, produces the various styles of pantheism.[1]

Once we realize that the *divine milieu discloses itself to us as a modification of the deep being of things,* it is at once possible to make two important observations touching the manner in which its perception is introduced and preserved within our human horizons.

In the first place, the manifestation of the divine no more modifies the apparent order of things than the eucharistic consecration modifies the sacred Species to our eyes. Since the psychological event consists, at first, solely in the appearance of an *inward ten-*

sion or *deep brilliance,* the relations between creatures remains exactly the same. They are merely accentuated in meaning. Like those translucent materials which a light within them can illuminate as a whole, the world appears to the Christian mystic bathed in an inward light which intensifies its relief, its structure and its depth. This light is not the superficial glimmer which can be realized in coarse enjoyment. Nor is it the violent flash which destroys objects and blinds our eyes. It is the calm and powerful radiance engendered by the synthesis of all the elements of the world in Jesus. The more fulfilled, according to their nature, are the beings in whom it comes to play, the closer and more sensible this radiance appears; and the more sensible it becomes, the more the objects which it bathes become distinct in contour and remote in substance. If we may slightly alter a hallowed expression, we could say that the great mystery of Christianity is not exactly the appearance, but the transparence, of God in the universe. Yes, Lord, not only the ray that strikes the surface, but the ray that penetrates, not only Your Epiphany, Jesus, but *Your diaphany.*

Nothing is more consistent or more fleeting—more fused with things or at the same time more separable from them—than a ray of light. If the divine milieu reveals itself to us as an incandescence of the inward layers of being, who is to guarantee us the persistence of this vision? No one other than the Ray of light itself. The diaphany . . . No power in the world can prevent us from savouring its joys because it happens at a level deeper than any power; and no power in the world—for the same reason —can compel it to appear.

That is the second point, the consideration of which should be used as the basis for all our further reflections on the progress of life in God.

The perception of the divine omnipresence is essentially a seeing, a taste, that is to say a sort of intuition bearing upon certain superior qualities in things. It cannot, therefore, be attained directly by any process of reasoning, nor by any human artifice. It is a gift, like life itself, of which it is undoubtedly the supreme experimental perfection. And so we are brought back again to the center of ourselves, to the edge of that mysterious source to which we descended (at the beginning of Part Two and watched it as it

welled up). To experience the attraction of God, to be sensible
of the beauty, the consistency and the final unity of being, is the
highest and at the same time the most complete of our "passivities
of growth." God tends, by the logic of His creative effort, to make
Himself sought and perceived by us: *Posuit homines . . . si forte
attrectent eum.* His prevenient grace is therefore always on the
alert to excite our first look and our first prayer. But in the end the
initiative, the awakening, always come from Him, and whatever
the further developments of our mystical faculties, no progress is
achieved in this domain except as the new response to a new gift.
Nemo venit ad me, nisi Pater traxerit eum.

We are thus led to posit intense and continual prayer at the
origin of our invasion by the divine milieu, the prayer which begs
for the fundamental gift: *Domine, fac ut videam.* Lord, we know
and feel that You are everywhere around us; but it seems that
there is a veil before our eyes. *Illumina vultum tuum super nos*—
let the light of Your countenance shine upon us in its universality.
Sit splendor Domini nostri super nos—may Your deep brilliance
light up the innermost parts of the massive obscurities in which we
move. And, to that end, send us Your spirit, *Spiritus principalis,*
whose flaming action alone can operate the birth and achievement
of the great metamorphosis which sums up all inward perfection
and towards which Your creation yearns: *Emitte Spiritum tuum,
et creabuntur, et RENOVABIS FACIEM TERRAE.*

B. Individual progress in the divine milieu: purity, faith and fidelity, the operatives

Ego operor . . . Pater semper operatur. The charm of the divine
milieu (heavy with responsibilities) is that it can assume an *ever
increasing* intensity around us. One could say that it is an atmosphere ever more luminous and ever more charged with God. It
is in Him and in Him alone that the reckless vow of all love is
realized: to lose oneself in what one loves, to sink oneself in it
more and more.

It could be said that three virtues contribute with particular effectiveness towards the limitless concentration of the divine in
our lives—purity, faith and fidelity; three virtues which appear to

be "static" but which are in fact the three most active and unconfined virtues of all. Let us look at them one after the other, and
examine their generative function in the divine milieu.

i. Purity

Purity, in the wide sense of the word, is not merely the abstaining from wrong (that is only a negative aspect of purity),
nor even chastity (which is only a remarkable special instance of
it). It is the rectitude and the impulse introduced into our lives
by the love of God sought in and above everything.

He is spiritually impure who, lingering in pleasure or shut up
in selfishness, introduces, within himself and around himself, a
principle of slowing-down and division in the unification of the
universe in God.

He is pure, on the other hand, who, in accord with his place
in the world, seeks to give Christ's desire to consummate all
things precedence over his own immediate and momentary advantage.

Still purer and more pure is he who, attracted by God, succeeds in giving that movement and impulse of Christ's an ever
greater continuity, intensity and reality—whether his vocation
calls him to move always in the material zones of the world
(though more and more spiritually), or whether, as is more often
the case, he has access to regions where the divine gradually re-
places for him all other earthly nourishment.

Thus understood, the purity of beings is measured by the degree of the attraction that draws them towards the divine center,
or, what comes to the same thing, by their proximity to the center.
Christian experience teaches us that it is preserved by recollection,
mental prayer, purity of conscience, purity of intention and the
sacraments. Let us be satisfied, here, with extolling its wonderful
power of condensing the divine in all around us.

In one of his stories, Robert Hugh Benson tells of a "visionary"
coming on a lonely chapel where a nun is praying. He enters.
All at once he sees the whole world bound up and moving and
organizing itself around that out-of-the-way spot, in tune with
the intensity and inflection of the desires of that puny praying

figure. The convent chapel had become the axis about which the earth revolved. The contemplative sensitized and animated all things because she believed; and her faith was operative because her very pure soul placed her near to God. This piece of fiction is an admirable parable.

The inward tension of the mind towards God may seem negligible to those who try to calculate the quantity of energy accumulated in the mass of humanity.

And yet, if we could see the "light invisible" as we can see clouds or lightning or the rays of the sun, a pure soul would seem as active in this world, by virtue of its sheer purity, as the snowy summits whose impassible peaks breathe in continually for us the roving powers of the high atmosphere.

If we want the divine milieu to grow all around us, then we must jealously guard and nourish all the forces of union, of desire, and of prayer that grace offers us. By the mere fact that our transparency will increase, the divine light, that never ceases to press in upon us, will irrupt the more powerfully.

Have we ever thought of the meaning of the mystery of the Annunciation?

When the time had come when God resolved to realize His Incarnation before our eyes, He had first of all to raise up in the world a virtue capable of drawing Him as far as ourselves. He needed a mother who would engender Him in the human sphere. What did He do? He created the Virgin Mary, that is to say He called forth on earth a purity so great that, within this transparency, He would concentrate Himself to the point of appearing as a child.

There, expressed in its strength and reality, is the power of purity to bring the divine to birth among us.

And yet the Church, addressing the Virgin Mother, adds: *Beata quae credidisti*. For it is in faith that purity finds the fulfilment of its fertility.

ii. Faith.

Faith, as we understand it here, is not—of course—simply the intellectual adherence to Christian dogma. It is taken in a much

richer sense to mean belief in God charged with all the trust
in His beneficent strength that the knowledge of the divine Being
arouses in us. It means the practical conviction that the universe,
between the hands of the Creator, still continues to be the clay
in which He shapes innumerable possibilities according to His
will. In a word, it is *evangelical faith,* of which it can be said that
no virtue, not even charity, was more strongly urged by the Saviour.

Now, under what guise was this disposition so untiringly revealed to us by the words and deeds of the Master? Above all
and beyond all, as *an operative power.* But, intimidated by the
assertions of an unproven positivism, or "put off" by the mystical
excesses of Christian Science, we are sometimes tempted to gloss
over the disconcerting promise that the efficacy of prayer is
tangible and certain. Yet we cannot ignore it without blushing
for Christ. If we do not believe, the waves engulf us, the winds
blow, nourishment fails, sickness lays us low or kills us, the
divine power is impotent or remote. If, on the other hand, we
believe, the waters are welcoming and sweet, the bread is multiplied, our eyes open, the dead rise again, the power of God is,
as it were, drawn from Him by force and spreads throughout
all nature. One must either arbitrarily minimize or explain away
the Gospel, or one must admit the reality of these effects not
as transient and past, but as perennial and actually true. Let us
beware of stifling this revelation of a possible vitalization of the
forces of nature in God. Let us, rather, place it resolutely at the
center of our vision of the world—careful, only, that we understand it aright.

When we say that faith is "operative," what do we mean? Is
divine action, at the call of faith, going to replace the normal
interplay of the causes which surround us? Do we, like the
"illuminati," expect God to bring about directly, upon matter or
upon our bodies, results that have hitherto been obtained by our
own industrious research?

Obviously not. Neither the internal inter-relations of the material or psychical world, nor man's duty to make the greatest
possible effort, are in any way undermined, or even relaxed, by
the precepts of faith. *Iota unum aut unus apex non praeteribit.*
All the natural links of the world remain intact under the trans-

forming action of "operative faith"; but a principle, an inward
finality, one might almost say an additional soul, is superim-
posed upon them. Under the influence of our faith, the universe
is capable, without outwardly changing its characteristics, of
becoming more supple, more fully animate—of being "sur-ani-
mated." That is the "at the most" and the "at the least" of the
belief expressly imposed upon us by the Gospel. Sometimes this
"sur-animation" expresses itself in miraculous effects—when the
transfiguration of causes permits them access to the zone of their
"obediential potency." At other times, and this is the more usual
case, it is manifested by the integration of unimportant or unfavorable events within a higher plane and within a higher providence.

We have already mentioned and analysed a very typical example of this second form of divinization of the world by faith (a
form no less profound and no less precious than more striking
prodigies). In considering the passivities of diminishment we saw
how our failures, our death, our faults even, could—through God
—be recast into something better and transformed in Him. The
moment has come to envisage this miracle in its most general sense
and from the particular point of view of the act of faith which is,
on our part, its providential condition.

In our hands, in the hands of all of us, the world and life (*our
world, our life*) are placed like a Host, ready to be charged with
the divine influence, that is to say with a real Presence of the Incarnate Word. The mystery will be accomplished. But on one
condition: which is that *we shall believe* that *this* has the will and
the power to become for us the action—that is to say the prolonga-
tion of the Body of Christ. If we believe, then everything is illuminated and takes shape around us: chance is seen to be order, success assumes an incorruptible plenitude, suffering becomes a visit
and a caress of God. But if we hesitate, the rock remains dry, the
sky dark, the waters treacherous and shifting. And we may hear
the voice of the Master, faced with our bungled lives: "O men of
little faith, why have you doubted . . . ?"

Domine, adjuva incredulitatem meam. *Ah, You know it Yourself, Lord, through having borne the anguish of it as man: on certain days the world seems a terrifying thing: huge, blind and brutal.
It buffets us about, drags us along, and kills us with complete in-*

difference. Heroically, it may truly be said, man has contrived to create a more or less habitable zone of light and warmth in the midst of the great, cold, black waters—a zone where people have eyes to see, hands to help, and hearts to love. But how precarious that habitation is! At any moment the vast and horrible thing may break in through the cracks—the thing which we try hard to forget is always there, separated from us by a flimsy partition: fire, pestilence, storms, earthquakes, or the unleashing of dark moral forces—these callously sweep away in one moment what we had laboriously built up and beautified with all our intelligence and all our heart.

Since human dignity, O God, forbids me to close my eyes to this—like a beast or a child—that I may not succumb to the temptation to curse the universe and Him who made it, teach me to adore it by seeing You concealed within it. *O Lord, repeat to me the great liberating words, the words which at once reveal and operate:* Hoc est Corpus meum. *In truth, the huge and dark Thing, the phantom, the storm—if we want it to be so, is You!* Ego sum, nolite timere. *The things in our life which terrify us, the things that threw You Yourself into agony in the Garden, are, ultimately, only the Species or Appearance, the matter of one and the same Sacrament.*

We have only to believe. And the more threatening and irreducible reality appears, the more firmly and desperately must we believe. Then, little by little, we shall see the universal horror unbend, and then smile upon us, and then take us in its more than human arms.

No, it is not the rigid determinism of matter and of large numbers, but the subtle combinations of the Spirit, that give the universe its consistency. The immense hazard and the immense blindness of the world are only an illusion to him who believes. *Fides, substantia rerum.*

iii. Fidelity

Because we have believed intensely and with a pure heart in the world, the world will open the arms of God to us. It is for us to throw ourselves into these arms so that the divine milieu should close around our lives like a circle. That gesture of ours will be one of an active response to our daily tasks. *Faith consecrates the world. Fidelity communicates with it.*

To give a worthy description of the "advantages" of the fidelity, that is to say of the essential and final part which it plays in our taking possession of the divine milieu, we should have to go back to what was said in the first two parts of this study. For it is fidelity which releases the inexhaustible resources offered by every passion to our desire for communion.

Through fidelity we situate ourselves and maintain ourselves in the hands of God so exactly as to become one with them in their action.

Through fidelity we open ourselves so intimately and continuously to the wishes and good pleasure of God, that His life penetrates and assimilates ours like a fortifying bread. *Hoc est cibus meus, ut faciam voluntatem Patris.*

And finally, through fidelity we find ourselves at every moment situated at the exact point at which the whole bundle of inward and outward forces of the world converge providentially upon us, that is to say at the one point where the divine milieu can, at a given moment, be made real for us.

It is fidelity and fidelity alone that enables us to welcome the universal and perpetual overtures of the divine milieu; through fidelity and fidelity alone can we return to God the kiss He is for ever offering us across the world.

What is without price in the "communicating" power of fidelity is that, like the power possessed by faith and purity, it knows no limit to its efficacy.

There is no limit in *respect of the work* done or the diminishment undergone, because we can always sink ourselves deeper into the perfecting of work to be achieved, or into the better utilization of distressing events. We can always be more industrious, more meticulous, more flexible. . . .

Nor is there any limit in *respect of the intention* which animates our endeavor to act or to accept, because we can always go further in the inward perfecting of our conformity. There can always be greater detachment and greater love.

And there is no limit, indeed there is still less limit, *in respect of the divine object* in the ever closer espousal of which our being can joyfully wear itself away. This is the moment to abandon all conception of static adherence; it can only be inadequate. And let us remember this: God does not offer Himself to our finite beings as a thing all complete and ready to be embraced. For us He is eternal discovery and eternal growth. The more we think we understand Him, the more He reveals Himself as otherwise. The more we think we hold Him, the further He withdraws, drawing us into the depths of Himself. The nearer we approach Him through all the efforts of nature and grace, the more He increases, in one and the same movement, His attraction over our powers, and the receptivity of our powers to that divine attraction.

Thus the privileged point which was mentioned a short time back—the one point at which the divine milieu may be born, for each man, at each moment—is not a fixed point in the universe, but a moving center which we have to follow, like the Magi their star.

That star leads each man differently, by a different path, in accord with his vocation. But all the paths which it indicates have this in common: that they lead always upward. (We have already said these things more than once, but it is important to group them together for the last time in the same bundle.) In any existence, if it has fidelity, greater desires follow on lesser ones, renunciation gradually gains mastery over pleasure, death consummates life. Finally the general drift throughout creation will have been the same for all. Sometimes through detachment of mind, sometimes through effective detachment, fidelity leads us all, more or less fast and more or less far, towards the same zone of minimal egoism and minimal pleasure—to where, for the more ecstatic creature, the divine light glows with greater amplitude and greater limpidity, beyond the intermediaries which have been, *not rejected,* but *overcome.*

Under the converging action of these three rays—purity, faith and fidelity—the world melts and folds.

Like a huge fire that is fed by what should normally extinguish it, or like a mighty torrent which is swelled by the very obstacles placed to stem it, so the tension engendered by the encounter between man and God dissolves, bears along and volatilizes created things and makes them all, equally, serve the cause of union.

Joys, advances, sufferings, setbacks, mistakes, works, prayers, beauties, the powers of heaven, earth and hell—everything bows down under the touch of the heavenly waves; and everything yields up the portion of positive energy contained within its nature so as to contribute to the richness of the divine milieu.

Like the jet of flame that effortlessly pierces the hardest metal, so the spirit drawn to God penetrates through the world and makes its way enveloped in the luminous vapours of what it sublimates with Him.

It does not destroy things, nor distort them; but it liberates things, directs them, transfigures them, animates them. It does not leave things behind but, as it rises, it leans on them for support; and carries along with it the chosen part in things.

Purity, faith and fidelity, static virtues and operative virtues, you are truly, in your serenity, nature's noblest energies—those which give even the material world its final consistency and its ultimate shape. You are the formative principles of the New Earth. Through you, three-fold aspect of a same trusting adoration, "we shall overcome the world": Haec est quae vincit mundum, fides nostra.

NOTE

1. In other words and more simply: Just as in the love of God (Charity) can be found, quite obviously, the human power to love in its supernatural state—so, in the same way, we believe that at the psychological origin of the "feeling of omnipresence," experiencd by the Christian can be found "the sense of universal Being" which is the source of the majority of human mysticisms. There is a soul which is *naturaliter christiana*. It should be remembered that these pages contain a psychological description, not a theological explanation, of the states of soul met with.

OUR TEMPTATIONS
CONCERNING THE CHURCH

HENRI DE LUBAC, S.J.

LOVE should, of course, be our only reaction to our Mother the Church; yet in fact there are many temptations which trouble us with regard to her. Some are clear enough, and violent; others are less clear, and all the more insidious. There are some that are perennial, and some that are peculiar to our time, and they are all too varied—even to the point of mutual opposition—for any one of us ever to think himself sheltered from the threat which they constitute.

There will always be men who identify their cause with that of the Church so totally that they end by equating the Church's cause with their own, and this in all good faith. It does not occur to them that if they are to be truly faithful servants they may have to mortify much in themselves; in their desire to serve the Church, they press the Church into their own service. It is a "dialectical transition," inside-out from *pro* to *contra,* as easy as unobtrusive. For them the Church is a certain order of things which is familiar to them and by which they live; a certain state of civilization, a certain number of principles, a certain complex of values which the Church's influence has more or less Christianized but which remain none the less largely human. And anything which disturbs this order or threatens this equilibrium, anything which upsets them or merely startles them, seems to them to be a crime against a divine institution.

Where there is question of a muddle of this sort, we are not always involved with those crude forms of "clericalism" which estimate the amount of honor paid to God by the privileges accorded to His ministers or measure the progress of divine rule over souls, and the social reign of Christ, by the influence, either hidden or open, of the clergy on the course of secular affairs. Here the whole order of thinking may well be on the loftiest plane—as when Bossuet, towards the end of his life, adjusted the whole Catholic order in accordance with a Louis-Quatorze pattern of things, and was unable to see anything but a threat to religion in the mixed forces which began to disintegrate that particular synthesis, which was, of course, a brilliant one, but was also matter for questioning in some aspects at least—a thing contingent, and by essence perishable. Against those forces he made his stand, and that with every ounce of his strength.

Bossuet was as perceptive as he was forthright; yet his perceptiveness did not go the whole way. "Together with an imperious will, he had a spirit by nature timid."[1] He wanted to maintain for ever (though courageously condemning certain faults and criticizing certain abuses) the mental and social world in which his genius found a natural ground for its unfolding. He could not imagine how the faith could survive it—rather like those ancient Romans (among whom were even some Fathers of the Church) for whom the collapse of the Empire could not be anything other than the heralding of the end of the world, so great an impression had the Roman power and majesty made upon the mind of the time.[2] But since Bossuet's dream was of something which was in fact impossible, he found himself involving with the moribund world in question the Church whose business it was to free herself from it in order to bring life to the coming generations. The inadequate defenses he threw up against the oncoming evil buried beyond hope of germination the seeds of the future; he was apparently victorious on every field which he fought but it was irreligion which profited from the way in which he won his victories.[3]

In the same way, we are sometimes all the more self-confident and strict in the judgments we pass in proportion as the cause we are defending is the more dubious. It is possible that we sometimes forget in practice something we know well enough in principle— that the intransigence of the faith is not a passionate unbendingness in the desire to impose upon others our personal tastes and personal ideas. A tight-clenched hardness of that kind is fatal to the supple firmness of truth, and is no defence to it whatsoever; a Christianity which deliberately takes up its stand in a wholly defensive position, closed to every overture and all assimilation, is no longer Christianity. Sincere attachment to the Church can never be used for the purpose of canonizing our prejudices, or making our partialities part of the absolute of the universal faith. It may thus be pertinent to recall that a certain confidence and detachment are part of the Catholic spirit. At the right time, the Church can find in the very shrines of the devil things to beautify her own dwelling; that particular miracle is always something new and unforeseen, but we know that it will happen again.[4] However rooted in history the Church may be, she is not the slave of any epoch or indeed of anything whatsoever the essence of which is temporal. The message which she is bound to pass on and the life which she is bound to propagate are never integral parts of "either a political régime or a social polity or a particular form of civilization," and she must forcefully remind people of the fact, in opposition to the illusive evidence to the contrary which in fact derives simply from the bonds of habit.[5] She repeats for us, in their widest possible sense, the words of St. Augustine: "Why are you dismayed when earthly kingdoms pass away?"[6] for she is founded upon no rock other than that of Peter's faith, which is faith in Jesus Christ; she is neither a party nor a closed society. She cannot resign herself to being cut off from those who do not yet know her simply for the sake of the comfortableness of those who make up her traditional faithful. She desires no opposition from the reality in men, since they are all her sons, at least virtually; on the contrary, she will make it her aim to set them free from all evil by giving them their Saviour.

We should therefore ourselves get into this frame of mind, which was that of Christ (Phil. 2:5), and we should if necessary impose on ourselves the mortifications fitted to this end. Far from failing in the intransigence of the faith, we shall in this way alone sound its depths. We must not relax in any way our zeal for Catholic truth, but we should learn how to purify it. We must be on our guard against turning into those "carnal men" who have existed since the first generation of Christians and who, turning the Church into their own private property, practically stopped the Apostles from announcing the Gospel to the Gentiles.[7] For if we do that we lay ourselves open to something yet more calamitous—collaboration with militant irreligion, by way of making it easier for it to carry out its self-assigned task of relegating the Church and her

doctrine to the class of the defunct; we provide irreligion with a
clear conscience, as it were, for it has no understanding of the
actuality of the eternal. Its attitude is: "Let the Church remain
what she is" (and one knows what sort of petrifaction such a wish
implies)—and then "she will receive all the appreciation always
accorded to historic relics."[8] An irreligion of this type mixes up at
will cases of the most widely differing kinds, confusing with dogma
opinions or attitudes inherited from situations which have ceased
to be, and takes up a firm stand over "concessions" in which it
detects "bad faith or irresponsibility."[9] It establishes its own lists
of what is suspect—in the fashion of religious authority itself—
and is ready to call that authority to order, if need be. Having
made up its mind once and for all that there can be nothing reasonable in Christian beliefs, it brands as "liberalism" or "modernism"
every effort made to disentangle Christianity in its real purity and
its perpetual youth, as if this were an abandonment of doctrine. It
can never see in the thought of men like Justin or Clement of Alexandria or their modern disciples anything but the concessions of an
apologetic which sacrifices the "tough" element in dogma to the
desire to please those whom it wishes to win over; Tatian and
Hermias are the favorites, and their method alone is regarded as
the only Christian one.[10] It maintains that "the Church can never
cut loose from her past . . . religion is a whole which must not be
touched . . . as soon as you reason about it, you are an atheist."[11]
The principle is "All or nothing"—provided that the "all" is understood in the terms dictated—which are not those of the Church;
thus, for example, Renan, making the Catholic faith involved for
ever with the historicity of the Book of Daniel and other things of
the same kind.[12] And it is a day of rejoicing in this quarter when
voices are raised within the very heart of "this poor and aged
Church"[13] which sound like approval. A false intransigence can
certainly cause an enormous amount of harm in this way—quite
in opposition to its own intentions.

The vistas opened up by all this should be yet one more motive
for our distrusting ourselves. We should be wary of a certain kind
of humility which borders on pride, cultivating a healthy fear of
sacrilegious usurpation, and taking to heart the exhortation of St.
Augustine to his fellow-fighters in the thick of the Donatist contro-

versy: "Take your stand upon the truth without pride."[14] We have
to bear in mind that our knowledge is always partial and that in
this world we only glimpse the divine truth "through a glass in a
dark manner" (1 Cor. 13:12); like Newman, instead of settling
ourselves into the Church as our private property and personal
possession and more or less identifying her with ourselves, we
should rather make it our business to identify ourselves with the
Church, and without expecting any personal triumph from it.[15]

But there is another temptation from the opposite direction,
which is certainly more frequent today, and sometimes more aggressive in the provocation which it offers—the critical temptation. This also very frequently advances itself cunningly under the
camouflage of the good; it can easily put itself forward to the
apostolically-minded as a necessary concern for clarity. And for
this reason it cannot, in most cases, be avoided save by a preliminary "discernment of spirits."

The very word "criticism" means discernment, and there is, of
course, a kind of criticism which is good—particularly self-criticism. That kind is a striving for realism in action—a determination
to bar all that cannot justify its claim to genuineness. It is an examination carried out in humility, capable of recognizing the good
achieved, but arising out of an essentially apostolic discontent and
a perpetually restless spiritual dynamism. It is born and grows from
attitudes such as the inability to be satisfied with work done and a
burning desire for the best; integrity of judgment on matters of
method; independence of will to break with customs that cannot
be justified any more, to get out of ruts and put right abuses; above
all, a lofty idea of the Christian vocation and faith in the mission
of the Church. It stimulates an intensified activity, inventive in-
genuity and a sudden outburst of exploration and encounter which
must, doubtless, be brought under control on occasion—and which
certainly often disturbs our habits a little too rudely. Criticism of
this type is hard on the illusions which it tracks down, but can induce others which will soon be in turn the object of similar criticism. Yet how very much better it all is, still, than the naïve self-
complacency which admits of no reform and no healthy transformation—that certain comfortableness which gradually digs itself deeper and deeper into its dream-world, that obstinacy which

thinks that it is preserving things when all it is doing is piling up
the ruins of them.[16]

We should be wrong if we wished to prevent on principle all
public expression of this kind of criticism. When the Church is
humble in the persons of her children she is more attractive than
when they show themselves dominated by the all-too-human concern for respectability. Jacques Maritain once said, not entirely
without his tongue in his cheek, that many Christians of today
find any admission of our deficiencies "somehow indecent." "It
will be said," he adds, "that they are afraid of putting difficulties in
the way of apologetic. . . . The ancient Jews and even the Ninivites
didn't stand on ceremony in that way."[17] No more did the saints in
the past. Think of St. Jerome's famous address to Pope Damasus,[18]
or St. Bernard's broadsides against bad pastors[19] and the programme of reform which he outlines in his *De Consideratione*,[20]
or diatribes like that of St. Catherine of Siena against certain
highly-placed ecclesiastical dignitaries: "O men who are no men
but rather devils incarnate, how you are blinded by your disordered
love for the rottenness of the body, and the delights and bedazzle-
ments of this world!"[21] Or again, remember for a moment people
like St. Brigid, and Gerson, and St. Bernardino of Siena, and St.
Thomas More; or, to come nearer to our own day, St. Clement
Hofbauer. Or think of the struggles of the "Gregorians" to tear
the government of the Church free from the system which was enslaving it; or the audacity of a man like Gerhoh of Reichersberg,
addressing to Pope Eugenius III his work *On the Corrupt State of
the Church*, like St. Bernard; or Roger Bacon, demanding of
Clement IV that he should "purge the Canon Law" and cast out
of the Church the pagan elements which had been brought into her
with the ancient Civil Law;[22] or of William Durandus publishing
his treatise *De Modo Celebrandi et Corruptelis in Ecclesia Refor-
mandis;* of the Carthusian Peter of Leyden exhorting the Roman
Pontiff at the opening of the edition which he issued in 1530 of the
works of his fellow-Carthusian Denys.[23] This last example evokes
the whole great movement of Catholic reform which is all too inadequately described under the name of the Counter-Reformation;
an enterprise of that kind could not even have been outlined with-

out an effective determination on self-criticism, of which history shows us more than one brilliant example.

Yet for every constructive complaint and each clear-headed and fruitful analysis there is all too much excess and recklessness. Each really courageous act is counterpoised by a mass of futile agitation. There is all too much purely negative criticism. Sanctity is not common, and the sincerest goodwill has neither the same rights nor the same privileges. And both competence and opportunity may be lacking; even if a given criticism is a fair one, we are, nevertheless, not always justified in making it. In addition, we have to bear in mind this important fact; that today we do not have the same situation as existed in what we call the Christian centuries. Then, everything happened within the family circle, as it were; and irreligion was not perpetually on the lookout to turn this, that and everything to account in argument. Today, when the Church is in the dock, misunderstood, jeered at for her very existence and even her sanctity itself, Catholics should be wary lest what they want to say simply in order to serve her better be turned to account against her. We have to be on our guard against misunderstandings of a fatal kind; and this is a filial delicacy which has nothing to do with prudery or hypocritical calculatingness. It is not possible to give a hard-and-fast rule, but the Holy Spirit will not be miserly with the gift of counsel to the really "ecclesiastical" man, as I have tried to depict him above—that is, to the man who cannot but be truly spiritual.

We must in any case make a distinction between healthy self-criticism, even when it is excessive or ill-directed, and all sterile complaining—everything that stems from a loss, or even a diminishing, of confidence in the Church. It would certainly be impious to use one or two unfortunate occurrences as an excuse to run down "contemporary Christianity's excellent and laborious task of diagnosing its own deficiencies, and trying to understand, love and preserve all that has grown up of value outside its own direct influence, and to venture out into the storm to collect the first materials for its new dwelling."[24] But if an attempt of this kind is to be carried out and bear fruit, we have to be careful that it is not contaminated by the breath of a spirit very different from that which is its own principle.

There are certain times when one sees springing up in every
direction the symptoms of an evil which catches on like an epidemic—a collective neurasthenic crisis. To those who are afflicted
by it, everything becomes matter for denigration, and this is not
just a case of the irony, quarrelsomeness or bitterness which are at
all times a perpetual threat to a certain kind of temperament.
Everything gets a bad construction put upon it, and knowledge
of all kinds, even when accurate, only serves to intensify the evil.
Half-digested new discoveries and clumsily used new techniques
are all so many occasions for believing that the traditional foundations of things have gone shaky. The spiritual life goes but limp-
ingly—so much so that nothing is really seen in the light of it any
more. People think themselves clear-headed when all the time it is
precisely the essential that they have overlooked. We are no longer
capable of discovering, sometimes on our very doorsteps, the fresh
flowerings of the Holy Spirit's innumerable inventions—that Holy
Spirit which is always in Its own likeness and always new. And thus
discouragement creeps in by a thousand and one different ways;
things that might have given us a healthy shock simply have the
effect of paralyzing us. Faith may stay sincere, but it is undermined
here, there and everywhere, and we begin to look at the Church as
if from outside, in order to judge her; the groanings of prayer become an all-too-human recrimination.[25] And by this movement of
Pharisaism—a sort of interior falling-away—which may be un-
admitted but is none the less pernicious for all that, we set foot on
the road which may end in open denial.

That this should be realized in time and that the appropriate
reaction should take place, is something devoutly to be hoped for.
There is no question of blinding oneself to inadequacies; those are
always only too real. And there is no question of not feeling the
painfulness of them; indifference can be much worse than excess
of emotion. The total and burning loyalty of our holding to the
Church does not demand of us a puerile admiration for every possible thing that can be, or be thought, or done, within her. Christ
wished His Bride to be perfect, holy and without spot; but she is
this only in principle. If she does indeed shine with a spotless
radiance, it is "in the sacraments with which she begets and nur-
tures her children; in the faith which she preserves ever inviolate;

in the holy laws which she imposes on all, and in the evangelical counsels by which she admonishes; and, finally, in the heavenly gifts and miraculous powers by which out of her inexhaustible fecundity she begets countless hosts of martyrs, virgins and confessors."[26] Her soul is the Spirit of Christ but her members are men, all the same; and we know well that men are never up to the level of the divine mission which is entrusted to them. They are never wholly amenable and submissive to the inspirations of the Spirit of Christ, and if they do not succeed in corrupting the Church—since the source of her sanctifying power does not lie in them—she, on the other hand, will never succeed in stopping completely the source of evil in them—at least, as long as the conditions of this world hold good. Their good will is no guarantee of their intelligence, and intelligence is not always accompanied by strength. The best among them will always be setting up innumerable obstacles to the good which God wants to bring about through them;[27] so that we may as well get it well into our heads to start with that nothing which they do should surprise us—a lesson which is most healthily rammed home by history.

Yet we are all men, and there is none of us but is aware of his own wretchedness and incapacity; for after all we keep on having our noses rubbed in our own limitations. We have all, at some time or other, caught ourselves red-handed in the very act of contradiction—trying to serve a holy cause by dubious means. And we must add that our most serious shortcomings are those very ones that escape our notice; from time to time, at least, we see that we are without understanding in the face of the mystery which we are called upon to live out. So that there are scanty grounds for making exceptional cases of ourselves; and none at all for the withdrawal implied in a grimly-judging eye. If we behave in that way we fall into an illusion like that of the misanthrope, who takes a dislike to humankind, for all the world as if he himself were not a part of it: "In order to attain to a deep understanding with humanity it is enough to be a part of it, to cleave to the whole mass of it and all the intermingling of its members"—then "we have no more grievances left, no more standing-back, no more judgments and no more comparisons."[28] Then the staring contrast between the human wretchedness of those who make up the Church, and the greatness of her divine mission, will no longer be a scandal to us; for we shall first have become painfully aware of it in ourselves. Rather, it will become a stimulus. We shall understand how a certain sort of self-criticism which is always directed outwards may be nothing more than the search for an alibi designed to enable us to dodge the examination of our consciences.[29] And a humble acceptance of Catholic solidarity will perhaps be more profitable to us in the matter of shaking us out of some of our illusions. It will perhaps help us to fall in love once more, from a new standpoint, with those elements in the wisdom and the institutions and the traditions and the demands of our Church which we were coming near to understanding no longer.

Today, however, disquiet often takes forms more precise than this, and the most lowly of active Catholics does not entirely escape it. He may ask himself with painful anxiety: Is the Church's action on our age properly adapted to it? Surely indisputable experience shows that it is tragically ineffective? For some time past at least that kind of question has been asked in many quarters, and we should not underestimate its seriousness, or dismiss it hastily as if we refused to look at it. If we do that we shall only add to the troubles of those who (perhaps because they are more wide awake than we) are at grips with it in a real "dark night." But here again we must make a sober effort at the discernment of spirits.[30]

In many quarters people are asking themselves questions as to the real value, not, of course, of Christianity itself, but of many of the parts that go to make up, as it were, the religious instrument, as the centuries have forged it. They find its efficiency at too low a level, and point grimly to the worn cogs and tired springs; many practices are put in the dock and there is talk of out-of-date methods and institutions. It will scarcely be a matter for surprise if there is in all this more than one illusion of the inside-out kind, and if certain errors creep into both the diagnosis of the evil and the choice of remedies for it; a genuine intuition of new needs may be accompanied by inadequate knowledge and a certain lack of grip on reality. It is not always possible to make an accurate distinction between what ought to be preserved and what ought to be changed, at the first shot; sometimes we are over-quick to despair of forms which,though apparently dead, are capable of reanimation. However, if our inspiration is sound we shall not find it difficult to make the necessary adjustments to a programme rather hastily drawn up, and to round out a somewhat one-sided effort by others more calculated to balance it.

But it is that inspiration, precisely, which stands in need of control. For here the worst may go cheek by jowl with the best. What is the real source of this concern for adaptation, or—which is very much the same thing—the need felt for what is often called a more effective "incarnation"—a concern in itself wholly justified[31] and frequently encouraged of set purpose by the supreme authority of the Church?[32] Is it a pure overflowing of charity, as in the case of St. Paul who, following the example of Christ, wanted to make himself all things to all men? Or is there some admixture in it of this illusion, all too natural to the professional man which every priest must inevitably be to a certain extent—that it is enough to make a change of method, as all human undertakings may do, to obtain results which primarily suppose a change of heart? Realistic views, objective enquiry, statistics, the elucidation of sociological laws, the drawing up of methodical plans, breaks both big and small with the forms of apostolate belonging to the past, the perfecting of new techniques—all these things may be made use of by zeal that is really pure and upright, and anyone who belittles them puts himself in the right with a facility somewhat suspect if he makes a mere opposition between them and the methods of the Curé d'Ars. Yet all these things have to be kept in their proper place, in the service of the Spirit of God alone.

But—and this is something more serious—it may well be that there is mingled with our disquiet in some more or less subtle way a certain timidity, a certain deep-seated lack of assurance and secret revulsion against the tradition of the Church. We may, when we see ourselves as setting ourselves free from what seems a spirit of senility, and as struggling against ankylosis and sclerosis, be putting ourselves in the way of contracting "childish ailments";[33] what we take for an awakening of the personality may in point of fact be the end-product of a blind aberration, and we may set ourselves to judge all things in accordance with criteria which are superficially "modern" and no more. The secular values which the world spreads before our eyes may begin to dazzle us, and in the presence of those who stand for them we may, bit by bit, allow ourselves to be affected by an inferiority complex. Where things that should be most sacred to us are concerned, we may be on the way to accepting ideas about them held by men whose blindness should in fact be matter for our sorrow. We may be stupidly allowing ourselves to be imposed upon by the manifestations of the "pride of life"; to put it in a nutshell, although our faith may not be flagging, we may be beginning to lose our faith in our faith, if one may put it so.[34]

This should be an occasion for recalling with greater explicitness certain constant truths. "I, when I have been lifted up from the earth, will draw all things unto me"[35]—those words of Christ are not, doubtless, an invitation to literal imitation, and we are not Wisdom personified that we should be able to be content to say: "Come over to me all that desire me: and be filled with my fruits." (Ecclus. 24:26). St. Paul, conformed to Christ, traveled the world over, the precusor of a whole army of apostles, and the Church will always be a missionary. And this is at least the symptom of a certain spirit; in other words, we are quite right not to want to be separated from men who are to be led to Christ—if by that we understand the necessity of breaking down the barriers which would be put between them and ourselves by forms of living or thinking which are superseded, and even more so by ways of behaving whose sole justification is an ideal of comfortableness or peace and quiet. We are quite right not to allow ourselves to be shut up in any sort of ghetto, by ourselves any more than by anybody else. But we have to be on our guard against misunderstanding both the truly central position which our faith guarantees us, to the degree of its own strength, and that essential condition of being "set apart" from the world which belongs to every Christian, let alone every priest.[36] If we are really "turned to God" we have "abandoned idols" and cannot "bear the yoke" with those who are deceived by them (1 Thess. 1:9; 1 Cor. 6:9–12; 2 Cor. 6:14–17). And if we show real vitality in this sacred operation and the joyful practice of all that it imposes on us, others will certainly be drawn to this source of life and will not want to be separated from us. The miracle of the drawing power of Christ will continue in and through our lives.

We should, then, have no inhibitions about feeling a profound sympathy with the men who surround us. We should be fully human, for we are obliged to that by our duty of interior sincerity as well as of brotherly love; or rather, that disposition should be something so natural and congenital to us that there is no need to go looking for it. We ought not to get our loyalty to the eternal mixed up with an attachment to the past which is mischievous and even morbid. Yet at the same time we should beware of modern self-sufficiency; we should be wary of making our own the weaknesses and infatuations, the pretentious ignorance and the narrowness of the surrounding milieu, and of giving a welcome to worldliness, whether it be proletarian or middle-class, refined or vulgar. Or rather, we should be always extricating ourselves from it—for unfortunately we are always getting involved in it to a greater or a lesser degree. To sum up; we should always be adapted, and that as spontaneously as possible; but we must do it without ever allowing ourselves, either in behavior or thought, to adapt Christianity itself in the least—that is to say, to de-divinize it or lower it, make it insipid or twist it out of shape. We should have a great love for our age, perpetually as society changes. Psychologies, customs, and social relationships change; man remains, with his evil. This does not mean that we ought not to try everything in our search for betterment; the tenacity of evil can be nothing other than a challenge to a yet more determined and sustained struggle. But suppose for a moment something which we are, unfortunately, far enough away from—a more or less perfect functioning of society; that is, not an economic or political machine more or less adequately powerful, but an exterior order which is as human as possible. With all that granted, the Church's work would not, in a sense, have even started. For her business is not to settle us in comfortably in our earthly existence, but to raise us above it. Her bringing to us of the redemption of Christ means that she wants to tear us free from the evil that is in us and lay us open to another existence; and the other side of the same fact is that if she were to give temporal effectiveness top priority, that very thing would not be granted to her. If she were to wait, in order to carry out in the world the work of salvation, for temporal conditions to undergo an eventual improvement (whatever the terms in which the ideal state of affairs were actually conceived), she would be playing false to her mission, which is to bring safely home not a future humanity at some time to come, but the whole of humanity throughout time—not a mythical humanity but the actual men of each generation.

If, then, we want to be realistic, it is none the less indispensable that our realism should not mistake its object. And if we are anxious to be effective, it is essential that we should not build our foundation on means which are too extrinsic and thus calculated to turn us aside from our end. If we rightly may, and sometimes should, be strict with those who call themselves Catholics—with ourselves—it is essential that we should understand what we do and do it with reference to valid standards. We must not lose sight of the essential.

This essential, which cannot remain as even a distant objective on our horizon if we do not find a place for it in the heart of our present activity, is not something which can be judged from a quantitative point of view. God brings about the saving of us according to laws which are hidden from us as far as their concrete application is concerned, but which are imposed on our faith in principle—the mysterious laws of the community of salvation. And today the prayer of intercession and the sacrifice of charity have lost none of their secret power; moreover, the existence of one saint alone would be sufficient witness to the divine value of the principle by which saints live. But the question is whether our sight is clear enough, and whether we have sufficient knowledge of where to look, to discern among ourselves, in this order of sanctity, the effectiveness of the Church? Let us at least try to catch a glimpse of it. Massive appearance should not hide from us the central reality, nor noisy ideological debate prevent us from hearing the silent breathing of the Spirit. At a time when he was the head of a community which was made up of none but the poor and uneducated, and was without appreciable influence on the destinies of the Empire, the great St. Cyprian said: "As for us, we are philosophers not in word but in act; we do not say great things but we do live them."[37] And that saying remains true, in all its proud humility. The essential is very rarely something that can be much talked about; Christian vitality is in every age very much less dependent on all that is discussed and done and picked to pieces on the world's stage than we are often led to believe. There is a life which it is almost impossible to judge of from the outside; and that life keeps itself going, passes itself on and renews itself under all the turmoil of politics, all the swirl of public opinion, the currents of ideas and the controversies, far removed from the scene of public debate, unsounded and untabulated. The blind see, the deaf hear, the dead are raised to life and the poor have the Gospel preached to them (Luke 7:22); the Kingdom of God shines in secret. Here and there there are sudden glimpses; patches of light break through, widen, and join up with others. A point of light or two in the night suddenly shines more brightly; sometimes there will be patches of blood, to draw our attention. All are so many heralding signs.

Today, when there is so much discussion about Christianity and so much complaining about its "ill-adaptedness" or "ineffectiveness," we should always be returning again and again to these very simple considerations. The best Christians and the most vital are by no means to be found either inevitably or even generally among the wise or the clever, the intelligentsia or the politically-minded or those of social consequence. And consequently what they say does not make the headlines; what they do does not come to the public eye. Their lives are hidden from the eyes of the world, and if they do come to some degree of notoriety, that is usually late in the day, and exceptional, and always attended by the risk of distortion. Within the Church itself it is, as often as not, only after their deaths that some of them acquire an uncontested reputation. Yet these are responsible, more than anyone else, for ensuring that our earth is not a hell on earth. Most of them never think to ask themselves whether their faith is "adapted" or "effective." It is enough, for them, to live it, as reality itself, and reality at its most actual; and because the fruit of all this is often enough a hidden fruit it is none the less wonderful for that. Even if such people are themselves not engaged in external activity, they are the source of all initiative and action, all spadework which is not to be fruitless. It is these people who are our preservation and who give us hope, and it would be a bold man who said that they are less numerous and less active today than in the past.[38] We should not become

blind to the real fruitfulness of our Mother the Church for the sake
of a dream of efficiency which may be no more than a mirage.

But there is another temptation yet. This again is not that of the
simple soul, and it is the most serious of all.

Its point of entry is by way of an observation which was made
as early as in St. Paul's day: "For see your vocation, brethren, that
there are not many wise according to the flesh, not many mighty,
not many noble" (1 Cor. 1:26). The wise, the powerful and the
noble were to come, certainly, but the Apostle's words retain their
profound and many-sided truth none the less for that. Like her
Master, the Church cuts in the eyes of the world the figure of a
slave; on this earth she exists "in the form of a slave" (Phil. 2:7).
And it is not only the wisdom of this world, in the crude sense,
that is lacking in her; it is also—in appearance at least—the wisdom of the spirit. She is no exclusive club for spiritual geniuses or
supermen, no academy of the clever; in fact, she is the very opposite. The warped, the sham and the wretched of every kind
crowd into her, together with the whole host of the mediocre, who
feel especially at home in her and everywhere set the tone of
things. Her most magnificent advances merely serve to accentuate
this characteristic, both in the average run of her members and in
the stuff of her day-to-day existence; to show how, in detail, would
be only too easy. And as a consequence it is hard, not to say entirely impossible, for the "natural man" to find in such a phenomenon the consummation of the saving *kenosis* and the awe-inspiring
traces of the "humility of God"[39]—that is, in so far as his innermost thoughts have not been changed in direction.[40]

The Church has always drawn down on herself the contempt of
the élite. There are many philosophers and devotees of the spiritual life, much concerned about the sources of spiritual vitality,
who refuse her their adherence; some of them are openly hostile to
her, disgusted, like Celsus, by "this scrape-together of simple
minds,"[41] and they turn aside from her, either with the Olympian
serenity of a Goethe or in the Dionysiac fury of a Nietzsche. It is
as if they said: "So you claim to be the Body of Christ, do you?—
the Body of God? Could the Body of God really be made of such
coarse stuff as that? And to start with, how can Divinity have a
body anyhow?"[42]

There are others among these sophisticated men who feel that they are doing the Church full justice and protest when they are described as her adversaries. After all, they would stand up for her if need were; they think she plays a very useful part. "What!" says one of them, replying to some friends who considered him too favorable to the Christian schools. "Do you want me to explain Parmenides to my cook?"[43] But they keep their distance; they don't want for themselves a faith which would make them one with all the wretched creatures above whom they rank themselves in virtue of their aesthetic culture, their powers of rational reflection and their concern with the things of the spirit; they are an aristocracy who don't see themselves mixing with the herd. In their view, the Church leads men by ways that are altogether too well-trodden. They willingly concede her her skill in presenting higher truth under the veil of imagery;[44] but they distinguish themselves as those who know, from the mass of "those who believe," and claim to know the Church better than she knows herself. They "place" her, condescendingly, and grant themselves the power of disentangling the deeper meaning of her doctrines and actions—without her consent—by virtue of a "metaphysical transposition."[45] They place their own intuition above her faith, as they would place the absolute above the relative, or direct and active participation in the divine knowledge above indirect and passive participation. One might describe them as "specialists of the *logos*"[46]—but specialists who have not read, in St. Paul, how the Logos repulses "every height that exalteth itself against the knowledge of God (2 Cor. 10:5). They are the wise—but not wise enough to see how for twenty centuries the prophecy has been worked out: "I will destroy the wisdom of the wise" (Is. 29:14; 1 Cor. 1:19). They are the rich who have never taken in the first beatitude. Some of them, setting themselves up as the leaders of schools or sects, add to the attraction of the promise of knowledge that of the secret—like Valentine in the early days, or that Faustus under whose influence St. Augustine suffered for a time,[47] or, to quote an example from our own day, René Guénon—for the mirage of initiation has a fascination for minds at every level. Yet others remain in their solitude; and that is not always in virtue of a diabolical refusal—sometimes, and much less mysteriously, it is quite simply an absurd pretentiousness. It may be merely a case of the disgust felt by a lofty intelligence for ways of thinking and living which would get him mixed up with the common crowd; or the shivering recoil of the "sensitive soul." And thus there develops a "distinguished individualism which is, however, a closed one, admitting at most only a few chosen beings to a friendly sharing in interior experience."[48] There is a fear that just as the Church would hamper the freedom of investigation and put the curb on the adventurousness of spiritual impulse, so also strict adherence to her would surely involve something like regimentation and a kind of pigging in with the herd.

The Christian consciousness itself can give out a faint echo of these objections and this repugnance. Faith may not be shaken by them, but all the same they sometimes have the effect of straining the bonds that bind us into the Church and lessening their strength and holding power. Without going as far as making an actual break, we can come to forget the close correlation of ecclesiastical faithfulness and religious faithfulness, for the fact is that Christianity may, at the level of truth, emerge triumphant from the challenge, and the Church yet not appear correspondingly justified; at least, the theoretical justification may not win a downright victory over an experienced repugnance. Impartial enquiry may indeed establish that the wisdom she offers and infuses does not, in fact, consist of that collection of "puerile futilities" which St. Augustine believed it to be before the preaching of St. Ambrose opened his eyes.[49] It may lead a man to discover the solidity of her dogma, even to get a glimpse of the depth of her mysteries, and the orthodox interpretation of them given by the great Doctors of the Church. It may bring him to admire the artistic splendours and the cultural riches which have glorified the human aspect of her, at certain periods at least. But all that does not change the obvious commonness of the binding medium which all Catholic living has to use from day to day and in which we must ourselves be set.

André Malraux, confronted with the pictures in the Roman catacombs and their first graphic expression of the Word which was heard in Christ, was driven to exclaim: "How badly these poor figures answer to that voice and all its depths!"[50]—a reaction we may develop further. Won't it be so, and fatally so, with every expression of the Catholic reality, whatever its mode and its nature? What, in fact, does happen to revelation in current preaching—what becomes of the summons of God in the popular mind, or of the Kingdom of God in many an imagination among the devout or the theologically-minded? What becomes of the holy love of unity in hearts which are all too inadequately purified of human passion, or of mystery—all too often—in our textbooks? Pascal was much impressed by the fittingness of maintaining two extremes while covering the whole space that lies between, and thus uniting so many truths "which seem repugnant and yet all subsist in a wonderful order"—yet in practice this dynamic synthesis very often transforms itself into some flat-foot formula of the happy medium. The wonderful *complexio oppositorum* held out to us by every aspect of Catholicism does, in point of fact, cause considerable alarm and despondency in a great many believers. The Church herself does not as a rule encourage overbold thought or too-high-flying spirituality; for the forms which she approves most willingly must be such as can be accepted by the average Catholic environment—and that, one must admit, is always "something somewhat insipid and somewhat mediocre"[51]— which all provides perpetually rich matter for the *irrisio infidelium,* even from among the educated. And in truth, if we look at it realistically, not in the rarefied atmosphere of pure idea but in concrete reality, the Church is—as Newman pointed out—a humiliated body which calls forth insult and impiety, sharp revulsion or at best an indulgent reserve, from men who do not live by faith.

There is no question of simply suffering in silence the really destructive elements in all this, or of accepting it wholesale as something to be desired; it is a matter of *assuming* it, of taking it all upon ourselves, and that with a loyalty which will not deserve the name if it is of the surface only. There is no "private Christianity," and if we are to accept the Church we must take her as she is, in her human day-to-day reality just as much as in her divine and eternal ideality; for a separation of the two is impossible both in fact and by right. Loving the Church means loving her in the full massiveness of her tradition, all repugnance overcome, and burrowing deep, so to speak, into the massiveness of her life, as the seed goes deep into the earth. Equally, it means giving up the insidious drug of religious philosophies which would take the place of our faith, or offer to transpose it. For such is the Catholic way of losing oneself in order to find oneself. The mystery of salvation cannot reach us or save us without this final mediation; we have to push to its conclusion the logic of the Incarnation, by which Divinity adapts itself to human weakness. If we are going to have the treasure, then we must also have the "earthen vessels" which contain it (See 2 Cor. 4:7) and outside which it evaporates. We have to accept what St. Paul, who knew all about the contrary temptation, called "simplicity in Christ" (2 Cor. 11:3). We must be "the common people of God" with no reservations made. To put it another way: the necessity of being humble in order to cleave to Christ involves the necessity of being humble in order to seek Him in His Church and add to the submission of the intellect "brotherly love."[53]

He alone participates in Christ who keeps himself united to all the members of His body. Insofar as he is rich, he does not say to the poor man: "You are not necessary to me." Insofar as he is strong he does not say that to the weak: insofar as he is wise, he does not say it to the foolish. . . . He is a part of the Body of Christ, which is the Church. And it is necessary that he should know that those who, in the Church, appear weak, poor, foolish—like the sinners—should be surrounded with all the greater honour and watched over with all the more exacting care. On that condition he will be able to say to himself: "I am one of those who fear the Lord." It is necessary that he should have compassion on men of this kind, as opposed to showing himself embarrassed by them; that he should suffer with those who suffer, in order to learn by experience that we are all one Body with many different united members.[54]

Such is the price of a good thing which cannot have any price set upon it—Catholic communion. The point was made as early as by St. Clement of Rome, one of the earliest among Peter's successors, who thus went at one stroke to the very heart of the meaning of the Church: "Christ belongs to all those who have a humble attitude and not to those who set themselves above the flock."[55]

As far as the superior type of man can see, everything in the Church is low-grade. But "power sorts well with this poor quality"—in fact it sorts well with it alone. The idealized forms in which that kind of man finds such satisfaction seem higher and purer to him only because they are the product of his own thought. It does not matter whether he is seeking in them an instrument for the fashioning of a rich personality which is both integrated and forceful; or a reference frame for interpreting the universe with; or a springboard from which to project himself beyond the limits which enclose the human condition. In each and every case they are equally powerless; they cannot even begin to change his own heart. For all its apparent sublimity the thought of the superior man is no more than a mirror in which he admires himself and which in consequence holds him hypnotized in vanity. It sets up an idol in his heart (Ez. 14:3 and 7; Eph. 4:18) and when he throws himself into the arms of it his embrace finds nothingness—the One which is pure only if it is not being, or the Universal Possibility from which the multiple states of being are derived: "Id vanitate sentit humana non veritate divina."[56] We know all too well—unfortunately—that the profession of Catholicism, even militant Catholicism, does not automatically confer sanctity, and we must admit that amongst us (and even in surroundings distinguished by fervour and freedom from contamination) much human narrowness often places obstacles in the way of the action of the Spirit. Yet we also know well that the humblest of our saints is freer, interiorly, than the greatest of our masters of wisdom. The former speaks modestly of salvation while the latter is all ready to talk about deliverance; but it does not take long to see which of the two is, in point of fact, "delivered." The noblest and sincerest efforts, thrown awry by an initial *hubris,* end up in the hollowest of pretensions; the only depths which are not deceptive are those which the Spirit Himself hollows out within a man (1 Cor. 2:10), and they presuppose the ground of the common faith, accepted without second thoughts and never abandoned.[57] There, and there only, is the royal road.

"O humility, O sublimity! House of clay and palace of the

king, body of death and temple of light! A thing of scorn to the proud, and spouse of Christ."[58] In all her apparent crudity the Church is the sacrament—the true and effective sign—of these "depths of God." And by the same token there are opened to us the depths of man—"deep calls to deep."[59] That is why the passage from St. Paul commented on earlier is at one and the same time the statement of a scandal to the "natural man" and a cry of triumph to the believer—"For see your vocation, brethren, that there are not many wise according to the flesh, not many mighty, not many noble. But the foolish things of this world hath God chosen, that he may confound the wise: and the weak things of this world hath God chosen, that he may confound the strong. And the base things of the world and the things that are contemptible, hath God chosen; and things that are not, that he might bring to nought things that are: that no flesh should glory in his sight" (1 Cor. 1:26–29).

It takes a miracle of grace to enable us to see things so; without it, the most edifying sentiments and the richest spiritual gifts are merely obstacles, making men like the cedar of Lebanon which has not yet been broken by the Lord—they feed pride and close the heart to charity. And as we have said, they can become a temptation even in the heart of the Church herself. If something of the sort ever becomes the case with us, perhaps we shall benefit from recalling to mind the example of men who have heroically overcome such a situation, together with the concrete circumstances under which they did it.

When Newman, driven by an interior logic which was something much more than a "paper logic," knelt at the feet of Father Domenico Barberi and asked him to receive him into the Church, it was not just that he sacrificed a situation, and habits dear to him, and delightful friendships, and a spiritual home loved with a certain melancholy but always tenderly, and a reputation which was already a glorious one. The situation was even more unfavorable than that. It was an autumn evening in the year 1845, toward the end of the pontificate of Gregory XVI; to Newman, Catholicism had everywhere the appearance of a thing beaten by life, and all the sorrier a figure because it trailed after it so many ironic relics of a recent splendor. It could have no human attraction whatsoever for the one-time Fellow of Oriel; as he wrote later: "Ours is not an age of temporal glory, of dutiful princes, of loyal governments, of large possessions, of ample leisure, of famous schools, of learned foundations, of well-stored libraries, of honoured sanctuaries. Rather, it is like the first age of the Church, when there was little of station, of nobility, of learning, of wealth, in the holy heritage; when Christians were chiefly of the lower orders; when we were poor and ignorant, when we were despised and hated by the great and philosophical as a low rabble, or a stupid and obstinate association, or a foul and unprincipled conspiracy. It is like that first age, in which no saint is recorded in history who fills the mind as a great idea, as St. Thomas Aquinas or St. Ignatius fills it, and when the ablest of so-called Christian writers belonged to heretical schools. We certainly have little to show for ourselves; and the words of the Psalm are fulfilled in us: 'They have set fire to thy sanctuary, they have defiled the dwelling-place of thy name on earth. Our signs we have not seen; there is no prophet. . . .' "[60] Indeed, Newman found nothing attractive about Roman Catholics; he admitted that he did not find himself attuned to them, and that he expected little from them, and that in becoming one of their number he had made himself an outcast—he had, as he put it, turned to the wilderness. And, of course, at that time he could not know of all the other thorns which were to tear at him in the course of his long trek across that wilderness. Yet to his soul, full of faith, the step was inevitable, and he was never to regret it for a moment.[61]

Again, we may read what St. Augustine has to say in the eighth book of the *Confessions*. He had the story from his friend Simplicianus, and it is well known how deep an impression it made upon him at the moment when he also was in the process of making a similar decision. The aged Victorinus was a philosopher, "skilled in all the liberal disciplines"; yet he, who had taught so many noble senators and who, as a famous thinker, had seen his own statue set up in the Forum, eventually "thought it no shame to make himself the slave of Christ and bend his neck beneath the yoke of humility and his brow under the shame of the cross." But that did not come about without a long resistance, strengthened by a superb incomprehension—for which the example is none the less fine:

O Lord, Lord, who dost bow down Thy heavens and descend, dost touch the mountains and they smoke, by what means didst Thou find Thy way into that breast? He read, so Simplicianus said, Holy Scripture; he investigated all the Christian writings most carefully and minutely. And he said, not publicly, but to Simplicianus privately, and as one friend to another: "I would have you know that I am now a Christian." Simplicianus answered: "I shall not believe it, nor count you among Christians unless I see you in the Church of Christ." Victorinus asked with some faint mockery: "Then is it the walls that make Christians?" He went on saying that he was a Christian, and Simplicianus went on with the same denial, and Victorinus always repeated his retort about the walls. The fact was that he feared to offend his friends, important people and worshippers of . . . demons; he feared their enmity might fall heavily upon him from the height of their Babylon-dignity as from the cedars of Lebanon which the Lord had not yet brought down. But when by reading in all earnestness he had drawn strength he grew afraid that Christ might deny him before His angels if he were ashamed to confess Christ before men. He felt that he was guilty of a great crime in being ashamed of the sacraments of the lowliness of Your Word, when he had not been ashamed of the sacrilegious rites of those demons of pride whom in his pride he had worshipped. So he grew proud towards vanity and humble towards truth. Quite suddenly and without warning he said to Simplicianus, as Simplicianus told me: "Let us go to Church. I wish to be made a Christian." Simplicianus, unable to control his joy, went with him. He was instructed in the first mysteries of the faith, and not long after gave in his name that he might be regenerated by baptism. . . .[62]

If Victorinus had not made up his mind to take this decisive step and lose himself among the humble flock of the "practising" faithful, we should doubtless still remember him as a distinguished philosopher. Perhaps we should be able to admire him still as the thinker who first conceived the elements of that internal theory of the Trinity for which St. Augustine was to provide the West with the definitive formulae. We may even imagine that he would have been capable, without entering the Church, of composing his hymns to the Trinity, in which case his name would also live among those of the poets of dogma.[63] But if all that were so he would still have no better title than the one which he has, for he would not have deserved to be called by a name which is common indeed and in the eyes of many without distinction, yet is the finest of all when its significance is understood; he would not have been a "Catholic."[64]

NOTES

1. A. Molien, "Simon (Richard)," *Dictionnaire de Théologie Catholique,* vol. xiv, col. 2112.

2. Thus Tertullian, *Apologia,* ch. xxxii, no. 1; ch. xxxix, no. 2 (pp. 94 and 106 in Waltzing's edition): *Ad Scapulum,* ch. ii (vol. 1, p. 541 in Oehler's edition): Melito of Sardis, quoted in Eusebius, *Hist. Eccl.,* bk. iv, ch. xxvi, no. 11.

3. One cannot read without profound sadness the reflections of non-believing authors on this subject, however exaggerated they may be; for example, those of Leon Brunschvicg in his *Le Progrès de la Conscience dans la Philosophie Occidentale,* 1927, vol. i, pp. 221–2.

4. St. Hilary of Poitiers, *In Psalm.,* lxvii, no. 12 (pp. 287–8 in Zingerle's edition).

5. Bruno de Solages, *Pour Rebâtir une Chrétienté,* 1938, p. 174; cf. Leo XIII, Letter to His Eminence Cardinal Rampolla, Oct. 8, 1895: "Things human change, but the beneficent virtue of the supreme magisterium of the Church comes from on high and remains always the same. . . . Established to last as long as time, it follows with a loving vigilance the advance of humanity, and does not refuse (as its detractors falsely claim) to come to terms with the reasonable needs of the time as far as this is possible."

6. *Sermo CV,* no. 9 (PL, 38, 623).

7. St. Augustine, *Sermo CCLII,* no. 3 (PL, 38, 1173–4).

8. Renan, "Du Libéralisme Doctrinal," in *La Liberté de Penser,* May 15, 1848.

9. Renan, letter to the Abbé Cognat of Sept. 5, 1846, quoted in J. Cognat, *M. Renan Hier et Aujourd'hui,* 1886, p. 203.

10. Renan, Marc-Aurèle, 3rd ed., 1882, p. 109; cf. pp. 403–4.

11. Renan, *Questions Contemporaines,* p. 423: *Drames Philosophiques,* pp. 279–80 (Act 1 of *Le Prêtre de Némi*).

12. Letter to the Abbé Cognat, in J. Cognat, *M. Renan,* p. 203: *Souvenirs d'Enfance et de Jeunesse; Questions Contemporaines,* p. 457.

13. Proudhon, *De la Justice dans la Révolution et dans l'Eglise,* new ed., vol. iv, p. 332.

14. *Contra Litteras Petiliani,* bk. i, ch. xxix, no. 31 (PL, 43, 2509).

15. *Apologia Pro Vita Sua,* ch. v.

16. Cf. the panegyric on St. Rémi delivered at Rheims by Mgr. Chapoulie, Bishop of Angers; confronted with "the great upheaval which has been going on for more than a century in society," the duty of the Catholic is "to try to understand, and above all to desire to love." Certainly, "there are audacities we may not like, and certain 'discoveries' may seem to us to be

naive," but "when all is said and done, is it really preferable . . . to shut oneself up within a disdainful and immovable refusal, to continue to seek a timid refuge in love of the past?" If we are to succeed in disengaging the eternal truth of the Gospel from a crumbling past, "as did St. Rémi," we must have "a powerful faith in Jesus Christ and the coming of His Kingdom" ("Semaine Religieuse d'Angers," *Témoignage Chrétien*, Nov. 14, 1952).

17. *Du Régime Temporel et de la Liberté*, 1933, p. 139.

18. *Epist. XV* (PL, 22, 355).

19. *In Cantica, Sermo LXXVII*, nos. 1–2 (PL, 183, 1155–6).

20. Particularly in bk. iv (PL, 182, 771–88).

21. Letter cccxv.

22. *Compendium*, chs. i and iv.

23. Dedication to the *Opuscula* of Denis the Carthusian: "I address myself to Your Beatitude, not in my own name but in the name of many, not to say in the name of all. The act of solicitude which we ask for, we call reform of the Church. . . . What is there in the Church which is not contaminated or corrupted? What is there left of integrity among the clergy, of honour among the nobility, or of sincerity among the people? All is put to confusion, wounded, ruined, mutilated. From the soles of the feet to the crown of the head, there is nothing healthy left."

24. Emmanuel Mounier, "Un Surnaturalisme Historique," *Georges Bernanos*, p. 113.

25. Cf. Paul Claudel, letter to André Gide of Jan. 9, 1912.

26. His Holiness Pope Pius XII, Encyclical *Mystici Corporis Christi*.

27. This reflection appears several times in the correspondence of St. Francis Xavier, and he impresses it again upon his faithful disciple Gaspard Barzée in his final advice to him; cf. Catherine Ranquet's letter to Fr. de Bus of May 4, 1647: "Before God, I am nothing but an obstacle to His designs, and the destruction of his work . . ." (quoted in G. Gueudré, *Catherine Ranquet, Mystique et Educatrice*, 1952, p. 168).

28. *Paul Claudel Interroge le Cantique des Cantiques*, p. 277.

29. Cf. Cardinal Wyszynki's letter of Nov. 1952, published in the Cracow Catholic weekly *Tygodnik Powszechny*: "The active presence of Catholics in the universal Church needs a deepening . . . It ought to be the presence of *domestici fidei*, incorporated in Christ living in the Church . . . we must induce men to break with religious individualism; with the facile criticisms of far-off observers who impose on the Church (often conceived of in a highly abstract fashion) great demands, and forget that these demands should first be imposed upon oneself, since the Church . . . is ourselves" (*L'Actualité Religieuse dans le Monde*, April 1, 1953, p. 28). See also De Montcheuil, *Aspects de l'Eglise*, pp. 77–9.

30. Here I am not envisaging any of the objective problems which may really present themselves. It is not that I wish to question the importance of such, but that to do so would be to go beyond the bounds of my subject. All I am attempting here is to define the attitude without which such problems would of necessity be mispresented and would bear within their very formulation risks of misunderstanding or error.

31. There is a permanent value in what Fr. Alfred Soras wrote in 1938 in *Action Catholique et Action Temporelle* concerning the "law of incarnation," its depth, scope and problems.

32. One of the most recent examples of this is the allocution of His Holi-

ness Pope Pius XII to the superiors of female religious gathered in congress in Rome in Sept. 1952: ". . . Where things which are not essential are concerned, adapt yourselves as reason and rightly-ordered charity counsel you."

33. Cf. Joseph Folliet, *Presence de l'Eglise,* 1949, ch. iii: "Maladies Séniles et Maladies Infantiles des Catholiques Français": Fr. Louis Beirnaert's invitation "not to entrench ourselves in resentment" in his "Fidélité à l'Eglise et Fidélité à l'Homme," *Etudes,* vol. cli, p. 16.

34. This temptation will already be partly got rid of if we see how others before us have recognized and overcome it. Newman came close to giving way to it during his Anglican period—admittedly, within the framework of a situation very different from ours. It has been said of a certain type of politician: "He both believes in his truths and despairs of them" (Etienne Borne, in *Terre Humaine,* Oct. 1952, p. 7). It would be even more illogical for a Christian to harbor such an attitude of mind with regard to his faith.

35. John xii. 32; cf. Bengt Sundkler's stimulating study, "Jésus et les Paiens," *Revue d' Histoire et de Philosophie Religieuse,* 1936, pp. 462–99.

36. *Sanctus = segregatus;* cf. Acts xiii. 2; Rom. i. 1: ". . . called to be an apostle, separated unto the gospel of God."

37. St. Cyprian, *De Bono Patientae,* ch. iii: "Nos autem . . . qui philosophi non verbis sed factis sumus . . . qui non loquimur magna sed vivimus" (vol. i. p. 398 in Hartel's edition): Minucius Felix, *Octavius,* ch. xxxviii, no. 6 (PL, 3, 359a).

38. Cf. *Paradoxes,* pp. 89–117 (on the subject of efficacity). The reader should also consult Henry Dumery's *Les Trois Tentations de l'Apostolat Moderne,* 1948: Yves Congar, *Jalons Pour une Théologie du Laicat,* 1953, ch. ix: "Au Monde et pas du Monde."

39. That is, insofar as there has not been a *metanoia;* cf. Mark i, 15; Rom. xii. 2; Ephes. iv. 23.

40. St. Augustine, *Enchiridion,* ch. cviii: ". . . ut humana superbia per humilitatem Dei argueretur ac sanaretur" (PL, 40, 283): *Sermo CLXXXIV,* no. 1: "Teneant ergo humiles humilitatem Dei" (p. 74 in Lambot's edition of 1940): *Sermo LI,* nos. 4–5 (PL, 38, 336): *Sermo CXVII,* no. 17 (PL, 38, 671): *Sermo CXXIII,* no. 1 (ibid., col. 684): *Sermo CXLII,* no. 2 (ibid., col. 778): *De Doctrina Christiana,* bk. i, ch. xiv: no. 13 (PL, 34, 24): *Confessiones:* "Non enim tenebam Jesum, humilis humilem": *In Joannem,* tract. ii, no. 4; tract. xxv, no. 16 (PL, 35, 1390–1 and 1604): *De Trinitate,* bk. iv, ch. ii, no. 4 (PL, 42, 889): bk. viii, ch. v, no. 7 (ibid., col. 952): *De Agone Christiano,* ch. xi, no. 12 (PL, 40, 297): *De Div. Quaest.,* lxxxiii, q. 69, no. 9 (ibid., col. 79): Pope St. Leo the Great, *De Ascensione Domini Sermo II,* ch. i: "Sacramentum salutis nostrae . . . per dispensationem humilitatis impletum est" (PL, 54, 397a): Pope St. Gregory the Great, *Moralia in Job,* bk. ii, ch. xxxv, no. 58: "Dum ipse humilitatem carnis suscepit, in se credentibus vota humilitatis infudit" (p. 224 in the edition of De Gaudemaris): cf. Fr. Adnès' "L'Humilité, Vertu Spécifiquement Chrétienne, d'après Saint Augustin," RAM, 1952. Henri Bergson speaks of the "divine humility" in the *Deux Sources,* p. 249.

41. Celsus, *True Discourse,* i (quoted in Origen's *Contra Celsum,* bk. iii, ch. xliv; cf. chs. lv and lx); cf. Goethe's ". . . a narrow-minded mass, ready to cringe and be lorded over."

42. Celsus, *op. cit.;* cf. St. Hilary of Poitiers, *Tractatus in Pslam.,* i. no. 5: ". . . sacramentum Dei corporati" (p. 22 in Zingerle's edition).

43. Victor Cousin, quoted by Franck in his *Nouveaux Essais de Critique Philosophique,* 1890, pp. 43–4: ". . . he regarded it as sheer cruelty to deprive of their twilight those whose eyes were closed to light of another kind." And Proudhon mocked at the philosophers of his day who "on the strength of having unpicked one or two metaphysical tangles" considered themselves superior to the Church (*De la Justice dans la Révolution et dans l'Eglise,* vol. i. p. 275).

44. Cf. Victor Cousin, *Fragments Métaphysiques,* preface to the second edition, 1833: "Religion, which addresses itself to all men, would be wide of its aim if it were to present itself under a form which could be grasped by intelligence alone . . . It is different with philosophy. Philosophy speaks to intelligence alone, and in consequence to a very small number of men; but that small number is the élite and vanguard of humanity . . . It takes a bad philosophy and a bad theology to quarrel. Christianity is the cradle of modern philosophy; and I myself have pointed out more than one lofty truth hidden under the veil of Christian imagery" (pp. lxxi–xxii in the fifth edition of 1866).

45. René Guénon, *Autorité Spirituelle et Pouvoir Temporel,* 1930, p. 36: *L'Homme et son Devoir selon le Vedanta,* 1925, p. 51: *Introduction Générale à l'Etude des Doctrines Hindoues,* 1921, p. 151, etc. Cf. Schuon's *De l'Unité Transcendante des Religions,* 1948, pp. 61 and 10–22, where there is an attempt to persuade us to disengage the "naked truth" from the symbol or form which encloses it in faith and transcend dogma through penetrating to its "internal dimension."

46. Cf. Marcel Mery, *La Critique du Christianisme chez Renouvier,* 1953, vol. ii, p. 498.

47. St. Augustine, *Confessions,* bk. v, chs. iii–vii.

48. Dom Odo Casel, O.S.B. (he is talking about the hermetic books).

49. *Confessions,* bk. vi, ch. iv, no. 5: "Confundebar et convertebar et gaudebam. Deus meus, quod Ecclesia, tua unica, corpus Unici tui, in qua mihi nomen Christi infanti est inditum, non saperet infantiles nugas."

50. André Malraux, *La Monnaie de l'Absolu,* p. 160.

51. *Paul Claudel Interroge le Cantique des Cantiques,* p. 362; cf. his letter to Gabriel Frizeau, *Correspondance* (Claudel-Frizeau-Jammes), ed. Blanchet, 1953, p. 35.

52. Cf. E. Kaesermann, quoted by C. Spicq in his *L'Epître aux Hébreux,* p. 277: this Epistle "makes no mention of private Christianity, and faith, like obedience, is characteristic of the community as such."

53. 1 Pet. 1:22: ". . . with a brotherly love, from a sincere heart"; 2:17: "Love the brotherhood"; iii. 8: ". . . being the lovers of the brotherhood"; cf. 1 Thess. i. 4:9.

54. St. Ambrose, *In Psalm.,* cxviii, sermo viii, no. 54 (PL, 15, 1317c-d).

55. Epistle to the Corinthians, ch. 16.

56. St. Augustine. The vanity of all that which is *figmentum mentis* as distinguished from the truth which comes from God is a frequently-recurring theme in his thought; see, for example, *De Trinitate,* bk. iv, no. 1: "Satiavit illos phantasma eorum, non veritas tua, quam repellendo resiliunt, et in suam vanitatem cadunt . . . " (PL, 42, 887); cf. Rom. i. 18–22.

57. William of Saint-Thierry, *Aenigma Fidei* (PL, 180, 407–8); cf. Origen, *In Levit.*, hom. xii, no. 5, concerning the faith which "perseveres in its simple confession as in virginal integrity."

58. St. Bernard, *In Cantica*, sermo xxvii, no. 14 (PL, 183, 920d).

59. Cf. St. Ambrose, *De Isaac et Anima*, ch. viii, no. 67: "Philosophi curulia illa animarum in suis libris expressere certamina, nec tamen ad palmam pervenire potuerunt; quoniam summitatem Verbi et altitudinem illorum animae nescierunt, quam cognovit haec anima, in qua erat Verbi conversio" (PL, 14, 528b); also St. Bernard, *In Cantica*, sermo lxxx, nos. 2–3; "Celsa creatura, in capacitate quidem Majestatis . . . Eo anima magna est, quo capax aeternorum" (PL, 183, 1167c-d).

60. *Present Position of Catholics in England*, lecture ix.

61. Newman, letters to Coleridge (Nov. 16, 1844), Keble (Nov. 21, 1844) and his sister Jemima (Mar. 15, 1845); cf. Louis Bouyer, *Newman*, pp. 298–314.

62. *Confessions*, bk. viii, ch. ii, nos. 3–4. Concerning Simplicianus, who was to follow St. Ambrose in the See of Milan, see G. Bardy in his *Oeuvres de Saint Augustin*, 1952, vol. x, pp. 383–9.

63. In point of fact these hymns, like the other Christian works of Victorinus, come after his public conversion. On Marius Victorinus, see P. Sejourne, "Victorinus Afer," DTC, vol. xv, 2887–954. The three hymns to the Trinity are in PL, 8, 1139–46.

64. A more far-reaching examination of some of the problems discussed in this chapter will be found in Fr. Karl Rahner's recent work *Die Chancen des Christentums heute*, Cologne, Erzbischofliche Seelsorgeamt.

GOD OF WRATH OR GOD OF LOVE?

PHILIPPE DE LA TRINITÉ, O.C.D.

Love and Works

IN the Church of God there will always be actives and contemplatives, since both are necessary. The spiritual temperament of the first category tends to be aggressive; that of the second, loving. "Love tends to receive its object, for it desires one thing only: to be united to that which gives it pleasure. The irascible, on the other hand, is orientated towards action, since it tends to struggle to master whatever threatens it."[1]

Nevertheless, though action means struggle against the exterior obstacles arising from people and things, the solitary life also takes the form of struggle, in a grim attempt at self-mastery with the aim of attaining to divine contemplation. "At the beginning of the *Institutions* . . . Cassian portrays the monk as a soldier armed for battle; a little further on, he compares the novice who submits himself to his elders for the purposes of his education to a youth who longs to take part in the Olympic games. It is always combat that is involved; the comparisons being taken either from the military life or from athletics. . . . It was from the language of athletics that our word for spiritual labor, 'asceticism', was derived."[2] It would therefore be wrong to attempt to erect any fundamental opposition between actives and contemplatives. The contrary is true: love needs to be strong in both cases, both for doing and for contemplating, and the aggressiveness that is based on love has no supernatural value except according to the amount of love that is involved. That is why the contemplative life is eminently apostolic and superior to the life of action;[3] it is also the reason why the mixed life that comprises both action and contemplation is ultimately the best and the most harmonious of all. "It is better to give to others the fruits of one's contemplation than merely to contemplate."[4]

It would be quite ridiculous, in choosing one's vocation, to go against one's aptitudes and desires; this would simply be asceticism turned inside out. Grace does not destroy nature. The variety of the states and conditions of existence corresponds to the diversities of temperament and character. God is quite capable of raising His own obstacles in the way of those He chooses: it is sufficient to let Him act upon us.[5]

In any case, close scrutiny will show that there is no kind of existence from which all works can be entirely absent. Every existence necessarily implies, in some form or other, works arising from the duties of one's station in life and from brotherly love.

The entire spirituality of St. John of the Cross is based on the proper performance of the duties of one's station, which are to be fulfilled lovingly. Before he gives his nine spiritual "cautions"—three against the world, three against the devil and three against the flesh—he expresses himself quite simply as follows:

"With habitual care and with no further labour or other kind of exercise, failing not of his own part to do that which his state enjoins on him, he will progress very quickly to great perfection, gaining all the virtues together and attaining to holy peace."[6]

But if a living faith always produces works (whether these are insignificant or important from the human point of view makes no difference in the eyes of God), they are only valuable in proportion to the love that informs them. "Faith . . . worketh by charity" (Gal. 5:6). "The Lord does not look so much at the magnitude of anything we do as at the love with which we do it," as St. Teresa of Avila succinctly puts it.[7]

And St. John of the Cross adds: "More does God desire of thee the least degree of purity of conscience than all the works that thou canst perform."[8]

This is why St. Thérèse of the Child Jesus can even say, "God has no need of our works but only of our love." But this is an intentional paradox: her example proved that a genuine love of God includes works of brotherly love. In this she was a true daughter of Teresa of Avila, whose words have the genuine spirit of the Gospels: "When I see people very diligently trying to discover what kind of prayer they are experiencing and so completely wrapped up in their prayers that they seem afraid to stir, or to indulge in a moment's thought, lest they should lose the slightest degree of the tenderness and devotion they have been feeling, I realize how little they understand of the road to the attainment of union. They think that the whole thing consists in this. But no, sisters, no; what the Lord desires is works. If you see a sick woman to whom you can give some help, never be affected by the fear that your devotion will suffer, but take pity on her: if she is in pain, you should feel pain too; if necessary, fast so that she may have your food, not so much for her sake as because you know it to be your Lord's will. That is true union with His will. . . . I have said a great deal about this elsewhere, sisters, because I know that if we were to fail here we should be lost."[9] "If we have attained great perfection here [in our love for our neighbor], we have done everything."[10] The theological virtue of charity governs the two precepts of the love of God and the love of one's neighbor, and whatsoever we do unto the least of our brothers we do unto Christ.

"If I speak with the tongues of men, and of angels, and have not charity, I am become as sounding brass or a tinkling cymbal"

(1 Cor. 13:1). Faith, knowledge, prophecy, are nothing without
charity. And philanthropy without charity is nothing either. But
what exactly is love? "Charity is patient, is kind. . . . Charity . . .
rejoiceth with the truth; beareth all things, believeth all things,
hopeth all things, endureth all things. . . . Charity never falleth
away" (1 Cor. 13:4–8). Patience, says St. Francis de Sales,
best ensures our perfection. "The soul enkindled with love is a soul
that is gentle, meek, humble and patient."[11] This love—with its
works—is the only kind of love with which the heart of God is
concerned. "We do so much good when we give ourselves and all
that we have."[12]

Love and Penance

In practice the duties of one's station involve a whole complex
of compulsions and privations that enter quite naturally into line
with renunciation, with the will of God, and hence with love. But
this is not enough.

People who do no more than this do less than they should. We
must now turn to the aggressiveness of asceticism—not as it concerns others (this is the tactic of false piety), but as it concerns
ourselves. Anyone with any character must lay certain works of
supererogation upon himself. But the question arises, how to be
guided to discern aright, since not every inner prompting necessarily comes from the Holy Spirit. St. John of the Cross gives two
criteria: reason and faith:

"Enter into account with thy reason to do that which it counsels
thee on the road to God, and it will be of greater worth to thee
with respect to thy God than all the works that thou doest without
this counsel and than all the spiritual delights that thou seekest."[13]
What then, in this matter of asceticism, is the criterion of reason,
whereby one may discern the real value of an inspiration or a decision? St. Thomas answers with his usual clarity. "Can one sin
by fasting excessively or going without too much sleep?" he asks.[14]
Here is his reply:

According to Aristotle [*Pol.,* I], advice should vary according to
whether it is the end or the means with which we are concerned. The

end should be sought without qualification; the means should be employed according to the end: medicine improves health as much as it possibly can because health is its end, but it uses remedies only to the extent that they are beneficial to health.

In the spiritual life the love of God should be regarded as the end; fasting, denying oneself sleep and performing other bodily penances—these are not sought as ends, because, as St. Paul says in the Epistle to the Romans [xiv. 17], 'The Kingdom of God is not meat and drink'; these penances are used as means necessary for a certain end—to overcome the lusts of the flesh, according to the Apostle's words to the Corinthians [1 ix. 27]: 'I chastise my body and bring it into subjection.' They should therefore be used to a reasonable extent—for example, as a remedy against concupiscence—but without exhausting nature, in conformity with the words of the Epistle to the Romans [xii. 1]: 'Present your bodies a living sacrifice, holy, pleasing unto God, your reasonable service.'

But if, by fasting, and depriving oneself of sleep, and other practices of a like kind, the natural powers are weakened to such an extent that the actions required by duty are unable to be performed—as, preaching by the preacher, teaching by the teacher, singing by the singer—then there is no doubt that sin has been committed. Similarly, too, sin would be committed by anyone who was prevented by his voluntary privations from fulfilling his duties as a husband to his wife. Hence, Saint Jerome's sayings: 'Anyone who burdens his body immoderately with fasts and excessive watchings offers the sacrifice of a criminal, the holocaust of a robber,' and again: 'Anyone who considers fasting more important than charity, going without sleep more important than the proper exercise of his bodily faculties, forfeits his dignity as a reasonable human being.'

One is reminded of St. Francis de Sales' saying: I am a man above all things. How careful St. Thomas is here, as always, not to asphyxiate poor human nature by strangling love under aggressiveness. This is not Port Royal! But there can be special cases. Discussing the extreme forms of penance adopted by St. Margaret of Cortona, François Mauriac observes very justly: "A contemplative lacking in physical charm and untouched by carnal love cannot know this appetite for destruction, nor these audacities of a holy vengeance. In the case of a woman who is bent on a direct mortification of the flesh, the plough of penance must sink to the level of her former sensual satisfactions. The more delicious these have been, the deeper must the plough cut through. But apart from penance, mere prudence should oblige a sanctified soul to mortify the body that has been pampered for so many years."[15]

There are other calls made by Christ on the cross. There are saints like the Curé d'Ars who never knew the sins of the flesh and yet have left us frightening examples of penance, inspired as they were to unite themselves in this way through love to the redemptive sufferings of our Lord Jesus Christ.

But no one is a good judge of his own case. "He that desires to be alone, without the support of a master and guide, will be like the tree that is alone in the field and has no owner. However much fruit it bears, passers-by will pluck it all, and it will not mature."[16] "This is what happens when we perform excessive penances in order to make ourselves believe that, because of what we are doing, we are more penitent than others. If we conceal our penances from our confessor or superior, or if we are told to give them up and do not obey, that is a clear case of temptation."[17]

Studying the Gospels, weighing the circumstances, asking advice as to what best suits the love of God and the love of the neighbor—which together form one perfection, one and the same love—these are what is needed: the theological virtue of charity, in fact, the fullness of all perfection, embodied in the two great commandments, the second of which is like unto the first: Thou shalt love the Lord thy God with all thy strength, and thy neighbor as thyself for the love of God.

Let us learn from St. John of the Cross, then, how to distinguish renunciation from penance.

"Renunciation is love": self-renunciation means doing the will of God and being ready for any eventuality—without excluding in advance any divine invitation. Not loving father or mother, son or daughter, more than God, means being willing to say, if the necessity arises, "The Lord gave and the Lord hath taken away; blessed be the Name of the Lord." When St. John of the Cross counsels the harder, the more costing thing, in preference to the easier and more delightful one, he obviously means only in so far as the will of God demands it—only to that extent, but to the full extent of God's demand. We must love with all our might: this will mean

more for some than for others, but however much or however little
it may be, it is always the absolute that is demanded of us. "Thou
shalt love . . . with all thy heart and with all thy mind."

Mortification is, in itself, a punishment, a privation that hurts.
It belongs to the sphere of aggressiveness. It is simply a means, and
as such its value must be carefully estimated. There is no virtue in
any compulsion unless the resulting obedience comes from love.
"One of the criteria of health, of moral and physiological equilibrium, lies in the quantitative connection between these two antago-
nistic impulses (love and aggressiveness)."[18] A tree is only pruned
so that it will give more fruit—in this case the fruit of love.

A contemplative monk is obliged to mortify himself more than
the father of a family, obviously, but at the end of their lives both
will be judged by love. We all have to learn how to love greatly.
Only a love that is pure and disinterested will enable us to persevere to the end.

Pathological Cases

Unfortunately it is only too true that circumstances can arise in
which the natural equilibrium of the soul is upset, or even destroyed. In certain cases an individual may find himself, through
no fault of his own, subject to disorders of such a nature that they
are beyond his control. This does not mean that he will lose merit
in the eyes of Him who sounds the reins and the heart.

"The practice of psychoanalysis gives one the impression of
human illogicality," writes Roland Dalbiez. "It is an impression
which is too often lacking in jurists and moralists. We certainly
do not dream of denying the specific and irreducible value of law
and of morality, but we cannot refrain from regretting how completely most of their exponents neglect the study of the findings of
psychopathology. The result of this procedure is that the judgments they deliver often exhibit a shockingly unreal quality."[19]

A person who has lost his mental balance may be driven ir-
resistibly to perform actions which in other cases would be repre-
hensible (one has only to think of certain cases of suicide or attempted suicide, morbid habits of blasphemy, some kinds of
impurity). If such a person's mind was lucid, would he go on

hating God? Not necessarily. He may be the victim of some kind of mechanism over which he has no control. The disorder may be unable to stop him from wanting God. As has been very justly observed: "It may happen in rarer and more difficult cases, in which purely material sins are involved, that the director is obliged to tell his penitents not to bother about these sins, advising them not to go to confession and even in some cases refusing to allow them to go. In these cases, confession would only plunge them more deeply into despair.[20] For here one is faced with Christians who, burdened with the very heavy Cross of an unavoidable obsession, no longer dare to look God in the face. They drag their way through life without ever experiencing a moment's joy, either natural or supernatural, because they do not properly understand their condition, because they imagine that the physical depression following upon certain acts is a sign of reprobation, and finally because they believe that they are under an unavoidable compulsion to commit sin. No one is tempted beyond his strength; if the contrary seems to be true, there needs to be an enquiry into whether the 'fall' is really a fall in the moral sense."[21] This last remark is particularly relevant. It is a mistake to be so much "under the influence of a purely objective morality" that one forgets "the possibility of subjective non-imputability." The director should not neglect the "purely pathological territory"; "by reconciling himself to its existence," he "will prepare more happy souls for eternal life,"[22] at the same time doing all he can to estimate the extent to which the particular sick or unbalanced person in question may be made responsible for his condition through his own inner behavior.

Such people, as the author rightly insists, may by no means be without a longing for perfection or the gift of mystical prayer. This seems to be the opinion of the best theologians on the subject—for instance, Père de Guibert, Père Garrigou-Lagrange, Père de Tonquedec.[23] "There is nothing to prevent some unfortunate soul who is subject to fits of madness from rising during his lucid intervals to a very high level of love and sanctity, despite all the acts he may commit without being responsible for them; if he is conscious of these acts, they may be a rare source of humility and merit for him."[24] It is a mistake to think that "real sanctity" must always be "the kind of sanctity that can be proved in a court of

law and then set up for the faithful to venerate."[25] The Sacred
Congregation of Rites is in any case an essentially prudent body of
men. However difficult discernment may be in such cases, it is
all the more necessary for the spiritual director to be capable of it
"when in the soul of some abnormal person an efflorescence of
mysticism mingles with the artificial flowers of psychosis."[26]

"The world is so full of melancholy," wrote St. Teresa in the
sixteenth century (instead of "melancholy" we should say today
"depressive states"), "that confessors have very good cause to be
afraid of it and to watch for it very carefully."[27]

The director can sin by excess or defect in his estimate, by being
either too rigorous or too lax, and this is made all the easier for
him by the fact that there is no mathematical frontier between
neurosis and normality. "If the neurotic represents the typical
schema of the dualism between conscious and unconscious activities, the difference is frequently only one of degree between the
neurotic, the 'nervous' person in the ordinary meaning of the word,
and the genuine normal type."[28] "The same laws of psychic life
apply throughout the whole of psychology."[29]

Between the madman who has lost the use of his reason and
the healthy, vigorous, balanced personality, there is a chromatic
scale comprising an infinite number of cases.[30]

The philosopher and the theologian should aim to be psychologists too, and keep on the look-out not only for cases that are
explicitly pathological but for any case that shows the slightest
sign of neurosis. In serious cases "the joint action of psychothera-
pist, doctor and priest"[31] is eminently desirable. It is demanded by
the virtue of prudence. Spiritual directors "should not be semi-
educated and afraid of everything," like the ones who cost St.
Teresa "so much." She describes the torture experienced by the
soul who "comes to a confessor so careful and inexperienced
that he thinks nothing is certain"; "he is afraid of everything, he
doubts everything", she says[32]—and he is unbearable!

Some acquaintance with psychoanalytical knowledge is therefore highly desirable; more important still, however, is a receptive
attitude towards the gifts of the Holy Spirit, so that the smoking
flax may not be quenched, the bruised reed not broken. We must
not be sons of thunder; on the contrary, we must be kindly dis-

posed towards all who endure their share of human misery, whether this be physical, psychological or moral.

It is undoubtedly true that moral lapses have repercussions in the domain of faith, but it should also be realized that in this field too a loss of psychological balance may have a pernicious influence for which the individual is not necessarily, *a priori,* responsible. The physical nervous system can indirectly be the source of intellectual crisis—I say the source, since sense-impressions are only an incidental factor in the play of ideas, an image is an instrumental cause and the imagination is the mistress of error. Thus organic balance is necessary for a normal intellectual life.

"An intellect operating on the basis of elements that are subject to perturbations of a pathological kind will inevitably come to wrong conclusions, and as a result of this the will, in its turn, will be diverted into abnormal channels. . . . Anyone who is deficient in his natural faculties will have more difficulty, not perhaps in meriting, but in turning himself into a perfect example of morality, even of the supernatural kind."[33]

Conscience is our immediate and universal rule of action. A thing that is objectively good—such as abstaining from fornication and believing in Christ—St. Thomas teaches, becomes evil for anyone who considers it evil.[34] Hence the need to distinguish between the outer act and the inner motive when judging the morality of any act.

When the Vatican Council teaches that "those who have received the faith under the direction of the magisterium of the Church can never have any *just* cause for modifying this same faith or for putting it in doubt,"[35] it is taking its stand on a historical, philosophical and dogmatic objectivity, but it does not for all that mean to exclude the possibility of subjective non-imputability of a total or partial kind.[36] Objective truth is not involved here, but only the accidental psychology of the individual. So true is this that the Sovereign Pontiff himself, despite his ability to pass infallible judgment on any case of heresy, leaves to God alone the decision as to whether the heretic is guilty of mortal sin. So true is it, again, that between the instructed and well-balanced believer, on the one hand, who consciously preserves and strengthens his faith, and the imbecile who goes mad and loses all control of his mind, there is a whole scale of variations that includes the believer by logic and habit; the conscious believer who is illogical about some particular point of his faith; all the neurotics who have doubts and hesitations and are more to be pitied than blamed—victims, too often (in varying degrees of responsibility) of "an intellectual intoxication followed by vertigo, which—though these things are not in themselves able to cause the absolute destruction of the infused virtue of faith—nevertheless give those who experience them the impression that their belief is crumbling";[37] before we come down to the absolute renegades, the genuinely guilty.

Not every kind of moral or intellectual disorder, of course, is mere sickness, or entirely sickness; and that brings us to the question of sin.

Confidence and Sin

The way of spiritual childhood is not the prerogative of a privileged sect: it is open to all who have a genuine desire to keep, or discover, the soul of a child.

Far from being an insurmountable obstacle, sin can providentially, by way of permission, become a means to our soul's greater good. "To them that love God all things work together unto good", says St. Paul (Rom. 7:28); even sin, *etiam peccata*, adds St. Augustine.

The great principle of love dominating the mystery of the Redemption is announced by St. Paul in the Epistle to the Romans: "Where sin abounded, grace did more abound" (Rom. 5:20). It is easy to see how this applies in the economy that governs the Fall and Redemption of mankind. The liturgy for Holy Saturday says, "Happy fault, that won so holy and so high a Redeemer!" It is not so often realized that this scheme of merciful love is, by this very fact, valid for each one of us in particular, from the moment that we learn to have confidence and to be of goodwill. "There is no doctrine more appropriate to man," says Pascal, "than this, which teaches him his double capacity of receiving and of losing grace, because of the double peril to which he is exposed, of despair or of pride."[38]

The worst sin for any soul to commit is that which was committed by the angels and by Adam; or, again, the sin of despair, which is simply another form of their sin of pride.

The thing that is objectively intolerable is for a soul to admire itself and feel self-satisfied, as though its perfection or happiness came from itself alone. Cardinal de Bérulle said of the Blessed Virgin Mary: "In her the Sun of God has no shadow." Every soul should surrender itself to the divine light; its first beneficial effect will be to bring out the ugliness of its faults.

The proper function of falls and imperfections is, precisely, to reveal our own weakness to us. Sin is the surest sign of our wretchedness, and in the scheme of our sanctification its purpose is, quite simply, to humiliate us. In a sense sin is its own remedy. When a soul far advanced in virtue falls from grace, God permits this so that it may have a chance of extricating itself from the sticky webs of its own self-satisfaction.

And therefore, as St. Thérèse of the Child Jesus explains, when we have sinned, a kind of dual reaction should take place in us, so that in the first place we are sorry for the pain we have caused Almighty God (this being the negative aspect of our reaction) and then—on the positive side—we should go on to rejoice (yes, rejoice!) over our weakness rather than be annoyed by it. For annoyance would be a sign of pride and self-love; whereas joy means humility.

Like so many holy souls, St. Thérèse of the Child Jesus is profoundly convinced of her own weakness and misery. "All our acts of justice," she says, "are faulty in the eyes of God." "The greatest thing the Almighty ever did in me was to show me my own paltriness, my utter inability to do good." "To me too come many weaknesses, but they never surprise me." "O God, it is true, I rejoice to feel how small and weak I am in your presence: it brings peace to my heart."

To rejoice in one's own wretchedness is the key to the "Little Way." "For when I am weak, then am I powerful," (2 Cor. 12: 10), for I am strong with the strength of God in the abasement of my own nothingness.

When we have sinned—even though we have sinned mortally, and again and again—it always depends on our free consent to God's grace whether or not our sins turn to our greater good and thus cause in us a greater abundance of grace. For God is mercy. Our Lord tells us in the Gospels not to return evil for evil, and He exemplifies His teaching by forgiving us again and again after dying for us on the cross. In the Gospels there is an immense compassion for all forms of suffering and an infinite mercy towards sin.

"True love is shown in self-abasement, and if everyone were like the saintly doctors who adorn the Church, it would seem that God had not far enough to stoop when he came to them."[39] And so He had pity on thieves and publicans and died for them—for each and every one of us.

"It is not only because I have been preserved from mortal sin that I fly to Jesus with such confidence and love; even if I had all the crimes possible on my conscience, I am sure I should lose none of my confidence. Heartbroken with repentance, I would simply throw myself into my Saviour's arms, for I know how much he loves the prodigal son. I have heard what he said to Mary Magdalene, to the woman taken in adultery, and to the Samaritan woman. No one can make me frightened any more, because I know what to believe about his mercy and his love; I know that in the twinkling of an eye all those thousands of sins would be consumed as a drop of water cast into a blazing fire."[40]

A person who truly repents of his sins—even mortal sins repeated again and again—and rejoices in all sincerity at the realization of his own wretchedness (even to seventy times seven) will always receive far more in return—through being humiliated and forgiven—than he ever loses by thus falling from grace.

Is this quietism? or laxity?

"Shall we continue in sin that grace may abound?" asks St. Paul, voicing this objection. "God forbid. For we that are dead to sin, how shall we live any longer therein? Know ye not that all we, who are baptized in Christ, are baptized in his death?" (Rom. 6:1-3). No; for, whilst we accept our weakness joyfully, we have no desire to offend voluntarily One who died for us, and who thus gave proof of the greatest possible love. Love cannot wish to cause pain to the One it loves. Furthermore, nothing is more exacting or more devoted than love. It is always wanting to do more. If we are docile and persevering and generous-hearted, and abandon ourselves to the inspirations sent to us by God, we shall ultimately reach the haven of our sanctification.

What prevents us from ascending to God is not sin—even though it be mortal, and repeated again and again—if we are sincerely sorry each time we sin, and have a firm purpose of amendment, but a conscious, habitual determination not to break a certain binding link—it may be as light as a feather—that God wants us to break.[41] According to the virile teaching of St. John of the Cross, therefore, these habitual, voluntary attachments must be broken, even though they only involve slight imperfections. If the soul is attached to some imperfection against God's will, it has still not succeeded in uniting its will with His. If, consciously and obstinately, we hold on to a thing, or a function, or a person, that is against or outside the will of God, we are behaving like a bird that is unable to fly because it is caught in lime or held back by a thread, and it makes no difference how fine the thread is.[42]

When we go to confession or examine our consciences, therefore, the essential thing is not to be able to foresee with absolute certainty that we shall never again indulge in any repetition of our sin, but to wish with all our heart that this will be the case, and to ask God that it may prove to be so. At the moment of wishing, at least, our attachment to the sin is broken, no matter what weakness we may show afterwards; if it recurs, it must be broken again.

If we cannot manage to be sorry, if we cannot wish to amend, if, in fact, we are certain that we shall persist in an attachment that needs to be broken, then, faced with the difficulty of making the break, we must go on hoping against hope that we may discover a holy aggressiveness, and ask God, tell Him, that we must be delivered from it; then we are sure to be heard. "My God, I cannot do this thing, but You will do it." And indeed He will effect the renunciation, the liberation, for you. "God does not demand the impossible, but He tells us to do what we can and to ask for what we cannot do, then He helps us to be able."[43]

One thing we are sure to obtain by confident, persevering prayer —no matter what our failings and deficiencies may be—and that is our sanctification.

Any prayer of petition for our own personal perfection is bound to be absolutely in line with the will of God, and it will unfailingly be heard if it is made with faith and perseverance. There is no need to enunciate here the conditions that must inevitably accompany any petition for temporal objects (success, health, business, etc.); they can all be reduced to one: "If it be Thy will, O Lord"—for it is indubitably the will of God that we shall ascend to Him through love, rising higher and higher every day and being entirely freed from our slightest attachments. "Lead us not into temptation, but deliver us from evil."

Thus the theological virtue of hope is based on the mercy and omnipotence of an infinitely loving God. It is in no way dependent on the virtues, or the moral progress, or the spiritual effort, or the merits, of the petitioner, but it depends from first to last on the infinite love of God, which, as St. Thérèse of the Child Jesus says, is revealed just as clearly in the soul of a savage or a tiny child as in the soul of a man of learning or one who can work miracles. Ascending the way of perfection does not mean struggling, it means resting on God; it is not so much a case of acquiring things for oneself as of losing oneself: God is the One who gives. The motive of hope has to be divested of all human self-interest and directed towards God alone, until we become strong with the strength of God and powerful with His power. When they find themselves faced with this power, all our attachments will give way, because God is stronger than they are.

Undoubtedly there is a need for aggressiveness in the service of God: the Kingdom of Heaven is not taken by the lukewarm but by the violent. Only, the aggressiveness is not the fundamental thing, for it does not lead to love: love must come first in us as it comes first in God. Religion is not a "business"; it is not, in the first place, a "struggle"; it is the activity of the one true love.

To what extent may we have confidence in God, as regards our ultimate end?

Every Christian knows that he can and must avoid hell, but far too many Christians fail to realize that they can and should avoid purgatory too, however grave their sins may be and however great or small may be the degree of glory to which God has predestined them in His infinite wisdom—that wisdom which is a composite of independence and love.

The Mystery of Iniquity[44]

"The concrete facts of the problem that each individual has to solve for himself . . . can vary a great deal. It is required by justice, not that all the problems should be the same, but only that each problem should be soluble; in other words, that each person's particular difficulties should be taken into account, and that he should not be expected to do more than is reasonable. What counts towards retribution is precisely the way in which each person solves the entirely personal problem that has been set him. Divine justice does not mean that every soul shall be set the same problem, but that each person shall be set a problem proportionate to his character. And it means taking full account of the way in which each person solves this problem, considering the means at his disposal. . . . 'Let no temptation take hold of you, but such as is human. And God is faithful, who will not suffer you to be tempted above that which you are able, but will make also with temptation, issue, that ye may be able to bear it' (1 Cor. 10:13). We know that this must be proportionately true for every human life, and that at the last day none of the damned will be able to rise up and accuse God of injustice."[45]

Every damned soul, having refused God's grace, will witness to its own responsibility for the evil it has done and to the implacable hatred which it has freely assumed against the love that opposed its dastardly schemes. This witness will be given by the damned before One who shed His blood on the cross to purchase their redemption, One who had compassion on the poor, the sick and the sinful, who told the hight priests and the elders that the publicans and sinners would go before them into the Kingdom of Heaven (Mt. 21:31). One who condemned in the most violent terms the selfishness of the Pharisees, the proud, the avaricious, the hypocrites. Under the eyes of a just Judge who is at the same time merciful towards all forms of human weakness, sordid covetousness and conscious, intentional infidelity will be unmasked and revealed in all their nakedness, whilst genuine sincerity and purity of intention will appear in all their splendor, no matter what dark labyrinths of pathology, objective error and moral evil they may have been involved in against their will on earth. Those who refused to sacrifice to love—in so far as they could perceive it—will then persist in their refusal no less freely than they did during their last moments on earth, and they will receive from Christ the well-merited reply: Since this is the way you wish it to be, and will always wish it to be—"Depart from me, you cursed, into everlasting fire which was prepared for the devil and his angels. For I was hungry and you gave me not to eat: I was thirsty, and you gave me not to drink. I was a stranger, and you took me not in: naked, and you covered me not: sick and in prison, and you did not visit me. Then they also shall answer him, saying: Lord, when did we see thee hungry or thirsty, or a stranger, or naked, or sick, or in prison, and did not minister to thee? Then he shall answer them, saying: Amen I say to you, as long as you did it not to one of these least, neither did you do it to me. And these shall go into everlasting punishment: but the just, into life everlasting" (Mt. 25: 41 *et seq.*). We are dogged by our actions.

All the evil and privation that exist in hell have been created by angels and men who have misused their liberty in full consciousness of what they were doing; for hell is the creation of their own sinfulness—and sinfulness, from its very nature, cannot be the work of God. "The wicked do not perish because they are unable to be good, but because they do not want to be good."[46] "If anyone says that it is not within man's power to turn from his evil ways, and that evil works, like good works, come from God, meaning not only by way of permission but properly and essentially, so that the treachery of Judas is no less God's own work than the calling of St. Paul: let him be anathema."[47]

"Little by little, by the exercise of our free will, we construct our freedom"[48] and even in the beyond this freedom remains. Freely anchored in evil, the damned have not only sinned in the past, they go on sinning for ever. They are essentially in everlasting rebellion, incessantly repeating their refusal to love love, continually setting themselves up voluntarily against the love from which they separated themselves before they departed from this earth. The mystery is, that having always been free and perfectly lucid in mind, the damned will not repent; for this is something that they will never do. By their own free act they are immobilized in evil.[49] The violence and aggressiveness are not on God's side

—for God is by definition love—but on the side of hell, where hatred has always reigned and will reign for ever.

"The sin lasts for all eternity and the punishment should not come to an end so long as the sin lasts."[50] "It would be unjust if . . . punishment continued after . . . [the] will is good,"[51] but "the devils are obstinate in their wickedness"[52] and it will be given them to see "how justly"[53] they are damned.

Hell is not inhabited by beings who have repented, who are sorry for their sins and would like to lead a better life but have come to this conclusion too late. This would be a caricature of hell and an insult to the wisdom and goodness of God.

"In all ages writers on criminal law have asserted that the aim of lawful punishment is not revenge but that its severity is designed to prevent any recurrence of the crime that has been committed; and with this the Christian spirit is in entire agreement. If this is the Christian spirit on earth, why should there be a different spirit in heaven, giving rise to eternal torments which can only be the signs of an eternal vengeance?"[54]

Thus wrote Alfred de Vigny, but he assumed, quite wrongly, that there is no evil in hell; whereas evil persists there. Nicolas Berdyaev's words will meet with general approval: "There is something hideous and morally revolting in the idea of eternal torments as a just retribution for the crimes and sins of a short moment of life,"[55] but in reality it is not a moment's crime that is involved but an everlasting crime, willed in complete freedom for all eternity; and that is quite a different thing.[56]

Love of the creature easily changes into aggressiveness. We can put into the hearts of the damned when they stand face to face with God the feeling aroused in Dostoievsky's hero by the sight of the woman who made him suffer such torments: "I looked at her . . . with fearful hatred—that hate which is only a hair's-breadth from love, from the maddest love!"[57]—this hair's-breadth symbolizing the freedom of the damned. Thus "the pains of hell are not a punishment inflicted from outside but an ineluctable consequence of sin, the revelation of the sinner's conscience,"[58] torn in pieces, so to speak, between love and aggressiveness.[59]

The love that is rejected appears in the first place as justice towards those who voluntarily reject it—because it remains love, worthy of its name, a love which is not weakness, the only love worth loving, and worth loving infinitely since it is the supreme Good.

On the moral and psychological level, it is for us to choose between a proud rebelliousness and humble docility in our personal response to love's invitation. It is up to us, whether we transform our weakness into a means to our salvation or not.

We can reject love: such is the depth of our wretchedness. God died to save all men: such is the extent of His mercy. Let us get this firmly into our heads: we are not involved in a game of chance, in which we have no say.[60] He who created us without our assistance will not save us without our co-operation. If we work and struggle *as though* prayer were useless and—and this is even more important—pray *as though* our efforts were useless, we shall keep the necessary balance as we walk through the darkness of this mystery.

To the question, are many souls saved? no definite answer can be given. Christ and the Church have told us nothing about this question—and when all is said and done, that is surely something we can see the wisdom of.

St. Thomas Aquinas was pessimistic about the human race, most of whom he thought would be damned,[61] and optimistic about the angels, most of whom he thought had been saved.[62] There is no need to go into the reasons here for the difference between these two estimates,[63] but it is worth noting that in St. Thomas's view the number of the angels is incomparably higher than that of all the creatures in the universe put together, including not only the different species but all the individuals within the species;[64] altogether, therefore, even in the eyes of the "Angelic" Doctor, there are far more of the elect than of the damned, his rigorism applying only to human beings, and these being ultimately only a small proportion of the creatures endowed with intelligence and freedom.

This rigorism is itself generally rejected today,[65] and is certainly not in the spirit of the opening pages of such a book as *The Story of a Soul,* in which St. Thérèse of the Child Jesus speaks with such compassion of the infidels and pagans.

But "one dies alone, others have nothing to do with it."

"There was once a man who was very anxious, and wavered between fear and hope. One day, overcome with sadness, he lay prostrate in prayer before the altar in church, and pondering these matters in his mind, said, 'Oh, if only I knew that I should always persevere!' Then he heard within his heart an answer from God: 'If you knew this, what would you do? Do now what you would then, and all will be well.' "[66]

When Judas (not Iscariot) presented Christ with the problem of predestination in these words: "Lord, how is it, that thou wilt manifest thyself to us, and not to the world?" Jesus simply said in reply, "If anyone love me, he will keep my word, and my Father will love him, and we will come to him, and make our abode with him. He that loveth me not keepeth not my words. And the word which you have heard is not mine; but the Father's who sent me" (1 John 14:22–24).

"If anyone love me, my Father will love him." The essential thing is, therefore, to love greatly. But to what extent can we and should we love?

Confidence and Purgatory

"Love can only be paid back by love," says St. John of the Cross. Deeply wretched as we are, how near perfection will our response be to the love of God?

"That we may have confidence in the day of judgment," writes St. John the Evangelist, and goes on: "Fear is not in charity: but perfect charity casteth out fear, because fear hath pain. And he that feareth is not perfected in charity. Let us therefore love God: because God first hath loved us" (John 4:17–19).

St. Thérèse of the Child Jesus, who saw into the depths of this verse of Scripture, makes use of it to reveal one of the most audacious aspects of her "Little Way," gently insisting that whatever degree of the beatific vision God intends us for, He certainly does not will that any of us should endure the flames of purgatory. On the contrary, God wants to see us leaving this earth absolutely pure and purified, as abandoned to His will as the prodigal, repentant little child, who, having simply fallen asleep in her Father's arms, wakes up immediately in the light of heaven and thus throws herself without delay into the eternal embrace of the merciful love, and this immediately, and without delay.[67]

As regards this delicate point, here, from St. Thérèse's own pen, are a few statements made with all her amazing theological precision:

"You have not enough trust," she said to a timid sister, "you are far too afraid of the good God. I assure you that this hurts Him. You should not be afraid of purgatory because of the punishment there: you should try to aim not to go there and thus please the good God, who hates having to impose such a form of expiation. As soon as you begin to try and please Him in everything you do, if you have an absolutely unshakeable trust that you are being purified every moment in His love and that He will not let the slightest trace of sin remain in you, you may be perfectly certain that you will not go to purgatory."[68]

Not to go to purgatory "to please the good God", what a pearl of wisdom this is! "I would not pick up a straw to avoid going to purgatory. All that I have done, I have done to give God pleasure and to save souls."[69]

"I also know," she says elsewhere, "that the Fire of Love is far more sanctifying than the fires there" (i.e. in purgatory).[70]

"It seems to me that there will not be any Judgment for the victims of love."[71]

"In spite of your little failings you can hope to go straight to heaven . . . the good God wants this more than you do."[72]

And St. Thérèse is not afraid to assert as a consequence of this that the sufferings of purgatory are "useless."[73] What exactly does she mean by this? The theologians are unanimous in teaching the same thing: in purgatory one cannot merit any further, one cannot mount any higher in love; the sufferings endured there are therefore useless from the only point of view that ultimately counts towards the increase of our life of glory—growth in the love of Christ. We are judged on our love, and the judgment takes place at the end of this life.

By enduring their suffering, which God permits "as though turning a blind eye to it,"[74] the souls in purgatory expiate their sins—justly, since they did not do this, as they should have done, on earth; and, still more, mercifully, since in this way, despite their past half-heartedness, they are prepared to enjoy God face to face, and God brooks no impurity.[75]

St. Thérèse is quite precise about this: "Purgatory is only for souls who have disdained the merciful Love or had doubts about its purifying power."[76] Doubt is here an insult to God's goodness.

How does God use the flames of purgatory to purify souls consumed with divine love?

In the divine scheme purgatory, like hell, is not intended for anyone.[77] In God there is not the slightest trace of indifference or injustice or aggressiveness towards anyone. God is Justice and Mercy in a love that respects each person's freedom. It is always love that forms the hidden motive of His intention.

God, whose joy is infinite, whose peace surpasses all human imagining, whose power is unbounded, has absolute control over His creatures. Nevertheless, we are free to refuse the gift of love whenever we feel like it. Let us accept it with all our hearts. Let us trust in God, despite all appearances, like little children, and we shall not be disappointed. "The soul obtains from Him as much as it hopes for from Him,"[78] and "God is well pleased with those who hope in His mercy."[79]

Are there many souls who in fact do not pass through purgatory at all? The general opinion is that there are very few. St. John of the Cross says in the *Dark Night* that only a tiny number of souls go straight to heaven as soon as they die.[80]

St. Thérèse of the Child Jesus is no less precise on this point, but it is worth noting that it is "a multitude of little souls", "a legion of little victims,"[81] that she wants to draw after her in the shining wake of her spiritual childhood. Popes Benedict XV, Pius XI and Pius XII have done everything they could to emphasize the universality of her teaching and the demands it makes upon each one of us. "The 'Little Way' is the secret of holiness for all the faithful throughout the world."[82]

Let each of us remember in practice the words of St. John of the Cross that were so dear to St. Thérèse: "The soul obtains from Him just as much as it hopes for from Him." To ask for heaven "the moment we die" is not asking for the moon; it only means asking God "that His will be done on earth as it is in heaven, and that His Kingdom may come"[83] at the moment He desires.

"To live in an *act of perfect love,* I OFFER MYSELF AS A BURNT
OFFERING TO YOUR MERCIFUL LOVE, calling upon You to consume
me at every instant, while You let the floods of *infinite tenderness*
pent up within You flow into my soul, that so I may become a
Martyr to Your *Love,* O my God. . . .

"When that *martyrdom* has prepared me to appear before You,
may it cause me to die, and may my soul hurl itself in that instant
into the eternal embrace of *Your Merciful Love. . . .*"[84]

The Heavenly Mansions

Heaven is for everyone without exception, though in differing
degrees.[85]

"For a long time I had wondered why God had preferences, why
He did not give the same degree of grace to everyone," writes St.
Thérèse.[86] Jesus instructed her in this mystery. "If every little
flower wished to be a rose, nature would lose her Spring adorn-
ments, and the fields would be no longer enamelled with their
varied flowers. So it is in the world of souls, the living garden of
the Lord."[87]

The flowers are for the Master. We are Christ's joy. Our perfection is simply one spot of color bringing its own tiny contribution to the total composition of an immense flower bed. "The
happier they [the flowers] are to be as He wills, the more perfect
they are."[88]

"God is said to have equally care of all, not because by His care
He deals out equal good to all, but because He administers all
things with like wisdom and goodness,"[89] in an act of love that is
infinite, unique, simple and always consistent with itself.[90]

Two complementary truths are involved here and it is essential
that they should be properly grasped.

God distributes unequal gifts both in the order of grace and in
the order of nature. He shares them out as in the parable of the
talents; one receives more, another less. No one would be better
if God had willed to load him with more gifts; in this sense no one
would be better if he was loved more by God.

But in the eyes of anyone looking at the loving wisdom that

orders these gifts, God loves us all equally—and equally with the Blessed Virgin Mary herself.

Love means willing good to someone. And the way in which a thing is given is more important than the thing itself, so that the divine way of giving anything is to give whatever is given, great or small, with a love that is literally infinite.

This love is our hope and our strength. The best response that we can make to it is to have the confidence to abandon ourselves utterly to it. Loving God means allowing oneself to be loved by Him as He wills, in His own divine way.

Let us prepare ourselves for the contemplation of the Father and the Word in their ineffable light, according to the extent that we are personally called; whatever this may be, it is the only one that is possible for us, and it is the best—as it is the best for the splendor of the total Christ.

Having faith, let us from this moment onwards love the Father and the Son with the love with which they love each other. This love is the Holy Spirit, who also has been given to us. To live in the company of the divine Persons is the hidden treasure, the precious pearl of the Gospels, worth more than all the gold of the world and all the sacrifices put together.

"O souls created for these grandeurs and called thereto! What do ye do? Wherein do ye occupy yourselves? Your desires are meannesses, and your possessions miseries. O wretched blindness of the eyes of your souls, which are blind to so great a light and deaf to so clear a voice, seeing not that for so long as ye seek grandeurs and glories ye remain miserable and deprived of so many blessings, and have become ignorant and unworthy!"[91]

It is time we came out of the mists of Jansenism and rigorism and sailed in the full sunshine above a sea of clouds as white and shining in the light of God as they were grey and opaque down below, seen from the earth. "For that which is at present momentary and light of our tribulation, worketh for us above measure exceedingly an eternal weight of glory" (2 Cor. 4:17).

Let us have a good will and we shall be saved: this is the Gospel message, the good news. "Peace on earth to men of goodwill."

God is not a God of wrath: He is a God of love. "Where sin did
abound, grace does more abound."

In our hours of trial let us love repeating at the foot of the Cross
the Magnificat of pain, and Our Lady, Mother of God, will pray
for us sinners at the hour of our death:

My soul doth magnify the Lord:
And my spirit hath rejoiced in God my Saviour.
Because he hath regarded the humility of his handmaid:
For behold from henceforth all generations shall call me blessed.
Because he that is mighty hath done great things to me:
And holy is his name.
And his mercy is from generation unto generations,
To them that fear him.
He hath shewed might in his arm:
He hath scattered the proud in the conceit of their heart.
He hath put down the mighty from their seat,
And hath exalted the humble.
He hath filled the hungry with good things:
And the rich he hath sent empty away.
He hath received Israel his servant, being mindful of his mercy,
As he spoke to our fathers: to Abraham and to his seed for ever.

The Christian religion, says Pascal, "making those tremble
whom it justifies, and consoling those whom it condemns, so justly
tempers fear with hope through that double capacity of grace and
of sin, common to all, that it humbles infinitely more than reason
alone can do, but without despair, and it exalts infinitely more
than natural pride, but without inflating; thus making it evident
that alone being exempt from error and vice, it alone fulfils the
duty of instructing and correcting men."[92]

NOTES

1. *De Veritate,* q. 25, a. 2. St. Thomas is here speaking of the irascible
and concupiscible, but body and soul form a unity, the libidinous and aggressive functions also exist on the spiritual level of the will and, moreover,
grace does not destroy nature. The Kingdom of Heaven is taken by force.

2. Jean Brémond, *Les Pères du désert,* Gabalda, 1927, i, pp. 31-2 "A
religious, being the soldier of Jesus Christ and always ready for battle, must
always have his loins girded. The Scriptures show those who laid the foundations of this sacred profession in the Old Testament—Elias and Eliseus, for

instance—as wearing a belt" (Cassian, *Institutions*, i. 1., quoted in *op. cit.*, p. 36.)

3. II–II, 182, 3.

4. II–II, 188, 6.

5. There is the well-known quip attributed by the Bollandists to St. Teresa of Avila. "O, Lord," she exclaims, in her delightfully familiar way, "when will you stop spreading difficulties under our feet like this?" "Don't complain, daughter," replies the divine Master, "that's the way I always treat my friends." "Yes, Lord," replies Teresa, "and that's why you have so few!" (Bollandist *Histoire de Sainte Thérèse*, Paris, Retaux-Bray, 1888, vol. ii, p. 362).

6. *Cautions: Complete Works*, vol. iii, p. 220.

7. *Interior Castle*, vii: *Complete Works*, p. 350.

8. *Spiritual Sentences and Maxims: Complete Works*, vol. iii, p. 242.

9. *Interior Castle*, v: *Complete Works*, pp. 262–3.

10. *Ibid.*, pp. 261–2.

11. St. John of the Cross, *Spiritual Sentences and Maxims: Complete Works*, vol. iii, p. 244.

12. Père Jacques de Jésus.

13. *Spiritual Sentences and Maxims: Complete Works*, vol. iii, p. 246.

14. *Quodlibet* v, a. 18.

15. *Margaret of Cortona*, trans. Barbara Wall, Burns, Oates and Washbourne, p. 51.

16. *Spiritual Sentences and Maxims: Complete Works*, vol. iii, p. 241.

17. St. Teresa of Jesus, *The Way of Perfection*, ch. xxxix: *Complete Works*, vol, ii, p. 170.

18. See *supra*, p. 95.

19. *Psychoanalytical Method and the Doctrine of Freud*, trans. T. F. Lindsay, Longmans, Green and Co., vol. ii, p. 302. Spiritual directors will also find much useful information in *Les Deux Sources, consciente et inconsciente, de la vie morale*, by Dr. Charles Odier, Neuchâtel, éditions de la Baconnière, 1943.

20. Dr. Parcheminey observes very pertinently that a neurotic condition can be aggravated by too strict an attitude on the part of the director: "If the patient, faced with a growing feeling of guilt, has no other resource except one that accentuates his neurosis, he may be tempted to reject all constraint, and then his aggressiveness breaks through his defences with an iconoclastic rage that knows no bounds" (*supra*, p. 103).

21. Canon Dr. Adalbert Brenninkmeyer, "Défaitisme moral et victoire chrétienne," in *Le Risque Chrétien, Études Carmélitaines*, April 1939, pp. 170–1.

22. *Ibid.*

23. *Nuit Mystique, Études Carmélitaines*, Oct. 1938, p. 188.

24. Père de Guibert, "Le cas du P. Surin," *ibid.*, p. 187.

25. *Ibid.*

26. T.-L. Pénido, "Grâce et Folie," in *Études Carmélitaines*, April 1939.

27. *Interior Castle*, Sixth Mansion: *Complete Works*, vol. iii, p. 272.

28. *Supra*, p. 90.

29. *Supra*, p. 97.

30. "We are all mad, but we don't all manage to bring it off," as an excellent teacher at the Catholic Institute in Lille used to say jokingly.

31. *Supra*, p. 103.

32. *Interior Castle, Fifth Mansion.*

33. A. Gardeil, O.P., "A propos de la Madeleine de Pierre Janet," *Études Carmélitaines,* Oct. 1931, pp. 129, 131.

34. I–II, 19, 5.

35. Denzinger, 1794.

36. See L. de Grandmaison, *La Crise de la Foi chez les Jeunes,* 5th ed., Paris, Beauchesne, 1932, esp. pp. 92–102: Gardeil, *La Crédibilité et l'apologétique,* Paris, Gabalda, 1928, p. 299.

37. Grandmaison, *La Crise de la Foi chez les Jeunes,* p. 98.

38. *Pensées,* 523.

39. St. Thérèse of Lisieux, *Story of a Soul,* p. 6.

40. *Ibid.,* p. 181.

41. "Any one of these imperfections, if the soul has become attached and habituated to it, is of as great harm to its growth and progress in virtue as though it were to fall daily into many other imperfections and casual venial sins which proceed not from a common indulgence in any common and harmful attachment, and will not hinder it so much as when it has attachment to anything" (St. John of the Cross, *The Ascent of Mount Carmel,* bk. i, ch. xi: *Complete Works,* vol. i, p. 53).

42. "Even if it be slender, the bird will be as well held as though it were stout, for so long as it breaks it not and flies not away. It is true that the slender one is the easier to break; still, easy though it be, the bird will not fly away if it be not broken" (*ibid.,* p. 53). See Père François de Ste. Marie, *Initiation à Saint Jean de la Croix,* ed. du Seuil, pp. 83 et seq. "There is attachment when we take *pleasure,* knowingly, voluntarily and habitually, in the very things that God wants us to sacrifice."

43. Council of Trent, Denzinger, 804.

44. Thess. 2:7: "For the mystery of iniquity already worketh."

45. Charles Journet, "De l'inégale égalité des créatures," *Études Carmélitaines,* October 1939, pp. 200–2, *passim.*

46. Third Council of Valence, Denzinger, 321.

47. Council of Trent, Denzinger, 816.

48. Rondet, S. J., "Les Peines de l'enfer," in *Nouvelle Revue théologique,* April–May, 1940, p. 423.

49. Denzinger, 3028: "Iniquos autem arbitrio voluntatis propriae vasa irae apta in interitum permanentes"—"the wicked, remaining vessels of wrath fit for perdition and remaining such by the free motion of their own will."

50. St. Thomas, *In IV. Sent.,* dist., 46, q. i, a. 3, c.

51. *Contra Gentes,* iv, 93.

52. *In IV. Sent.,* dist. 46, q. 2, a. 3, sol. i, ad 1m.

53. III, 54, 4, "quam juste damnentur."

54. Alfred de Vigny, *Joural d'un poète.*

55. *The Destiny of Man,* Geoffrey Bles, 1937, p. 354.

56. This point is worth insisting on, as it is not sufficiently well known. " 'I could have avoided this dreadful misfortune,' they cry in despair, 'and now I can no longer get out': such will be the worm that dieth not of the damned" (Père Perroy, *La Montée du Calvaire,* p. 319). This is not so. "I *can* no longer get out," is not what the damned cry; that is not the way their psychology works. They do not want, they never will want, to get out, i.e. repent. That is their everlasting vice. "It is thus not necessary to accept

literally the naïve idea of the saintly Curé d'Ars" (is it really his? I have not verified it) "who used to say that if confessionals were placed at the gates of hell the damned would rush towards them to be forgiven and granted their freedom. With such an idea of hell and of the spiritual condition of the damned, how can one possibly not accuse God of cruelty and cruelty of an appalling kind?" (Lahitton, *Theologiae dogmaticae theses,* Beauchesne, vol. iii, p. 464). This is obviously true.

The following passages from St. Thomas, concerning the psychology and the immorality of the damned, leave no doubt about his opinion on this point.

"Since the demon has a perverse and obstinate will, he is not sorry for the evil of sin" (I, 64, 3, 3m).

"The devil's first sin still remains in him according to desire; although not as to his believing that he can obtain what he desired. Even so, if a man were to believe that he can commit murder, and wills to commit it, and afterwards the power is taken from him; nevertheless, the will to murder can stay with him, so that he would he had done it, or still would do it if he could" (I, 64, 2, 3m). "The minds of the damned are so firmly established in evil that every movement of their free will is disordered and is a sin . . ." (*De Ver.,* q. 24, a. 11, c.). "Just as the devil turned away from God voluntarily, so he is voluntarily fixed there, having made his choice: he goes on doing evil voluntarily but unchangeably" (*De Malo,* q. xvi, a. 5, ad 8m). "Diabolus habet libertatem servandi rectitudinem si eam haberet" (ibid., ad 19m); i.e., "The devil is free to remain good, but there is no goodness in him." "And this is in fact for St. Thomas the ultimate explanation of the existence of hell; hell is eternal . . . because sin is eternal" (Michel, art. "Enfer," *Dict. Théol. Cath.,* col. 97).

57. See above, p. 61.

58. Rondet. "Les Peines de l'enfer," *Nouvelle Revue théologique,* April–May, 1940, p. 401. This suffering is proportionate to the individual's wickedness. But St. Thomas tells us that it remains less than would be demanded by justice untempered by mercy (I, 21, 4, 1m).

59. Corresponding to aversion to God is the pain of damnation; to the unlawful pleasure found in sin, the pain of sense or the fire of hell—on the nature of which the Church has made no pronouncement.

60. It is of course an insoluble mystery because—amongst other things —two of the ideas that are vitally involved in it—the idea of power and the idea of freedom—are ultimately one (for a being is free to the extent that it can govern itself and its circumstances); but the idea of power is more accessible on the metaphysical level (active power means action), whereas the idea of freedom is more accessible on the psychological level (it can be described more easily than it can be evaluated from the ontological point of view). As these two aspects of the mystery are not equally clear to us, we shall never understand it absolutely.

Calvinism effects a unilateral systematization from the standpoint of the divine power—which means the end of any human freedom or any psychology of a God of Love.

Pelagianism effects a unilateral systematization from the standpoint of human freedom—which means the end of God's omnipotence or any influx of grace on human freedom.

I am not unacquainted with the learned controversies on these great questions. It will be sufficient to say here that I am neither on Bannez' side nor on Molina's.

I have considered it sufficient to emphasize in the text the personal responsibility of each damned soul and its eternal guilt, on the moral and psychological level. No system of thought has the least right to question these dogmatic assertions, for God is justice as well as love and wisdom and it would lead to frightful misunderstandings if St. Thomas's *metaphysical* assertions regarding the eternal immutability of heaven and hell were transposed on to the *psychological* level.

61. I, 23, 7, 3m.

62. I, 63, 9.

63. *Ibid.*

64. I, 50, 3.

65. See Capéran, *Le Problème du salut des infidèles,* Toulouse, Grand Séminaire, 1934, vol. i, p. 507. "Nothing would be easier than to draw from sermons, lectures, mystical treatises, even pastoral letters, expressions of tremendous hope for the millions of infidels who to all appearance have been left forsaken."

66. *Imitation of Christ,* bk. i, ch. 25.

67. The magisterium of the Church explicitly envisages the case of souls who do not need to pass through purgatory. According to the Council of Florence (Denzinger 693), these are souls who either did not commit any sins after baptism or purified themselves from their sins during their life on earth ("in suis corporibus . . . purgatae"). There is no more interesting, more readable and more concentrated piece of writing than St. Catherine of Genoa's little *Treatise on Purgatory.* It is a book that every Catholic should read. See particularly Chapter XII on the joy and suffering of souls in purgatory: "It is true that love for God, which fills the soul to overflowing, gives it, so I see it, a happiness beyond what can be told, but this happiness takes not one pang from the pain of the souls in Purgatory. Rather the love of these souls, finding itself hindered, causes their pain; and the more perfect is the love of which God has made them capable, the greater is their pain." It is precisely this love which, in the divine scheme, should not be delayed (*Treatise on Purgatory,* trans. Charlotte Balfour and H. D. Irving, Sheed and Ward, 1946).

68. Extract from a circular from the Carmel at Lisieux signed by the Rev. Mother Agnes and dated Feb. 17, 1924.

69. *Novissima Verba,* Burns, Oates and Washbourne, 1929, p. 93.

70. *Story of a Soul,* trans. Michael Day, Burns, Oates and Washbourne, 1951, p. 132.

71. *Conseils et Souvenirs,* p. 281.

72. *À l'École de sainte Thérèse de l'Enfant Jésus,* 5th ed., p. 37.

73. *Story of a Soul,* p. 132.

74. *L'esprit de sainte Thérèse de l'Enfant-Jésus,* p. 106. "It is great pain to Him thus to fill our cup with sorrows" (*Collected Letters of St. Thérèse of Lisieux,* ed. Combes, trans. F. J. Sheed, Sheed and Ward, 1949, p. 49).

75. Do the souls in purgatory suffer and pray for us? The theologians are not agreed on this point, but one thing is certain in the opinion of St. Thérèse of the Child Jesus: if they do suffer and pray for us, it is not, ideally, according to the divine scheme that they should do so. They should have accepted their Cross of redemption more generously beforehand, on

earth (and on earth the Cross is not so hard to endure as the sufferings of purgatory); immediately, as soon as they die, the incense of their prayers should ascend into the glory of heaven.

76. À l'Ecole de sainte Thérèse de l'Enfant Jésus, 5th ed., p. 36.

77. It is not always realized—and this ignorance is much to be regretted —that the main purpose of Extreme Unction is to help us to arrive directly and immediately at the beatific vision, as soon as we die. St. Thomas says: "In Extreme Unction man is prepared for the immediate attainment of glory" (III, 65, I 4m). This doctrinal point is developed in Vie Spirituelle, Jan.–Feb. 1945: "Even after a long and sinful life, the Christian who receives the last sacraments with the requisite dispositions goes immediately to paradise without passing through purgatory" (Père Philipon, pp. 16–17).

78. St. John of the Cross, Dark Night of the Soul, bk. ii, ch. xxi: Complete Works, vol. 1, p. 273.

79. Psalm 32:18 (author's rendering).

80. Bk. ii, ch. xx.

81. Story of a Soul, trans. Michael Day, Burns, Oates and Washbourne, 1951, p. 196.

82. Benedict XV, Allocution of Aug. 4, 1921.

83. This petition, made with humility, confidence and perseverance, is bound to be answered.

84. From the "Act of Offering" drawn up by St. Thérèse of the Child Jesus (Collected Letters, ed. Combes, trans. F. J. Sheed, Sheed and Ward, 1949, pp. 330–1). The same thought is to be found in the venerable Abbot Blosius: "He who is about to die . . . should offer himself to the greater glory of God, to the Lord Himself, as a living victim, to bear patiently according to His most acceptable will, with true love, all pain and languor and death itself, in one word whatever the Lord may will to send in time or in eternity. If he can really do this, if from pure love, with perfect resignation of himself, he can offer himself with a will ready to bear every pain in honor of the justice of God, he will go neither to hell nor even to purgatory, though he himself had committed all the sins of the whole world. No exercise then can be more useful at death than to resign oneself absolutely to the divine Will, humbly, lovingly and fully trusting in the mercy and goodness of God.

"This is certain, that anyone who, in a spirit of true and perfect resignation and holy confidence in God, goes forth from this world, will fly immediately to the Kingdom of Heaven. For just as no pain, no touch of the fire of purgatory, could possibly affect God, so also would it be powerless to affect a man perfectly united to God in entire and loving conformity of will.

"In this spirit did that repenting thief dying on a cross become a righteous man. He asked not from the Lord the healing of his body, nor did he pray to be delivered from purgatory, but willing to die for his sins and for the glory of God he resigned himself wholly to the will of God, and offered himself entirely to Christ that He might do with him whatsoever would be pleasing to Him. He asked for nothing except mercy and grace, saying 'Lord, remember me when Thou shalt come into Thy kingdom'" (Comfort for the Fainthearted, trans. B. Wilberforce, Art and Book Co., 1908, pp. 98–9).

85. Denzinger, 693.

86. *Story of a Soul,* trans. Michael Day, Burns, Oates and Washbourne, 1951, p. 5.

87. *Ibid.,* p. 6.

88. *Ibid.*

89. I, 20, 3.

90. *Ibid.*

91. St. John of the Cross, *Spiritual Canticle,* stanza xxxviii: *Complete Works,* vol. ii, p. 178.

92. *Pensées,* 435.